Turning Brownfields Into Greenbacks

Developing and Financing Environmentally Contaminated Urban Real Estate

Robert A. Simons

ULI
Urban Land Institute

About ULI–the Urban Land Institute

ULI–the Urban Land Institute is a nonprofit education and research institute that is supported and directed by its members. Its mission is to provide responsible leadership in the use of land in order to enhance the total environment.

ULI sponsors educational programs and forums to encourage an open international exchange of ideas and sharing of experience; initiates research that anticipates emerging land use trends and issues and proposes creative solutions based on this research; provides advisory services; and publishes a wide variety of materials to disseminate information on land use and development.

Established in 1936, the Institute today has more than 13,000 members and associates from more than 50 countries representing the entire spectrum of the land use and development disciplines. They include developers, builders, property owners, investors, architects, public officials, planners, real estate brokers, appraisers, attorneys, engineers, financiers, academics, students, and librarians. ULI members contribute to higher standards of land use by sharing their knowledge and experience. The Institute has long been recognized as one of America's most respected and widely quoted sources of objective information on urban planning, growth, and development.

Richard M. Rosan
President

Project Staff

Rachelle L. Levitt
Senior Vice President, Policy and Practice

Michael Pawlukiewicz
Director, Environmental Land Use Policy
Project Director

Nancy H. Stewart
Director, Book Program
Managing Editor

Barbara M. Fishel/Editech
Manuscript Editor

Betsy VanBuskirk
Art Director
Book, Cover Design

Joanne Nanez
Book Layout/Design

Diann Stanley-Austin
Associate Director of Publishing Operations
Production Manager

Kim Rusch
Artist

Maria-Rose Cain
Word Processing

Recommended bibliographic listing:

Simons, Robert A. *Turning Brownfields into Greenbacks: Developing and Financing Environmentally Contaminated Urban Real Estate.* Washington, D.C.: ULI--the Urban Land Institute, 1998.

ULI Catalog Number: TO5
International Standard Book Number: 0-87420-851-3
Library of Congress Catalog Card Number: 98-85109

1025 Thomas Jefferson Street, N.W.
Suite 500 West
Washington, D.C. 20007-5201

About the Author

Robert A. Simons is associate professor of real estate and urban planning at the Levin College of Urban Affairs at Cleveland State University. He teaches graduate courses in planning, environmental finance, real estate, and public economics. Simons received his master's and Ph.D. degrees in planning and economics from the University of North Carolina–Chapel Hill and a bachelor's degree in anthropology from Colorado State University.

Simons's research and consulting interests include brownfield development, retail and residential urban redevelopment, housing policy, environmental damages and impact analysis, and general real estate. Details on current activities are available at *www.rasimons.com.*

Contributing Writers

Rodney L. Jefferies
Senior Lecturer
The University of Auckland
Auckland, New Zealand

Todd S. Davis
President
Hemisphere Corporation
Cleveland, Ohio

Kevin Margolis
Vice President
Hemisphere Corporation
Cleveland, Ohio

Donald T. Iannone
Executive Director
Great Lakes Environmental Finance Center
Cleveland, Ohio

Paul M. Syms
Professor
School of Urban and Regional Studies
Sheffield Hallam University
Sheffield, UK

ULI Review Committee

George B. Brewster
Executive Director
California Center for Land Recycling
San Francisco, California

David C. Feltman
AEGON USA Realty Advisors
Cedar Rapids, Iowa

Peter Linneman
Director
Samuel Zell and Robert Lurie Real Estate Center
Wharton School of Business
University of Pennsylvania
Philadelphia, Pennsylvania

Glen E. Sibley
Managing Director
Mile High Properties
Denver, Colorado

Frank H. Spink
President
Lambda Alpha International
Annandale, Virginia

Acknowledgments

I wish to thank ULI and Cleveland State University for their financial support of this project and the travel expenses and for sabbatical leave. A number of people were helpful in developing this project, and they deserve thanks and have my deepest appreciation. First, Michael Pawlukiewicz, ULI's director of environmental land use policy, was project director for the book. He provided invaluable support and guidance as well as useful contacts. My overseas coauthors, Paul Syms and Rodney Jefferies, were a pleasure to work with. They picked fine sites to write about and showed extraordinary hospitality on my visits to their cities. Todd Davis and Kevin Margolis were wonderful to work with on the Ohio case. On the selection of other domestic cases, Steve Noble (New Jersey), Peter Simmons (Connecticut), and Debbie Fisher and Regis Carozza (Detroit) all gave me great advice and support. Ignacio Dayrit and Ravi Arulanantham in Emeryville, California, helped make my case study there successful. John Payne taught me a thing or two about minimizing stigma, and Nelson Chan in Sydney, Australia, was very gracious with his hospitality and was instrumental in helping me name the book. David Feltman, Peter Linneman, Glen Sibley, George Brewster, and Frank Spink provided excellent feedback during review of the manuscript. My family was supportive, and I appreciate the patience of DJ, Marc, and Joey when their dad was away from home, or at home tuned in only to the computer screen.

ULI's staff was extremely supportive. Rachelle Levitt, ULI's senior vice president for policy and practice, introduced me to the ULI system and helped get this project started on the road to publication. I am grateful to the ULI publications staff, who showed great skill and patience in bringing this book together: Nancy Stewart, who managed production of the book; Barbara Fishel, who edited the manuscript; Joanne Nanez, who did the layout; Diann Stanley-Austin, who coordinated production of the book; Betsy Van Buskirk, who designed the book and cover; and Maria-Rose Cain, who provided word processing support.

And the following people, in addition to a few who wish to remain anonymous, willingly shared their time and expertise about the development of brownfields in interviews conducted over several months:

James Adams, director of environmental services, Catellus Corp.

Randall Airst, principal, American Land Recycling Co.

Ravi Arulanantham, toxicologist, San Francisco Bay Regional Water Quality Control Board

Virginia Aveni, Cuyahoga County Planning Commission

Ed Bailey, director, facilities planning, Chiron Corp.

Tony Botelho, Connecticut Development Authority

George Brewster, executive director, California Center for Land Recycling

John C. Brown, vice president–acquisitions, Mars Equities

Carol Campman, Ecol Science

Kent Carlson, Ryan Construction

Regis Carozza, attorney

Nelson Chan, lecturer, Univ. of Western Sydney

Paul Christensen, project director, Neighborhood Progress, Inc.

Andrew Clark-Clough, City of Oakland

Colleen Connor, environmental counsel, GE

Barbara Cook, chief, Site Mitigation Branch, California Dept. of Toxic Substances Control

Jeffrey Cugno, director, Naugatuck Valley Development Corp.

Todd Davis, president, Hemisphere Corp.

Ignacio Dayrit, project director, Emeryville Dept. of Economic Development

Steven M. DeCamp, account executive, Neace Lukens Insurance Brokers

Paul Dickson, ERIIS

David Driver, executive director, Science Park Development Corp.

Cathy Dyer, manager, Contaminated Sites Section, New South Wales Environmental Protection Authority

Andy Evans, Richard Ellis

Derek Farmer, Trafford Park Development Corp.

David C. Feltman, AEGON USA Realty Management

Debbie Fisher, attorney, Detroit Planning and Development Dept.

Keith Ford, Minneapolis Redevelopment Authority

Michael Friedman, Ecol Science

Wayne Gibbens, risk manager, Westpac Trust

Richard Gimello, assistant commissioner for site redevelopment, New Jersey Dept. of Environmental Protection

Carl Goldberg, project director, Roseland Property Co.

Eddie Grogan, Auckland Regional Council

Mohammed Hassan, Woodward-Clyde Environmental Consultants

William Haubold, U.S. EPA Region 5

Susan Hollingshead, principal, LandBank, Inc.

Michael Holt, Irvin, Cohen & Jessif

John Housman, principal, HRP Associates

Sandra Karinen, California EPA, Dept. of Toxic Substances Control

Claudia Kerbawy, Michigan Dept. of Environmental Quality

William Kinnard, principal, Real Estate Research Group of Connecticut

Bob Kurtz, manager, Credit Policy and Risk Management, Colonial State Bank

Jenifer Kwasniewski, manager, Ohio Environmental Protection Agency, Voluntary Action Program

Ian McGowan, Seagars Valuers

Kevin Margolis, vice president, Hemisphere Corp.

Hardy Merrill, comptroller, USRAC

Tom Mitchell, City of Richmond

M. Morgan, commissioner, City of Milwaukee

Stephen Morse, chief, Toxics Div., San Francisco Bay Regional Water Quality Control Board

Randy Muller, environmental service manager, Bank of America (Chicago)

Bob Myers, U.S. EPA Superfund office

Willie Ng, Auckland City Council

Steve Noble, PNC Bank

Ric Notini, project director, Chiron Corp.

Patrick O'Keefe, director, Emeryville Dept. of Economic Development

Craig Parks, Connecticut Dept. of Environmental Protection

John Payne, corporate property manager, ICI/Dulux Australia

Ed Penhoet, CEO, Chiron Corp.

Richard Pennings, deputy director and chief underwriter, Michigan State Housing Development Authority

Penny Pirrit, planning manager, Auckland City Council

Lary Rand, project director, V.I.S.I.O.N.S.

Hal Reisenfeld, Reisenfeld & Co.

Rudy Salcedo, City of Milwaukee

Ramon Scoble, Auckland Regional Council

Mike Selby, risk manager, ASB Bank

Kathleen Shields, project director, GGP/Brass Mill, Inc.

Susan Phinney Silver, deputy director, The Development Fund

Peter Simmons, Connecticut Dept. of Economic and Community Development

Tom Stabell, facilities manager, Science Park Development Corp.

Redding Thompson, Olin Corp.

Alfred Wanger, California EPA, Dept. of Toxic Substances Control

Elizabeth Ward, president, Washington Advisors

Chris Warren, director, Cleveland Economic and Community Development Dept.

Betsey Wingfield, Connecticut Dept. of Environmental Protection

Alan Wolken, City of Richmond

Kevin Wood, Worleys Environmental Consultants

Neil Yoskin, attorney, Bennett & Yoskin

Robert A. Simons

Contents

Foreword

In 1980, Congress enacted the Comprehensive Environmental Response, Compensation, and Liability Act, which among other things, established the Superfund to underwrite the costs of environmental cleanups. The legislation was intended to eliminate the health and environmental threats posed by hazardous waste disposal sites. At the time of its passage, observers were optimistic that this nation could correct the toxic mistakes of the past and make our communities safe from the threat of hazardous waste. Unfortunately, it would not be that easy. Because Superfund's provisions for liability were so strict, no one wanted to be involved with contaminated land, or even with land that is *perceived* to be contaminated. Why invest in a risky venture in the city when the suburbs have plenty of safe, cheap land available? Thus, Superfund, instead of making our communities safe, has contributed to the decline of older industrial cities.

Recently, however, many states have adopted voluntary cleanup programs to attract new capital and facilitate the development of lightly contaminated land, making it possible for lenders to invest in brownfield projects without fear of exposure to the cost of final cleanup if the property should fall into their hands. With these changes, deals involving brownfields can be put together more readily.

Now public officials, especially at the state and local levels, are deeply engaged in promoting the development of brownfields in their jurisdictions. The U.S. EPA is learning that the best way to get contaminated land cleaned up and redeveloped is to facilitate deals and keep the regulatory "hammer" off the table. In other words, EPA is fading into the background and allowing states to develop incentives for brownfield development, realizing that the old model using threats and penalties is not the best tool for the job. State and local officials are doing what they can to make sites attractive for investment.

While state and local boosters are euphoric about the development potential of their brownfields, Robert Simons, the author of this book, advises caution. First, based on his research, the supply of brownfield real estate in most cases far exceeds the demand for it for the foreseeable future. Moreover, a brownfield site must have true value as real estate if it is to be developed. This statement may sound elementary, but many advocates of developing brownfields seem to believe that if we just get the right institutional framework in place, the brownfields will start marching down the development pipeline. This clearly is not the case.

Nevertheless, plenty of good news exists. Some great opportunities for development are available, opportunities that did not exist just a few years ago. They have come about because of a new, more cooperative regulatory environment for brownfield deals. More cooperative attitudes in the public sector and the lending community, and among environmental groups really are helping to put deals together and to succeed. Along this line, the case studies in this book offer a great deal of encouragement, documenting how outstanding projects can yield solid returns. This growing trend has the potential to really bloom when state voluntary programs mature and federal reforms and financial inducements are fully in place.

Michael Pawlukiewicz
Director, Environmental Land Use Policy

Glossary

***Brownfield*—**A formerly industrial or commercial site that is prevented from attaining its highest and best use as a result of perceived or actual environmental contamination.

***Cap*—**Partial encapsulation of contaminated soil, involving removal of most undesirable contamination and containment of less contaminated soil under clay, building structures, or a plastic barrier covered with soil.

***Closure document*—**A final document issued by some state environmental protection agencies when a site has been successfully remediated, stating that cleanup has been satisfactorily completed and listing further possible regulatory actions. Includes "no further action" letters, "certificates of completion," and "covenants not to sue."

***Comfort letter*—**A nonbinding document issued by the U.S. EPA to replace a memorandum of understanding, essentially stating that EPA has no plans to investigate a project further.

***Covenant Not to Sue*—**A strong form of closure document, binding all state and local agencies, promising that no further legal action or remediation is needed once the approved remediation plan for a site has been satisfactorily completed, subject to certain conditions.

***Delisting*—**Isolating residual contamination on site but outside the property used for a bank's collateral; clean portions used or sold to finance remediation of contaminated property.

***Encapsulation*—**Completely covering contaminated soil by paving the surface for use as, for example, a parking lot if the soil below is clay or prevents contamination of groundwater. Not for use if soil is contaminated by a volatile substance.

***Greenfield*—**A piece of virgin land, usually in the suburbs.

***Look-up database*—**A reference provided by local governments that records approved cleanups, required remediation practices, and soil conditions. Nearby property owners whose property has similar conditions to a remediated site can "look up" past practices and successful development conditions and use them to remediate their own sites.

***Memorandum of understanding*—**An agreement between the U.S. EPA and state environmental protection agencies indicating that the U.S. EPA will not be involved in a state EPA–approved voluntary cleanup action except under extremely restrictive circumstances. Also called a "state memorandum of agreement" or a "memorandum of agreement."

***No Further Action (NFA) letter*—**A closure letter stating that no further action is required on the site with regard to the remedial action just completed.

***Potentially responsible party*—**An entity in the chain of title who could be responsible for cleanup under CERCLA.

***Remediation*—**The cleaning up of contaminated land so that it can attain its highest and best use.

***Reopener*—**An action, such as fraudulent activity or a change in land use, that invalidates a closure document for a remediated site.

***Responsible party*—**A company or other entity that willingly or under duress as the result of court action cleans up a site its past business practices contaminated.

***Strict, joint, and several liability*—**A phrase meaning that anyone in the chain of title or who otherwise contributed to an environmental problem could be liable for the entire amount of cleanup, regardless of which portion of the problem it actually caused.

***Superfund*—**A revolving trust fund established by the U.S. Congress in the Comprehensive Environmental Response, Compensation, and Liability Act of 1980 to cover the cost of cleanups.

Abbreviations Used in This Book

BTEX	Benzene, toluene, ethylbenzene, xylene
CBD	Central business district
CDBG	Community development block grant
CDC	Community development corporation
CERCLA	Comprehensive Environmental Response, Compensation, and Liability Act
CERCLIS	Comprehensive Environmental Response, Compensation, and Liability Information System
CNTS	Covenant not to sue
EPA	(U.S.) Environmental Protection Agency
FAR	Floor/area ratio
HRS	Hazard ranking system
IDB	Industrial development bond
IRA	Industrial remediation account
IRR	Internal rate of return
LLC	Limited liability corporation
LTV	Loan-to-value (ratio)
LUST	Leaking underground storage tank
MOA	Memorandum of agreement
MOU	Memorandum of understanding
NFA	No further action (letter)
NFRAP	No further remedial action planned
NNN	Triple net
NOI	Net operating income
NPL	National Priorities List
OSHA	Occupational Safety and Health Administration
PAH	Polyaromatic hydrocarbon
PCB	Polychlorinated biphenyl
PRP	Potentially responsible party
QUANGO	Quasi-autonomous nongovernmental organization
R&D	Research and development
RBCA	Risk-based corrective action
RCRA	Resource Conservation and Recovery Act
REIT	Real estate investment trust
RP	Responsible party
SARA	Superfund Amendments and Reauthorization Act
TIF	Tax increment financing
TSD	Treatment, storage, and disposal (site)
UST	Underground storage tank
VCP	Voluntary cleanup program

Part I

1 Introduction and Overview

Most urban areas today face difficulty in redeveloping contaminated urban lands, or brownfields. At least half a million sites in the United States qualify as brownfields. Some are on government lists of contaminated sites, but many are not formally recognized as brownfields. Development of uncontaminated, agricultural greenfields over the past few decades has been a major contributor to urban sprawl, leaving abandoned center cities and former industrial sites. Thanks in part to new state legislation, however, it is now possible to reap substantial profits from these contaminated lands, turning brownfields into greenbacks.

A brownfield can be identified as such through a number of routes:

- A private developer or not-for-profit developer inadvertently stumbles across one while assembling a property for development.
- A seller or potential buyer seeking financing discovers that contamination exists when the property is marketed for sale.
- A developer actively seeks such properties, hoping to buy them at a reduced price, remediate real or perceived contamination, and later sell the properties at or close to market value for "clean" property.
- Government agencies or financial institutions become the owners of last resort or have an opportunity to acquire a brownfield or finance one.

The purpose of this book is to guide real estate practitioners in the development of brownfields. In other words, how can you maximize your gain while keeping the shirt on your back? Because part of this process involves working with the public sector to obtain grants, loans, or other aid, the public perspective is intermingled with the developer's throughout many parts of this book. A secondary goal is to inform public players and other real estate professionals about the steps involved in developing brownfields.

Definition and Extent of Brownfields

Because recognition of brownfields is relatively new, experts cannot agree on what a brownfield is. The narrowest definition includes formerly industrial or commercial land, with or without an existing building, that is actually contaminated. (The property may or may not be on one of the many federal or state lists of known contaminated sites.) As a result, the property cannot be financed or developed, which can be accompanied by financial distress, such as flagrant delinquency on property taxes or default on the mortgage. If observers believe that contamination has migrated off-site (e.g., groundwater contamination from leaking underground storage tanks), then nearby properties could be classified as brownfields by default. A brownfield could be an existing industrial property with a partly contaminated site whose on-site business cannot get a loan to expand (although actual contamination is not necessary to make it difficult to obtain financing, as a *perception* of or uncertainty about contamination can hinder marketing). A vacant, formerly residential lot with the old building plowed into the basement and covered over with dirt could also be a brownfield. Some insist that demand for development as the former use or another, higher use be present for the property to be a brownfield. Some brownfields have multiple sources of contamination. Therefore, the definition of brownfield used in this book is *a formerly industrial or commercial site prevented from attaining its highest and best use as a result of perceived or actual environmental contamination*.

Such properties, including those on one of the U.S. Environmental Protection Agency's (EPA's) lists or the list of leaking underground storage tanks (LUSTs) kept by most states, may become stigmatized. That is, their ability to be sold is reduced, and if they do sell, it would probably be at a price that is lower than its true market value minus any future cost of cleanup. While this situation is unfortunate for current owners, a profit is possible for shrewd real estate investors who can envision the market value of the property after cleanup, buy it for a very low price, clean up the property, obtain the correct approvals, and sell (or develop and finance) a former brownfield.

Not all contaminated lands are likely to be developed. For example, EPA's Superfund sites, which have the highest priority on EPA's National Priorities List (NPL), are not regular brownfields, because they entail public health problems and are not economic development opportunities. Likewise, active landfills, although contaminated by design, have presumably reached their highest and best use as public waste depositories and therefore are not "prevented from attaining [their] highest and best use." Likewise, many smaller, poorly located, and functionally obsolete brownfields may never be developed.

Why Is Developing Contaminated Land a Problem?

Before the recent enactment of state legislation, brownfields were very hard to develop because of the cost and risk involved, that is, the additional expense of cleaning up contaminated land as part of site preparation and the unknowns related to the adequacy of remediation from the perspective of regulators, possible users, and lenders.

Cost of Cleanup

The cost of cleanup reflects the actual or perceived cost to clean the site to acceptable standards (assuming they are known). Because the net price of urban land possibly contaminated by a prior use would be higher than a comparable suburban property on virgin farmland (for example, a three-acre industrial parcel in a midwestern city with all utilities available for $2.00 per square foot plus expected cleanup costs of $4.00 per square foot versus a greenfield for $4.00 per square foot and no cleanup cost), urban sites have long been overlooked based solely on cost. At one time, the only way to convince a bank to finance a brownfield was to haul away all possibly tainted soil to a landfill and bring in fill dirt that was "clean enough to eat"—which of course killed all but the rarest of real estate deals, such as a small part of a larger commercial site in a prime location. And this cost factor does not address other concerns: additional risk, fear of crime, small parcels, for example. Chapter 2 covers cost comparisons in detail.

Reduction of Liability

The second major reason most brownfields have been vacant for years is liability. As of the mid-1990s, any party involved with a brownfield could typically be held liable for the cleanup, regardless of who actually contaminated the land or whether or not the party knew of the contamination—the so-called "strict, joint, and several liability" clause under the Comprehensive Environmental Response, Compensation, and Liability Act (CERCLA) and the Superfund Amendments and Reauthorization Act (SARA) managed by EPA. Liability traditionally included lenders who foreclosed on a defaulted loan and took possession of a property. Moreover, the uncertainty about cleanup and the value of contaminated real estate as collateral for a potential loan meant lenders were reluctant to extend credit without thoroughly checking borrowers' creditworthiness.

Gridlock in Developing Brownfields

The cumulative effect of these factors has been gridlock in developing brownfields. The old "dig-and-dump" approach of hauling out debris and bringing in clean fill dirt was too expensive for all but the best-located, easy-to-remediate sites. Potential developers and lenders were scared off by the strict, joint, and several liability clause that could hold any party liable for some or all contamination on site, whether or not it caused the contamination or contributed to its current condition. EPA is still involved, however, and many state programs are incomplete or have not yet been tested. With some notable exceptions in a few states, brownfields have been a failure on the market, which local governments may be able to rectify with appropriate subsidies. The risks of developing brownfields have not been quantifiable, so environmental insurance and lending capital have not been available at reasonable cost. Banks have generally avoided brownfields, at least under regular real estate lending practices where the real estate secures a mortgage at a loan-to-value ratio of 0.7 to 0.8. Demand for brownfields is uncertain; community leaders hesitate to give up the idea that old jobs are coming back and generally avoid systematically analyzing or rezoning brownfields to their best use. This inaction has allowed the oversupply of brownfields to persist, softening their price. The good news is that new state legislation covering voluntary cleanup programs is beginning to alleviate the problem, and the situation should get better fast.

State Initiatives

Many states (30 as of January 1, 1997) have enacted some form of law addressing brownfields, usually a voluntary cleanup program (VCP) that encourages the cleanup and development of brownfields. The status of these laws in individual states is one of the most critical factors for a developer to ascertain for efficient management of a brownfield. The U.S. EPA has contributed to the reform by removing most of the sites on the NPL and turning over control of these and future sites needing remediation to the states. Many states in response passed legislation clarifying the necessary level of cleanliness required for different uses and different soil conditions. Whether soil is clay (good) or sand (usually very bad) makes a big difference, for example, in reducing migration of contamination through groundwater. These so-called risk-based corrective action (RBCA) standards help in two ways. First, they serve to substantially reduce the cost of cleanup in many cases. Second, they answer the question of what clean enough is. Some states act as coordinators between agencies when a multifaceted problem is encountered (involving, for example, LUSTs and heavy metals). States have also, by statute, exempted new lending and equity capital from liability, provided site assessment is conducted in advance and followed. When sites are successfully remediated, many state EPAs issue closure documents, including no further action (NFA) letters and covenants not to sue (CNTSs), which state that the cleanup has been satisfactorily completed and lists further regulatory actions that are possible in the future. (Other agencies may be bound by these letters.) Some states and localities also award site assessment and site remediation grants to determine the extent of the contamination in an effort to get the property cleaned up and back on the market. These changes are discussed in Chapter 3.

Given the working definitions of "brownfield," Chapter 4 looks at the extent of the problem nationally, based on information from many sources, including 384,000 known contaminated sites on over a dozen active federal EPA lists and state lists of LUSTs and hazardous waste sites. At least another estimated 75,000 formerly industrial sites in 31 large U.S. cities are probably not on any official list but are likely nevertheless to be brownfields based on a lack of current productive use and suspected contamination from prior use. The chapter shows sites by state and by type; every community includes some type of brownfield.

The Demand for Brownfield Sites

As development of brownfields moves out of the hands of the environmental regulators, who consider the remediation of a contaminated site the end of the process, to the hands of private and public real estate developers interested in economic development and profit, the issue of demand for sites becomes the next hurdle. Virtually no published evidence is available about this issue, and the analysis of supply and demand in Chapter 5 shows how out of balance the picture is in four cities. Three of the four cities contain three to ten decades worth of central city brownfield properties relative to annual nonresidential real estate demand, even with improved voluntary cleanup programs in the states. The fourth city defines brownfields very narrowly, implying that many brownfields will not be developed any time soon and that many jobs will not return. Further, some brownfields are economically obsolete, regardless of how clean the site is, unless new roads and infrastructure are built and parcels are assembled into marketable sites for development. Even smaller, formerly industrial parcels, which could be used for housing, would be more expensive to remediate for housing under new RBCA rules in many states. Fully half the existing brownfields may be best suited for long-term interim uses or for permanent open space, parkland, or buffers between incompatible land uses. As city leaders recognize this reality and the fact that jobs will not return, they should rezone brownfields and concentrate support of developing brownfields on the most competitive areas, letting the others revert to lower-intensity uses.

Tools for Developing Brownfields

In many markets, the table is set for substantial development of brownfields. This process requires real estate players to become familiar with the various tools and strategies available for developing brownfields. These tools and strategies (more than 50 in all) are described in Chapter 6, which is organized around the sequence required for developing brownfields: trying to exclude the brownfield from the development project, becoming familiar with the state's voluntary cleanup program, preparing a preliminary remediation and financing plan, controlling the site, remediating the site, obtaining permanent financing, and monitoring the site after completion to preserve environmental conditions. The brownfield developer can employ a financial and remediation strategy as needed to move the process forward. The tools include government regulations, financial resources for remediation (grants, loans, equity, and tax incentives), real estate strategies to lower liability by isolating low-level contamination on site, remediation strategies, sources of permanent financing (grants, loans, equity, and tax incentives), and loan guarantees and assurances. The case studies in Part II demonstrate how developers have successfully used many of these tools in developing brownfields.

Overview of Brownfield Development Projects

Chapter 7 presents an overview of the 13 case studies in seven venues that represent a cross section of future conditions developers are likely to encounter regarding brownfields. Both for-profit and not-for-profit developers and various types of soil and groundwater contamination are discussed. The venues include five states and two countries overseas. Only "successful" projects with favorable outcomes (under construction or already developed) are described. The cases represent diverse conditions and a spectrum of end uses, including retail stores, for-sale and rental housing, industrial sites, R&D, and a health clinic. Regulatory environments range from state-led, tightly controlled programs with substantial subsidies to initiatives led by the private sector with the state's concurrence. The overseas cases feature mostly city-led environmental permitting.

Chapter 7 also provides an overview of lessons learned from the cases. All cases were recognized as an opportunity for economic development rather than as a public health issue. The main lesson learned is the success of the new remediation paradigm: acceptance of appropriately clean sites through use- and site-specific RBCAs and the spreading of costs and risks among developers, users, financiers, and all levels of government. Creative remediation can reasonably ensure users' safety, isolate contamination on site so that lenders are satisfied with the quality of the brownfield to be used as collateral, and quantify any residual financial risk so financial products can be created to meet the needs of all parties.

Each case study is analyzed four ways: 1) site development, including the background of the site, final use, the development team, and remediation; 2) financial aspects, including financing, risk allocation, subsidies, and outcomes; 3) strategies that made the project work; and 4) a comparison of U.S. cases with the overseas ones.

Some interesting patterns emerged. For example, public subsidies for the projects depended on local land values. Where land prices were high, subsidies were low. The average public subsidy was about 20 percent. Remediation costs typically represented about 10 percent of a project's total value, but some projects using innovative remediation techniques kept the cost of remediation below 5 percent. Private sector financing was available for most projects but typically required indemnification and loan-to-value ratios of 0.5 to 0.6.

Allocating Costs and Risks Among the Players

Chapter 8 focuses on the activities and abilities of private, not-for-profit, and public entities in the brownfields arena and their current and potential roles in reducing site development costs, communicating with other players, and absorbing risk. It explores the equity players, which include developers and not-for-profit entities that seek out opportunities to develop brownfields, as well as private and public lenders; the role of responsible parties and hybrid consultants who can communicate with one or more disciplines in the brownfields process; and public and private insurers.

The chapter also briefly describes the activities of representative entities within each segment. The subsequent analysis highlights activities currently undertaken by each group and those that need to be considered more vigorously in the near future. With the exception of insurance products (where change is rapid), participation in cost reduction appears to be essentially complete. What is needed is for developers, equity players, state administrators of VCPs, and local governments to become more familiar with the needs of other players and to improve their communication with those players, in part by providing information in the way it needs to be seen or heard. The main shortfall is in the area of risk. Lenders and real estate appraisers need to take on a larger share of the risk. And lenders' risk can be partially offset by more responsive indemnification and insurance products and services from both the public and private sectors.

The Prescription for Brownfields

Chapter 9 contains recommendations for brownfield developers and their public partners. The strategies for developers are intended to provide guidance on how to deal best with constraints in each stage of development. It also discusses public policy for federal, state, and local governments, and offers suggestions for the real estate industry, including appraisers, lenders, and insurers.

Recommendations for Developers

Chapter 9 enumerates activities pertaining to site development and design, and offers strategies for acquisition of a brownfield (obtain a deeply discounted price for a previously remediated site with high demand and then build a high-density project), for dealing with environmental regulators (ask for a single lead agency for the contact and attain the highest level of closure possible), and for remediation (remove hot spots, contain the contamination on site, and design the site and construction around existing constraints). Recommendations address access to public funds, donated clean land, tax relief, and loans and grants, and methods for acquiring private financing (segment the contamination on site, use land leases, and lower risk for lenders by obtaining indemnification and loan guarantees). In all, the chapter includes about 50 strategies for developers.

Suggestions for Public Policy

The chapter also addresses the implications for public policy on brownfields for federal, state, and local governments. Policy issues are considered in light of risk-related market failure and by the evidence and trends suggested by the limited demand for brownfield sites, progress in state VCPs, and the successful case studies. In general, public subsidies appear to exceed expenses purely for remediation, indicating that other, presumably market-related, costs are being supported. Subsidy should be made available in whatever form is most useful to the developer but should not inadvertently exceed a predetermined amount, say 15 to 20 percent of the project's cost. Industrial projects and low-income housing, because of their lower real estate value, require larger subsidies. Amortizing remediation costs that accrue to the site (soil contamination) as opposed to the regional or local environment (groundwater) and regulating and financing them separately may become more popular in the coming years.

Specific items for consideration by the federal government include standardizing the memorandum of understanding between EPA and the states, providing remediation tax credits, and acting as information broker for the states. Most of the actions recommended for state governments are related to expanding voluntary cleanup programs to serve more subcomponents of brownfield sites, supporting markets for demolition materials to reduce net expenses of site remediation, and facilitating local control of brownfield development in areas where it is warranted. Local governments should play a larger role in rezoning, finding and targeting brownfields, firming up land markets for urban real estate, and providing creative local financing, including loan guarantees.

Recommendations for the Private Real Estate Community

The chapter concludes with suggestions for appraisers, lenders, real estate investment trusts (REITs), and the insurance industry. Appraisers need better information in valuing contaminated property before remediation so bankers can assign a realistic loan-to-value ratio. Lenders need to invest in more research to quantify the risks to both themselves and the borrowers of site cleanup, residual asset value, and regulatory changes. Insurance companies need to provide environmental insurance for an entire portfolio, not just for selected properties, to keep transaction costs more reasonable.

The Case Studies

Part II contains case studies of 13 successful brownfield remediation projects: two in Connecticut (Chapter 10), two in Michigan (Chapter 11), one in Ohio (Chapter 12), one in New Jersey (Chapter 13), one in California (Chapter 14), three in New Zealand (Chapter 15), and three in England (Chapter 16).

- *Regional mall in Waterbury, Connecticut.* Connecticut has several voluntary cleanup programs, including one oriented toward urban sites needing very large subsidies. This 1.2 million-square-foot regional mall on 90 acres received over $40 million in public funds. Construction of the mall, on the site of a former brass-rolling mill, is complete, and the grand opening was held in September 1997.
- *Winchester factory in New Haven, Connecticut.* The U.S. Repeating Arms Corp. (Winchester rifles) was the beneficiary of a new 225,000-square-foot state-of-the-art manufacturing building on 15 acres. Olin Corp., the former owner, voluntarily remediated the extensively developed former armaments site with help from the state of Connecticut and a local not-for-profit corporation.
- *Low-income housing in Detroit, Michigan.* Michigan is known for its strong leadership, regulatory stance, and financial support of brownfield remediation. The Helen Butler Odean apartments contain 96 low-income rental housing units on an 8½-acre former urban renewal site. V.I.S.I.O.N.S., the not-for-profit developer and apartment manager, has fully leased and occupied the project, and is moving on to the project's second phase.
- *Health clinic in Detroit, Michigan.* The Detroit Community Health Connection is a not-for-profit entity that recently opened a 14,000-square-foot health clinic on the one-acre site of a former gas station. Federal grants guaranteed the bank loan.
- *EastRock shopping center near Cleveland, Ohio.* Ohio's new permanent environmental regulations recently took effect. EastRock is a 19-acre expansion of a retail mall in a suburb of Cleveland. The site is under remediation, and the project is in the leasing phase.
- *Housing complex in West New York, New Jersey.* This 158-acre master-planned housing complex overlooks midtown Manhattan across the Hudson River. The former rail yard and transfer station was mildly contaminated with nonvolatile hydrocarbons, which are to be contained on site.
- *Chiron life sciences center in Emeryville, California.* Emeryville, a small suburb of Oakland, has emerged as a leader in local brownfield development. This 2.2 million-square-foot R&D facility on 25 acres is one example of how the risk can be spread among all parties.
- *Three projects in Auckland, New Zealand.* New Zealand is known for its clean, green environment, but it also has its share of formerly contaminated property. Case studies include a 13-acre shopping center on the site of a former paint factory, a 40-unit, four-story condominium project on a coal gasometer storage facility, and a 26+-unit residential project on the site of a former bus garage. Dense development and robust land prices drove the finances on these projects, which were developed without government subsidies.
- *Three projects in Manchester, England.* The British are several years ahead of even the most progressive states in the United States, having already grappled with brownfields and their problems by the early 1990s. Greater Manchester, which is very similar to many U.S. cities in the Rustbelt, has completed more than ten large (over 100 units) housing projects on brownfields and a 2,600-acre, internationally competitive industrial and business park. The descriptions include two successful housing projects (one for-sale and one rental) and the industrial park.

2 Development Costs: Why Most Brownfields Are Still Brownfields

Most brownfields have not yet been developed because the additional expense of cleanup makes the net price of contaminated urban land (after site cleanup) too expensive in comparison with greenfield properties in the suburbs. This situation is ironic, because many brownfields have excellent "location, location, location." The additional liability and uncertainty about cleaning up brownfields may also affect financing by altering loan-to-value and debt service coverage ratios, depending on how the remediation was handled. Probable delay in cleanup may also incur more carrying costs. In many areas, market rents in the central city are lower than in the suburbs. This chapter analyzes these challenges, which until recently faced brownfield developers—not to deter the reader from tackling a brownfield but to present useful information for exploring likely government responses to market failure and for dealing with an unenlightened seller or competing developer without a clear picture of how to develop a brownfield.

Other factors, considered during the predevelopment stage, could also affect the development of brownfields. Perhaps the quality of the labor force, earning power of nearby households, lack of information about the demand for brownfields, and a perception of high crime rates apply to the central city in general and prevent even the consideration of brownfields for development. These factors, however, do not necessarily pertain to suburban brownfields such as sites of former gas stations, where the demographics are often more desirable.

After briefly introducing the general issues behind the "nondecision" affecting brownfields, this chapter focuses on the cost of remediation and financing, demonstrating why brownfields have not been able to compete in the marketplace. It looks at three examples of financing for the same ten-acre piece of land with a moderate and identifiable brownfield problem, analyzing hypothetical brownfield and greenfield pro formas for a retail/commercial shopping center, a small industrial park, and residential lots for sale (see Figures 2.1, 2.2, and 2.3). It then advances reasons for brownfields' poor performance. The next part of the chapter summarizes the issues of liability that until recently plagued brownfield properties in the form of a lack of legislation and the threat of legal action by participants and third parties.

The cumulative effect of the lack of brownfield development has been to accelerate urban sprawl and contribute to urban blight and fiscal stress. The failure of developed brownfields on the market has taken several forms, including a lack of information and regulatory certainty. This market failure justifies partial government support for the development of brownfields, an area where such support can be most effective. It has created opportunities for developers knowledgeable about the problem who may find undervalued properties they can turn into profit.

The Predevelopment Decision: Why Brownfield Deals Have Not Made It to the Back of the Envelope

The irony of the situation is that central cities offer many advantages of location to properties that are properly developed to their highest and best use, such as proximity to businesses downtown and to a high concentration of activity. Retail projects offer access to local ethnic markets, and retail centers in many central cities enjoy a higher market concentration than their suburban counterparts.[1] Despite a strategic location in the center city and overall cheaper land costs, however, brownfields have competed poorly with greenfields based on several factors.

Difficulties in Site Assembly

Existing brownfields are often too small to be useful. The average size of industrial brownfields in Cleveland, for example, is one to one-and-a-half acres. In Milwaukee, the average size of a parcel on the city's list of tax-delinquent, contaminated nonresidential properties (the "do not acquire list") is four-tenths of an acre. The industrial market today demands sites of three to five acres, and if a developer wants to assemble a larger industrial site, problems are likely to arise in writing purchase options because the net proceeds to the seller are uncertain. This delay and uncertainty means developers avoid assembling brownfield sites.

Inadequate Highway or Road Access

Despite a good general location, not all inner-city properties are near enough to an interstate highway interchange to be competitive for the industrial market. Ideally, industrial properties should be within one-half mile, or five minutes, of an interstate interchange and should be able to reach that interchange via a truck route. The vast majority of new highways built since 1960 are in the suburbs.

The same lack of access applies to commercial properties. A successful retail project should be near an intersection of two major streets, and an intersection of a major and a minor street is generally required. Central cities contain many arterial roadways that are former streetcar routes, and while they often have four lanes, two are taken up with on-street parking and many have no turning lanes. After the streetcars were removed, much of the property, especially in the middle of blocks, became functionally obsolete.

A Perception of Crime

The perception or fear of crime is a major reason that people leave center cities. For example, homesellers in Cleveland in 1990 listed crime as the second major reason that they were moving, behind poor schools and just ahead of poor city services.[2] The same trend applies to industrial decision makers. Presidents and CEOs of smaller companies might want to remain in the center city or find an inexpensive site there to be able to offer competitive prices but fear for their and their employees' safety.

The Labor Force

The perception that the labor force in the center city is underskilled with a below-average education is generally correct. In 13 cities shown to have a large number of brownfields, center city residents over the age of 25 have a lower rate of high school graduation (66 percent, compared with the national average of 76 percent), and fewer have finished college (16 percent versus 20 percent)—helping to explain why many employers choose to locate their plants in the suburbs.[3]

Uncertain Demand

Information about the supply of and demand for brownfields in general is unavailable, as very few cities keep records on the sites' location and characteristics and calculating demand for center city real estate is a problem. Most readily available data, such as census statistics, could understate the buying power of inner-city niche markets by ignoring in-kind "income" such as food stamps, and

FIGURE 2.1

ANALYSIS OF BROWNFIELDS VERSUS GREENFIELDS FOR A RETAIL PROJECT

Factor	Brownfield	Greenfield
Land Use Information		
Lot Size (acres)	10 (435,600 square feet)	10 (435,600 square feet)
Floor/Area Ratio	0.25	0.25
Building Area (square feet)	108,900	108,900
Number of Current Owners	10	1
Development Cost Information		
Land Acquisition Cost	$871,200 ($2 psf)	$1,742,400 ($4 psf)
Site Preparation Costs		
Remediation (one-half the site at $5 psf)	$1,089,000	0
Other site preparation ($2 psf of land)	871,200	$871,200
Construction Costs		
Building hard costs	$5,445,000 ($50 psf of building)	$5,445,000 ($50 psf of building)
Other (shrink)	163,400 (3%)	54,500 (1%)
Soft Costs		
Legal	$100,000	$20,000
Other soft costs (architect, planner)	250,000	250,000
Environmental consultants	100,000	5,000
Construction loan/carrying costs	400,000	300,000
Subtotal	$9,289,800	$8,688,100
Developer's fee (5%)	464,500	434,400
Total Development Cost	**$9,754,300**	**$9,122,500**
Total Development Cost per Building Square Foot	**$89.57**	**$83.77**
Operating Cash Flow		
Number of Tenants	20	20
Market Rent	$1,089,000 ($10 psf NNN)	$1,306,800 ($12 psf NNN)
Market Vacancy	12%	6%
Security Costs	$108,900 ($1 psf)	$27,225 ($0.25 psf)
Environmental Monitoring	$50,000	0
Net Operating Income	**$799,400**	**$1,201,200**
Financing and Investment		
Value (NOI/0.1)	$7,994,000	$12,012,000
Loan Amount (loan-to-value ratio)	$4,796,400 (.60)	$8,408,400 (.70)
Debt Service (15 years at 10%)	$630,600	$1,105,500
Debt Service Coverage Ratio	1.27 (OK)	1.09 (OK)
Before-Tax Cash Flow	$168,800	$95,700
Equity Requirement	$4,957,900	$733,200
Return on Equity	3.4%	13.0%
Site Preparation Time	18 months	6 months
Future Liability	Unknown	None
Indemnification Letter from Seller?	Yes	No

the undercounting of income could be substantial.[4] Thus, despite fairly high density and substantial buying power, many center city retail niche markets cannot be easily and cheaply analyzed, and few have been developed.

Uncertainty about Possible Liability for Cleanup

Regardless of the cost of development, developing brownfields may incur additional risk to the developer, buyer, and seller, compared with greenfield deals. Additional difficulties with site assembly and remediation may delay a project's timing, which could cause it to miss a market window. Legislation in many states still includes a strict, joint, and several liability clause for cleanup of contaminated sites. Such a clause tends to frighten away new capital, because developers (through voluntary acquisition) or lenders (through foreclosures) wish to avoid

FIGURE 2.2

ANALYSIS OF BROWNFIELDS VERSUS GREENFIELDS FOR AN INDUSTRIAL PROJECT

Factor	Brownfield	Greenfield
Land Use Information		
Lot Size (acres)	10 (435,600 square feet)	10 (435,600 square feet)
Floor/Area Ratio	0.35	0 35
Building Area (square feet)	152,460	152,460
Number of Current Owners	4	1
Development Cost Information		
Land Acquisition Cost	$217,800 ($0.50 psf)	$609,800 ($1.40 psf)
Site Preparation Costs		
Remediation (one-half the site at $5 psf)	$1,089,000	0
Other site preparation ($1 psf of land)	435,600	$435,600
Construction Costs		
Building hard costs	$4,878,700 ($32 psf of building)	$4,878,700 ($32 psf of building)
Other (shrink)	146,400 (3%)	48,800 (1%)
Soft Costs		
Legal	$50,000	$20,000
Other soft costs (architect, planner)	250,000	250,000
Environmental consultants	100,000	5,000
Construction loan/carrying costs	400,000	300,000
Subtotal	$7,567,500	$6,547,900
Developer's fee (5%)	378,400	327,400
Total Development Cost	**$7,945,900**	**$6,875,300**
Total Development Cost per Building Square Foot	**$52.12**	**$45.10**
Operating Cash Flow		
Number of Users	3	3
Market Rent	$724,200 ($4.75 psf NNN)	$ 838,500 ($5.50 psf NNN)
Market Vacancy	10%	7%
Security Costs	$76,200 ($0.50 psf)	$38,100 ($0.25 psf)
Environmental Monitoring	$50,000	0
Net Operating Income	**$525,600**	**$741,700**
Financing and Investment		
Value (NOI/0.1)	$5,256,000	$7 417,000
Loan Amount (loan-to-value ratio)	$3,679,200 (.70)	$5 933,600 (.80)
Debt Service (20 years at 9%)	$403,000	$650,000
Debt Service Coverage Ratio	1.3 (OK)	1.15 (OK)
Before-Tax Cash Flow	$122,600	$91,700
Equity Requirement	$4,266,700	$941,700
Return on Equity	2.9%	9.7%
Site Preparation Time	18 months	6 months
Future Liability	Unknown	None
Indemnification Letter from Seller?	Yes	No

paying for pollution caused by others. And brownfield sites in general are stigmatized because of the uncertainty about their potential for development and financeability, implying a price discount beyond actual cleanup costs that is difficult for lenders and buyers to quantify. Partly because of this stigma, lenders have had difficulty in determining the market value of real estate as collateral for a prospective loan. In the absence of firm figures, lenders look to the borrower's creditworthiness. Onerous requirements for credit or collateral mean financing for the development of brownfields is essentially unavailable on a par with that for greenfield properties.

For these reasons, developers typically have overlooked brownfields in the city and turned their attention to easier projects on suburban greenfields. But

FIGURE 2.3

ANALYSIS OF BROWNFIELDS VERSUS GREENFIELDS FOR A HOUSING LOTS PROJECT

Factor	Brownfield	Greenfield
Land Use Information		
Lot Size (acres)	10 (435,600 square feet)	10 (435,600 square feet)
Dwelling Units (3.5/acre)	35	35
Floor/Area Ratio (2,800-square-foot house)	0.23	0.23
Final Lot Size (square feet)	12,450	12,450
Number of Current Owners	20	1
Development Cost Information		
Land Acquisition Cost	$108,900 ($0.25 psf)	$435,600 ($1 psf)
Site Preparation Costs		
Remediation (one-half the site at $5 psf)	$1,089,000	0
Other site preparation ($1 psf of land)	435,600	$435,600
Construction Costs		
Building hard costs	0	0
Other (shrink)	$13,100 (3%)	$4,400 (1%)
Soft Costs		
Legal	$100,000	$20,000
Other soft costs (architect, planner)	20,000	20,000
Environmental consultants	100,000	5,000
Construction loan/carrying costs	140,000	25,000
Subtotal	$2,006,600	$945,600
Developer's fee (5%)	100,300	47,300
Total Development Cost	**$2,106,900**	**$992,900**
Total Development Cost per Square Foot of Land	**$4.84**	**$2.28**
Development Sales		
Number of Lots Sold	35	35
Lot Sale Price (15% of total house)	$22,500 ($150,000)	$33,750 ($225,000)
Revenue from Sales	$787,500	$1,181,200
Security Costs during Sales	$25,000	0
Environmental Monitoring	$50,000	0
Net Income from Lot Sales	**$712,500**	**$1,181,200**
Profit and Return on Investment		
Net Income from Lot Sales	$712,500	$1,181,200
Development Costs	$2,106,900	$992,900
Net Profit (Loss)	($1,394,400)	$188,300
Equity Requirement	$1,671,300	$557,300
Return on Equity	(83.4%)	33.8%
Site Preparation Time	18 months	6 months
Future Liability	Unknown	None
Indemnification Letter from Seller?	Yes	No

brownfields with market potential are available for development under the right conditions.

Relative Costs of Developing Brownfields and Greenfields

From the perspective of development costs, brownfields, as potential real estate deals, incur low costs for site acquisition, very high costs for site preparation, and longer development periods compared with greenfield properties. Because rents in the center city are also usually lower than for comparable space in the suburbs, financial feasibility is threatened by a shortfall of revenue. For example, according to annual surveys by the Society of Industrial and Office Realtors (SIOR), the price to buy a square foot of developed industrial land averages $1.50

in center cities and $3.50 in the suburbs. The lease rate for a square foot of light industrial space averages $3.50 in the city, compared with $5.50 in the suburbs. In-line retail space in a strip or neighborhood retail center in Cleveland rents for $8.00 to $11.00 per square foot (triple net), compared with $13.00 to $15.00 in a similarly sized suburban center.[5]

Add to these numbers possible liability, and brownfield projects become too expensive. Some liability is incorporated into the cost structure of the deal, in the form of a lower loan-to-value ratio and higher debt service coverage. Other, contingent liabilities could affect recourse to the developer but may not directly affect the projected rate of return.

Three Comparisons of Development Costs For Brownfields and Greenfields

The following analysis of development costs looks at one brownfield site and one greenfield site for three different development scenarios. The size is held constant at ten acres to point out differences between brown and green sites and among three different land uses (retail, industrial, and housing, shown in Figures 2.1, 2.2, and 2.3, respectively).[6]

All three scenarios assume a well-located, ten-acre brownfield site with an identifiable, moderate, and finite environmental remediation problem, and that the correct zoning is in place or rezoning is not an issue. Cleanup costs can be estimated with reasonable certainty in advance. It is assumed that half the site is tainted and that all contaminated materials must be removed, transported to a landfill, and buried there. It is also assumed that clean fill brought in and the migration of off-site impacts amount to $5.00 per surface square foot for the contaminated portion of the site plus $100,000 for an environmental consultant. The remediation period is assumed to take 18 months. Costs of land acquisition do not include any site-assembly game playing or excessive problems to threaten the deal. No public subsidy is assumed. The developer is motivated to address the problem and therefore requires only a modest fee and rate of return.

Each figure shows the information for brownfields on the left side and that for greenfields on the right side. Each analysis covers four parts: land use information, development cost information, operating cash flow, and financing and investment. The first brief section, "land use information," contains information about the project's size, floor/area ratio, and number of owners and users.

The first few items in the second part, "development cost information," include costs for land acquisition, remediation, and other site preparation. In these examples, the total cost of acquiring land is less than expenses for cleanup. For example, some parcels can be acquired for almost no expense, while others can command top dollar. Some properties may be heavily contaminated, while others may be virtually clean. This situation does not necessarily imply negative equity on the part of the sellers. Acquisition costs are usually lower for brownfield sites than for greenfield sites. On the other hand, greenfield sites incur virtually no expense for remediation. The last few items under "development cost information" reflect hard costs for construction, soft costs for other (nonenvironmental) services, and expenses for construction financing. In all cases, a project's carrying costs (financing charges during the holding period) are higher for brownfields because of a longer development period and as a result of construction materials stolen from the site (shrink).

The third section provides a financial analysis of net operating income (NOI) or net revenue. For the retail and industrial analyses in Figures 2.1 and 2.2, market rents and vacancy must be determined. To simplify the analysis, rents were assumed to be triple net (NNN) except in a few cases where brownfields incur extra costs, such as ongoing environmental monitoring. Rents in the center city brownfields are lower and vacancy rates higher than for their greenfield counterparts. The result of this section is NOI for each project in a stable year. In Figure 2.3, which shows lots for sale for a housing project where the developer is assumed to sell "retail" lots to homebuilders, this part of the analysis pertains to net proceeds of lot sales over a one- or two-year sellout period.

The last section in Figures 2.1 and 2.2 shows the lender's appraised value, based on income. Normally, this amount reflects the present value of net cash flow before debt service and taxes. In this case, however, it has been proxied by taking NOI and dividing by a capitalization rate of 0.1. The permanent lender's loan-to-value ratio is applied next, resulting in an amount for the permanent loan and debt service at industry standard rates for each type of land use. When the debt service coverage ratios are satisfactory, the result is before-tax cash flow (BTCF). The equity requirement is the difference between actual project costs (paid for by the developer's equity) for the remediation and a construction loan, still outstanding, for built improvements "at the end of the day" upon closing the permanent loan. BTCF divided by the equity requirement is the measure used for the rate of return in this analysis. Some outstanding liability issues are also left dangling. In Figure 2.3, upon the sale of lots for single-family detached housing, the net proceeds are divided by equity required to estimate the rate of return. No permanent financing to the developer is assumed in this case.

Analysis of Brownfields versus Greenfields for a Retail Project

Figure 2.1 contains the first analysis of brownfields versus greenfields. The proposed ten-acre project is a 108,900-square-foot neighborhood shopping center anchored by a supermarket. The analysis assumes that the anchor and other tenants are regional firms with strong balance sheets and that their space has been preleased. The developer intends to develop and hold the center. The FAR is 0.25, consistent with normal patterns of retail development. Ten owners are currently involved in the brownfields deal, so the developer should plan on some extra time and legal costs to gain control of the site.

Acquisition costs of the brownfield site are cheaper than those for the greenfield site; at $2.00 per square foot, totaling nearly $900,000, they are half the cost of the greenfield site. The extra cost of site remediation ($1.1 million) is a major issue, however, particularly because it is an out-of-pocket expense. Banks are generally reluctant to finance remediation because of its effect on cash flow and the liability involved.

Hard costs, estimated at $50.00 per building square foot, are comparable except for the extra cost of construction materials and carrying costs for the construction loan. After construction is complete, the brownfield project costs a total of $9.8 million, or $90.00 per building square foot, compared with $9.1 million ($84.00 per building square foot) for the greenfield center.

The brownfield property's NOI of $800,000 compares poorly with the greenfield site, at $1.2 million per year. The different NOIs are the result of lower triple net rents ($10.00 versus $12.00 per square foot) and higher vacancy rates in the center city. Higher security and environmental monitoring costs for the brownfield site also slightly reduce NOI—market factors that are largely beyond the developer's control. These NOIs generate bank appraised values of $8 million and $11.9 million for the brownfield and greenfield properties, respectively.

Permanent financing at 10 percent for 15 years is available to both developers, but because of environmental concerns, the lender for the brownfield deal is required to meet a higher debt service coverage ratio (1.25 versus 1.10) and is allowed a lower loan-to-value ratio (0.6 versus 0.7) than for the greenfield deal. The equity requirement (total development cost minus the amount of the permanent loan) for the brownfield deal is huge: $5 million, compared with a modest $700,000 required for the greenfield deal. The rate of return for the brownfield deal is 3.4 percent, positive but well below any reasonable private sector rate of return. And the issue of who is liable for any future contamination is unresolved. It could be resolved if the developer/borrower has an indemnification letter from the seller. For the greenfield deal, the rate of return is 12.9 percent before taxes, without considering income taxes or upside potential. While not a stellar rate of return, many developers consider it acceptable in today's market. The bottom line: The brownfield deal fails, but the greenfield deal is a go.

Analysis of Brownfields versus Greenfields For an Industrial Project

The proposed ten-acre project in Figure 2.2 would contain 152,460 square feet of light industrial/office/showroom space with three different tenants. Two of the three buildings have been preleased to established companies with other locations and solid balance sheets. The developer intends to develop and hold the buildings. The FAR is 0.35, consistent with normal patterns of industrial development. Four owners are currently involved in the brownfield deal. Extra time and legal costs are expected to gain control of the site.

Acquisition costs for the brownfield site are cheaper than for the greenfield site: $0.50 per square foot for a total of $220,000 versus $1.40 per square foot or $610,000. Environmental remediation for the brownfield is a $1.1 million out-of-pocket expense.

Hard costs, except for the extra cost of construction materials and carrying costs for the construction loan, are comparable, at $32.00 per building square foot. After construction is complete, the industrial brownfield project costs a total of $7.9 million, or $52.00 per square foot, compared with $6.9 million, or $45.00 per square foot, for the greenfield industrial complex.

The industrial brownfield project's NNN market rents are lower ($4.75 versus $5.50 per square foot) and vacancy rates higher (10 percent versus 7 percent) than for the greenfield project. Higher security and environmental monitoring costs for the brownfield project also serve to slightly diminish NOI. Thus, the industrial brownfield property's NOI of $530,000 compares poorly with that for the greenfield site, at $740,000 per year. These NOIs generate bank-appraised values of $5.3 million and $7.4 million for the brownfield and greenfield properties, respectively.

Permanent financing at 9 percent for 20 years is available to both developers, but because of environmental concerns, the lender on the brownfield deal is required to meet a higher debt service coverage ratio (1.3 versus 1.15) and is allowed a lower loan-to-value ratio (0.7 versus 0.8) than for the greenfield deal. The equity requirement (total development cost minus the amount of the permanent loan) for the brownfield deal is very large: $4.3 million, compared with a modest requirement of $900,000 for the greenfield deal. The rate of return for the brownfield deal is 2.9 percent, positive but again well below any reasonable private sector rate of return. The same issue of who is liable for any future contamination is unresolved. For the greenfield deal, the rate of return is 9.7 percent before taxes, without considering income taxes or upside potential. While this rate of return is modest, some developers consider it acceptable in today's market. The bottom line: The brownfield deal fails, but the greenfield deal is a go for a specialized developer.

Analysis of Brownfields versus Greenfields For a Housing Lots Project

The proposed ten-acre project in Figure 2.3 would contain 35 single-family detached houses in the middle to upper-middle part of the price spectrum, in a medium-sized urban market. The developer is interested in developing the lots and selling them retail directly to homebuilders, which assumes no real estate sales commission is paid. The developer wants to be out of the deal in two to three years. The density is 3.5 units per acre. Twenty owners are currently involved in the brownfield deal, compared with a single owner for the greenfield deal. Extra time and legal costs are expected to gain control of the site, and the project may still end up with outparcels and scattered sites in the inner city, which would not help marketing.

This residential example is admittedly simplistic. For example, a developer might choose instead to be a merchant builder and sell the lots wholesale to contractors, but this strategy would likely make the deal appear even less affordable because revenues would be decreased. Alternatively, the developer might try a higher-density project. While some areas appear to have considerable demand for housing in the central city in this price range (many midwestern cities, such as Chicago and Cleveland, for example), development of new housing there requires substantial public subsidy. In Cleveland, for example, the local public subsidy exceeds $25,000 per new lot.[7]

In this case, acquisition costs for the brownfield site are a bargain: $0.25 per square foot, for a total of $110,000, compared with those for the greenfield site at $1.00 per square foot, or $440,000. Environmental remediation of $1.1 million for the brownfield site is an out-of-pocket expense for the developer. Site preparation costs are virtually identical, $440,000 per project. Site preparation, extra construction materials, soft costs, and carrying costs for the construction loan are not large, because the lots are sold to builders. No other hard costs are involved. After the lots are ready for marketing to builders, the brownfield housing project costs $2.1 million, or $4.80 per square foot of land, compared with $1 million, or $2.28 per square foot of land, for the greenfield development.

The brownfield project is for houses that sell for $150,000, which is much more than double surrounding residential values. Houses on the greenfield site are right in line with the market at $225,000. Assuming that 15 percent of a house's value lies in the finished lot, the sale prices for residential lots would be $22,500 for the brownfield lots and $33,750 for the greenfield lots. Higher security and environmental monitoring costs for the brownfield site also slightly diminish net proceeds. When they are all sold, the 35 lots have brought the brownfield project a total of $700,000, far less than the $1.2 million from the greenfield sites. The residential property sale disclosure required by some states could further depress the sale price and lengthen the time to sell all the lots for the brownfield site.

No permanent financing is assumed for this project. The equity requirement (total development cost minus site preparation costs of $430,000, which was assumed to be leveraged) for the brownfield deal is large: $1.7 million, compared with a modest requirement of $600,000 for the greenfield deal. Loss in dollars for the brownfield deal is very large compared with required funds, $1.4 million, and the rate of return is a negative 83 percent. The greenfield deal is a winner: a profit of $200,000 yields a leveraged rate of return of nearly 34 percent. Even if the developer pays for site improvements out of equity, the return would be about 19 percent, clearly a go. The bottom line: The brownfield deal never makes it past the back of the envelope, and the greenfield deal is going, going, gone!

Conclusions from the Cost Comparisons

Several conclusions can be drawn from these cost comparisons of brownfields and greenfields. The brownfields in these examples are assumed to be moderately contaminated, and site cleanup costs are known with reasonable certainty in advance. The following conclusions refer to markets where no subsidies are available, so readers can use these arguments to obtain subsidies from governments and to negotiate the purchase price of a brownfield property downward.

Return on Investment Is Too Low

First, and most important, the rate of return for brownfields is well below a reasonable hurdle rate of return (large negative to 3 percent), depending on what type of development is attempted. The rates of return on greenfield deals in these examples vary (10 percent to 34 percent), but all are within reach of developers in that development niche. Brownfield deals, to nobody's surprise, are a no go. Development of housing lots in inner cities, in particular, is very far from being feasible for private sector developers without substantial public subsidies. The lower rates of return for brownfields are caused not only by higher site development costs, but also by tougher financing terms and often by weaker market conditions in center cities. More debt could help boost rates of return, but private sector lenders have been unwilling to provide it. As is, adding more debt would fail the debt service coverage test and violate lenders' loan-to-value ratios that provide them with the cushion they may need if the properties must be foreclosured.

Equity Requirements for Brownfields Are Too High

Developers have had little real leverage because banks may require lower loan-to-value ratios to protect themselves from the possibility of having to own and manage stigmatized properties. Brownfield deals involve a gap between actual development costs and appraised value, which raises requirements for equity well beyond the point of reasonable expectations and also serves to drive down the rate of return on invested equity. Greenfield deals, on the other hand, involve normal leverage for the real estate industry. Further, if a developer is clever and efficient, the bank's appraised value (for the purpose of permanent financing) can exceed actual project development costs by a modest margin, just the opposite of the problems associated with the gap in financing brownfields.

The Silver Lining

These considerations present substantial opportunities for savvy real estate developers to acquire properties at low cost. These arguments can be presented to sellers as a demonstration of the property's low value and can increase profit by keeping acquisition costs low.

Liability for Past Contamination

CERCLA, the federal legislation enacting the Superfund, contained provisions to ensure strict, joint, and several liability on potentially responsible parties associated with past activities on a potentially contaminated site. Before the recent flurry of state voluntary cleanup programs, it was the law of the land, and it still applies to sites with the Superfund designation and especially to states without voluntary cleanup programs. Thus, under certain conditions (for example, material involvement), a lender who foreclosed on a real estate asset that secured a mortgage could be responsible for all costs of cleanup, especially if no other financially viable entities were to be found and the lender has deep pockets. This situation was exacerbated by the *Fleet Factors* case in the mid-1990s. This risk was so high that, for about two years, many lenders just threw the keys to defaulting borrowers to avoid potential liability for industrial or other high-risk properties, leading to reduced profits for them as assets were written off as uncollectible. The same basic situation applied to new owner capital. Anyone in the chain of title could be held responsible for "orphaned" shares of cleanup costs. Thus, even owners of last resort, municipalities taking properties through property tax foreclosures, were wary of acquiring properties with known contamination. Cleveland, for example, according to the Economic and Community Development director, took only formerly residential lots into its land bank, avoiding gas stations or properties with curb cuts or vent pipes. Milwaukee had its "do not acquire" list of brownfields that the municipality does not want, even though the properties are available.

Large private sector firms had similar concerns about liability. For example, General Electric, which owns hundreds of sites in many states through its 12 companies, has conducted environmental assessments of over 70 of these sites, many of which are needed for current or near-term business operations. Despite this surplus of assets, however, GE has not yet released any for development because of the fear of liability. The company is so large that the positive benefit of selling property could not influence the bottom line, and the potential liability from future problems is daunting, from both a public relations and a financial point of view. Further indemnification is not really a viable option, because GE is virtually in a league by itself financially. Those properties that could be considered for development would be highly polluted, and GE would likely maintain a veto over occupancy.[8] Other large firms have had similar experiences.[9]

On the surface, state exemptions from liability for lenders and new owners should defuse these problems. But if one reads the fine print, not all of these exemptions have the same effect for present or future owners. The good news is that virtually all states are headed toward "proportional liability" for past contamination rather than strict, joint, and several liability in their voluntary cleanup programs. Moreover, the federal government recently enacted legislation that provides a safe harbor for lenders' liability under CERCLA.

The potential for third-party lawsuits by off-site property owners has also been a concern. For example, location on the same block as a leaking underground storage tank can reduce residential property values by an average of 17 percent.[10] Similar effects have been observed for properties near landfills and Superfund sites. Although state insurance funds are available, so far no programs can fully protect new owners against this kind of liability, and some funds, like Michigan's UST fund, have experienced bankruptcy. Overall, the area of future liability is still a weak link in the development and financing of brownfields, mostly because it has not yet been quantified.

Market Failure and Expected Subsidies

The development of greenfield properties rather than brownfields has contributed to urban sprawl. Federal and state government policies are partially to blame. Building new suburban highways has encouraged industry to locate at the periphery of the urban area, improving the relative location of greenfield sites. Brownfields have not competed well with greenfields because the playing field has not been level.

Until now (with a few exceptions), state and federal environmental regulators have generally not paved the way for developers with a common-sense, financially feasible way to develop brownfields. The standards for risk or cleanliness have not been clear, so developers lacked the necessary information to make informed decisions involving quantifiable risks.

Stringent federal bank regulators have also discouraged lenders' participation, forcing banks to take an overly conservative posture with respect to brownfields and leading to inadequate financing for otherwise worthy projects and to credit rationing. Thus, government has been part of the problem. The good news is that a lack of capital has kept the competing supply at a minimum in many urban markets.

Local governments stand to gain if brownfields are developed. Politically, the gains are large: the appearance of taking positive measures, which could lead to reelection. But local government can also benefit from increased property, sales, and income taxes, which could more than offset investment. Developers do not consider these factors in making investment decisions, so brownfields that fail in marketing justify intervention by the government.

The Need for Governments To Be Partners

Some public funds are needed to help finance the development of brownfields, but they should be limited, leveraged, and a rational use of the government's money, priming the pump for the private sector's participation. Voluntary cleanup programs are part of this effort.

The other part is a financial role. Land subsidies are already in place in some cities. Public, subordinated debt may also be beneficial in certain instances. More important, grants, especially upfront grants for site assessment or remediation, appear to be a very good use of public funds for worthy deals. Grants would go a long way toward reducing the financing gap between actual project cost and appraised value. The following chapters set the stage for substantial development of brownfields in many urban areas.

Notes

1. Michael Porter, "The Competitive Advantage of the Inner City," *Harvard Business Review*, May/June 1995, pp. 55–72

2. Tom Bier, "Survey of Cleveland Home Sellers," Cleveland State Univ., Housing Policy Research Program, 1991.

3. U.S. Bureau of the Census, *Social and Economic Characteristics of the United States*, CP-2-1 (Washington, D.C.: U.S. Dept. of Commerce, 1990).

4. Robert A. Simons and John Brennan, "Development and Issues of Inner-City Retail Niche Markets," in *Megatrends in Retail Property*, edited by John Benjamin (Boston: Kluwer, 1996).

5. Hal Reisenfeld, Reisenfeld & Co. Leasing Agents, Cleveland, Ohio, telephone interview, September 1996.

6. See also Charles Bartsch and Elizabeth Collaton, *Coming Clean for Economic Development: A Resource Book on Environmental Cleanup and Economic Development* (Washington, D.C.: Northeast Midwest Institute, 1995), for a less comprehensive comparison of development costs for brownfields and greenfields.

7. Robert A. Simons and David Sharkey, "Jump Starting New Housing Markets: Do Public Housing Subsidies Justify the Cost?" *Housing Policy Debate*, Spring 1997, pp. 143–71.

8. Colleen Connor, environmental counsel, General Electric Corp., personal interview, November 1996.

9. Robert A. Simons, "Supply and Demand for Brownfields in Great Lakes Cities: Implications for Community Involvement," paper presented at the Brownfields '96 Conference, September 1996, Pittsburgh Pennsylvania.

10. Robert A. Simons, W. Bowen, and A. Sementelli, "The Effect of Leaking Underground Storage Tanks on Residential Sales Price." *Journal of Real Estate Research*, forthcoming.

3 The Regulatory Quagmire: Light at the End Of the Tunnel

A revolution—albeit an imperfect one—is occurring in the area of environmental law. Since at least 1980 and the passage of the Comprehensive Environmental Response, Compensation, and Liability Act, landowners and businesses have suffered nearly two decades of complex, unfair, and often incomprehensible or contradictory environmental regulations addressing the required cleanup of contaminated property. As a result, not many of these properties were developed. Recently, however, this complicated web of regulations has begun to be replaced by state voluntary cleanup programs, a more practical set of laws aimed at developing brownfields.

As of January 1997, 30 states had passed some form of legislation covering VCPs. Most of the programs were adopted during the last few years and perhaps have not yet received the recognition they deserve. This lack of recognition could be caused by many factors, including the novelty of the programs, the wide differences in the types of programs established, and many stakeholders' skepticism that they could actually use the programs to accomplish cost-effective remediation and obtain releases from liability from the government for their contaminated properties.

Certainly, a number of the VCPs will be improved over time. It is hoped that state and federal regulators will borrow the best ideas from the most comprehensive and creative programs. In fact, the federal government has indicated that it views the rise of state VCPs as a national incubator program, and it is anticipated that future federal legislation to assist the development of brownfields will be modeled on the most successful state VCPs.

This chapter briefly introduces prospective brownfield developers to the basics of two important federal environmental acts: CERCLA and the Resource Conservation and Recovery Act (RCRA). Many observers believe that these statutes have led to the creation of a large inventory of brownfield sites in the United States, primarily centered in urban areas. More important, this chapter also synthesizes and identifies the most critical elements of the existing state VCPs and highlights the best programs, based on an evaluation of these basic regulatory keys to the development of brownfields. The chapter includes two figures summarizing and ranking state VCPs enacted as of January 1, 1997.

The Federal Approach to Contaminated Properties

Although the disposal of industrial and hazardous wastes was largely unregulated for nearly a century, once it became evident that federal involvement was necessary, it came with a vengeance. Congress passed RCRA in 1976 and CERCLA in 1980. Along with legislation reauthorizing EPA's Superfund (SARA), these statutes provide an aggressive federal program for remediating contaminated sites and ensuring that waste is disposed of safely and in accordance with strict standards. The lead agency for these programs is the U.S. EPA.[1]

The Resource Conservation and Recovery Act

RCRA's primary purpose is to regulate the generation, transport, treatment, and disposal of hazardous wastes. Stringent statutory requirements mandate that persons or organizations that generate hazardous wastes identify themselves to the state and federal environmental protection agencies and ensure, through a tracking system, that their hazardous wastes end up in licensed recycling, incineration, or disposal facilities. Operators of these "treatment, storage, or disposal" sites must obtain a permit and meet hundreds of pages of onerous requirements for bonding, safety, record keeping, training, and design.

Underground Storage Tanks. RCRA's impact on the development of brownfields typically follows two avenues. The first is through its regulation of underground storage tanks (USTs) used to store gasoline and other hazardous substances; frequently, they are located on properties selling gasoline or have been put to some other commercial or industrial use. RCRA Subchapter I sets forth comprehensive requirements for liability and compliance for owners and operators of USTs if the tanks contain regulated substances (petroleum and an extensive list of other hazardous substances). Addressing problems stemming from leaking USTs may be the most commonly identified source of environmental liability associated with brownfield sites.

RCRA requires the states to designate a lead agency to regulate USTs and to enforce tightened antileak standards that are to be in place by 1998. These state agencies are required to maintain an inventory of sites where registered and leaking underground storage tanks are located. They also oversee site cleanup and issue closure letters when cleanups are completed.

Sites Posing an Imminent Hazard under RCRA. RCRA's other main component provides authority for governments or citizens to require cleanup at sites that "may present an imminent and substantial endangerment to health or the environment" or where hazardous wastes are released in violation of a permit or other requirement of RCRA. Landowners or operators and, in cases of an "imminent hazard," all other persons who contribute to the contamination are typically held responsible under RCRA for conducting the cleanup or reimbursing the state or U.S. EPA for expenses associated with cleaning up that facility.

The Comprehensive Environmental Response, Compensation, and Liability Act

In contrast to RCRA, CERCLA does not create a regulatory program but instead establishes an elaborate liability scheme for the remediation of virtually all contaminated properties. In the wake of several environmental disasters like the infamous Love Canal in Niagara Falls, New York, where hazardous substances were identified as leaking into area residents' houses, Congress hurriedly passed CERCLA in 1980. To ensure that private parties bear the burden of cleanup costs, Congress imposed expansive liability on a diverse number of parties who contributed to the hazardous substances present at a facility and on the owners of the sites, even if wastes were deposited before the passage of CERCLA. Unlike RCRA, liability for cleanup is not limited to sites containing an "imminent hazard" but extends to all sites contaminated with even modest amounts of one or more "hazardous substances." The term "hazardous substances" includes hundreds of listed substances as well as unlisted pollutants and contaminants but expressly excludes most petroleum products.

The courts, guided by Congress's desire to have those responsible for careless disposal pay for cleanup whenever possible, have interpreted CERCLA to impose full liability on covered parties, regardless of fault and regardless of the presence of other responsible parties. Thus, liability under CERCLA is often referred to as "strict, joint, and several." Since CERCLA's passage, this liability structure has been a major impediment to the development of brownfields, because liability was attached to anyone in the chain of title, including lenders if they chose to foreclose on a loan in default. At the end of 1996, Congress acted to ameliorate some of lenders' concerns by amending CERCLA to provide a "safe harbor" from federal liability, primarily to lenders, trustees, and other fiduciaries. This amendment effectively codifies a prior EPA rule covering lenders' liability that was overturned on procedural grounds by a federal court.

To make certain that the worst contaminated sites in the country are addressed first, Congress required EPA to rank the most severely contaminated sites in the nation on the National Priorities List (discussed in Chapter 4) and provided EPA with many tools to ensure their prompt cleanup. When private parties cannot be found to finance or perform these cleanups, EPA is authorized to use money from the Superfund, a revolving trust fund financed initially by a tax on chemical feedstocks and reimbursed in part with recoveries from settlements and lawsuits brought by EPA against potentially responsible parties (PRPs). Private parties may also use CERCLA's definition of expansive liability to recover cleanup costs from other responsible parties through private actions.

EPA can delegate regulatory authority for sites that have been determined not to pose a substantial threat to human health (sites not on the NPL). These sites, where no further remedial action is planned, are turned over to the states for follow-up, a trend consistent with development of voluntary cleanup programs.

Parallel State Superfund Programs

Many states have developed their own "mini-CERCLAs," which typically provide the state with authority to force potentially responsible parties to clean up contaminated sites, and establish a state fund to finance state-led cleanups when immediate action is necessary to protect the public health and environment or when solvent responsible parties cannot be located. Although state statutes often parallel CERCLA, several states have different standards for liability or provide enhanced measures to encourage voluntary cleanups. Some states have also been delegated authority under RCRA to require corrective actions and closures and to regulate USTs. State programs typically adopt federal regulations verbatim but occasionally impose more stringent requirements on the regulated community. In states with no explicit voluntary initiatives addressing brownfields, these state laws serve as the default brownfield development process.

Properties Subject to Liability for Cleanup

The broad jurisdictional reach, comprehensive provisions for liability, and uncertain and typically costly cleanup standards of RCRA, CERCLA, and parallel state programs have been blamed for impeding the development of many brownfield sites, whether they are on a formal list or not. Prospective purchasers who want cleanup costs quantified before buying a contaminated site are dismayed to learn that government entities have often been unable or unwilling to determine what constitutes an acceptable cleanup (how clean *is* clean?), even though the ultimate development of a property may serve the public interest. Familiarity with the requirements for cleanup of applicable federal and state laws is thus imperative for successful development of brownfields.

Under federal and parallel state laws, virtually any site that is even mildly contaminated can create liability for cleanup. Liability for remediating a brownfield site pursuant to these laws and regulations applies to:

1. Any place where a hazardous substance that does not occur naturally has "come to be located," if that hazardous substance is entering or threatens to enter the environment without a permit;
2. Any site where petroleum has been disposed of if the petroleum presents an "imminent and substantial endangerment to health or the environment";
3. Any UST that is leaking a hazardous substance or petroleum product; and
4. A building containing asbestos that will be subject to renovation or demolition or that contains friable asbestos posing a health hazard to workers in the building or violating state or local regulations.

The remedial purpose of CERCLA has reinforced the courts' generous reading of what constitutes a contaminated site subject to liability for cleanup. The courts have held that a site where any detectible amount of a hazardous substance has been released or where concentrations of hazardous substances exceed background levels may be the subject of a cleanup action.

Mandatory Cleanup

Added to the sweeping jurisdictional reach of what constitutes a brownfield potentially subject to statutory requirements for cleanup are the tremendous number of possible plaintiffs who can insist that the site be cleaned up. For many sites, RCRA and CERCLA provide legal mechanisms for federal, state, and local governments and private citizens to file suit for cleanup of a brownfield or for reimbursement of their own costs of cleanup. This multitiered enforcement authority makes it virtually impossible for a purchaser to obtain liability waivers from all potential plaintiffs before the transaction and can create legal uncertainties that are potentially so costly that risks of liability presented by a brownfield often outweigh the potential benefits or profits to be gained from its development.

If the federal government is the plaintiff, the U.S. EPA typically requires and oversees cleanups only at those sites on the NPL or in states without an authorized hazardous waste program where the contamination presents an "imminent hazard" or has been released in violation of RCRA. At all such sites, EPA can force a potentially responsible party to conduct the cleanup, or it can seek reimbursement for its costs of cleanup, including overhead and litigation expenses.

States may take similar actions pursuant to CERCLA or their own mini-CERCLA at sites that present an "imminent hazard" or are in violation of RCRA and involve the unpermitted release of a hazardous waste. The possibility of a state as plaintiff can create significant trepidation for developers, given the possibility that a moderately or even mildly contaminated site will rank among the state's priorities for enforcement and lead to a costly cleanup.

Finally, a private party may determine that a cleanup is necessary and force an owner or other potentially responsible party to conduct or pay for cleanup under CERCLA, RCRA, or state law. Private parties typically fall into two categories. The first is citizens who are concerned about the risks posed by a contaminated site. Under federal law, such citizens usually file only injunctive claims under RCRA for cleanup—commonly known as "citizen suits." They must prove either that the site presents an "imminent and substantial endangerment to health or the environment" or that the disposal of wastes occurred in violation of RCRA.

The second, more frequent type of private party actions is contribution suits brought by the current owner of a contaminated site or other responsible party. These plaintiffs bring suit against other responsible parties, either to receive reimbursement of their cleanup costs or, less frequently, to force responsible parties to undertake the cleanup if an "imminent hazard" exists at the site. Contribution actions have proven very popular over the past 15 years, even though most private party plaintiffs ultimately bear some of the cleanup costs themselves, including legal costs.

Other Government Agencies Involved in Brownfields

A few other agencies may be involved tangentially in the problem of brownfields. For example, the U.S. Occupational Safety and Health Administration (OSHA) sets standards for safety at job sites, including regulating workers' exposure to asbestos and other substances. Because asbestos is a carcinogen that could create potentially major health problems for exposed workers, only specified contractors may remove asbestos. OSHA can also require certain activities to take place during remediation (for example, dust control) to protect workers. But while OSHA sets and assists in the enforcement of standards of exposure, it does not generally regulate site cleanups or grant closure letters.[2] Lead in the soil and drinking water, primarily from leaded gasoline, lead pipes, and old lead-based paint, has long been recognized as having a detrimental effect on human health, especially on younger children who might ingest flakes of paint at home. EPA and HUD promulgated regulations regarding disclosure of the presence of lead in 1996 that could affect development of residential brownfield sites.[3]

In the local arena, municipal, county, or private landfills could play a role in their policies for accepting contaminated soil, and it can have a major effect on costs, because how material is classified (as, for example, construction and demolition debris, sanitary material, or hazardous waste) can mean the difference in costs for disposal of $6.00 to $200 or more per cubic yard. In some places, city or county health departments also play an important, although usually not a lead, role. Interestingly, in some countries (New Zealand and Australia, for example), environmental permits are a local matter, and municipal planning authorities exercise most of the discretion over development of brownfields.

The Rise of State Voluntary Cleanup Programs

Fortunately, a majority of states in the United States have enacted some form of legislation, generically termed voluntary cleanup programs, that encourages cleanup and development of brownfields. These recent state reforms may help to counteract the broad reach of liability and the uncertainty about expected cleanup costs that currently deter development of brownfields. The creation of state VCPs, usually administered by state environmental protection agencies, is emerging as one of the most innovative trends in environmental law. Many such programs have been designated specifically to address obstacles to developing brownfields, recognizing that public health must coexist with economic development as primary objectives. Therefore, the goals of these programs include integrating issues involving legal liability, technical requirements, and economic incentives. Many of the programs provide technical assistance from regulators, assurances about the extent of liability through covenants not to sue, and financial incentives, including tax abatement, not available through other state regulatory programs.

Voluntary programs are gaining in popularity because they allow private parties to initiate cleanup and to work cooperatively with state agencies, thus avoiding some of the costs and delay that would likely occur if the sites were subject to enforcement-driven programs. While many of these programs have developed independently of one another, it is possible to compare and contrast them based on a number of critical elements necessary to the development of brownfields:

1. The use of risk-based corrective actions to form the basis for remediation, including explicit standards for the presence of certain substances and an allowance for characteristics of the site and its users;
2. The availability of no further action or other closure letters and governmental releases from liability in the form of covenants not to sue;
3. The presence of a memorandum of understanding (MOU) between the state that established a VCP and EPA;
4. The establishment of financial inducements to encourage development of brownfields, including loans, grants, tax credits, property tax abatement, and other local initiatives;
5. The presence of state-codified exemptions for the liability of lenders; and
6. The overall depth and comprehensiveness of a particular state's VCP.

Overview of State Activity

As of January 1997, 30 state programs had been initiated.[4] Of that number, ten had initiated voluntary cleanup programs with all the necessary pieces in place to stimulate substantial development (on the order of 100 deals or more per state). A few states, notably California, Illinois, New Jersey, and Washington, have already seen a substantial number of sites clear their systems. These states, and other leaders such as Connecticut, Indiana, Massachusetts, Michigan, Minnesota, and Wisconsin, generally have the following characteristics: a well-defined system for RBCA, a closure letter (NFA or CNTS), a formal MOU with the U.S. EPA concerning any future EPA actions about the state's closure letter, specific state (not just federal) exemptions from liability for new lenders and owners, and financial inducements for site investigation and cleanup. Each state may define eligibility in its own way and may have different approaches to fees, consultants from the private sector, and public participation. Figure 3.1 contains an analysis of the state voluntary cleanup programs and their attributes, and Figure 3.2 ranks the overall environment for development of brownfields in each state for the near future.

Program Startup, Activity, and Overall Rankings

Thirty states have initiated some form of VCP, leaving 20 states and Washington, D.C., without any formal brownfield legislation. Notable laggards among the higher-growth, medium-sized states are Georgia, North Carolina (which has an informal program only), and Florida.

Of the 30 states with VCPs, the ten mentioned in the preceding subsection have all necessary legislative pieces in place. Some of their programs were initiated as far back as the early 1990s. Four of the states have more than one program, with newer programs often oriented toward urban sites requiring extensive subsidies, creative remediation, and a major governmental role upfront. All the other states have just one brownfield program in place.

Twelve more states, including Arizona, Colorado, Maine, Missouri, Ohio, Oregon, Pennsylvania, Rhode Island, Tennessee, Texas, Virginia, and West Virginia, have made substantial progress toward developing a brownfield program. These states, however, are usually missing a memorandum of understanding with EPA and part of another important piece, such as a strong CNTS. Typically, these states have brand new programs, passed in late 1995 or 1996.

A few states, including Arkansas, Delaware, Nebraska, and Vermont, have just passed partial brownfield legislation, but the pieces enacted to date are most likely insufficient to induce development and more progressive laws are needed. Maryland enacted brownfield legislation as part of its "Smart Growth" program in 1997. Three more states, Kentucky, New York, and Utah, are just developing legislation, with nothing officially on the books yet. New York, however, does have a substantial informal program.

Risk-Based Corrective Action Standards

Explicit and flexible standards are critical to keeping down the costs of remediation and to lending certainty to the finality of cleanup. The best programs include not only procedures for investigation, but also specific maximum standards for each contaminant and for combinations of contaminants after cleanup. A good RBCA should also consider specific site conditions (type of soil, groundwater, background contamination levels) and the site's end use. Progressively cleaner standards should be stated for land uses such as industrial ("dirtiest"), commercial, and residential ("cleanest") development. The most flexible stan-

FIGURE 3.1

STATUS OF STATE VOLUNTARY CLEANUP PROGRAMS AS OF JANUARY 1997

State	Depth of VCP	NFA	CNTS	MOU	RBCA	$$$	Lender Exempt	Overall
Alabama	1	1	1	1	1	1	1	1
Alaska	1	1	1	1	1	1	1	1
Arizona	3	4	1	1	3	2	3	3
Arkansas	3	1	1	1	2	1	3	2
California	5	5	4	4	5	3	3	5
Colorado	3	5	1	4	4	1	1	4
Connecticut	5	5	5	2	5	4	3	5
Delaware	3	4	4	2	1	3	1	3
District of Columbia	1	1	1	1	1	1	1	1
Florida	1	1	1	1	1	1	1	1
Georgia	1	1	1	1	1	1	1	1
Hawaii	1	1	1	1	1	1	1	1
Idaho	1	1	1	1	1	1	1	1
Illinois	4	4	4	5	4	1	4	4
Indiana	4	4	5	5	4	2	4	4
Iowa	1	1	1	1	1	1	1	1
Kansas	1	1	1	1	1	1	1	1
Kentucky	3	3	1	1	2	1	1	2
Louisiana	1	1	1	1	1	1	1	1
Maine	3	4	1	2	3	1	4	3
Maryland	2	2	1	1	2	2	2	2
Massachusetts	4	3	4	1	4	3	3	4
Michigan	5	4	5	5	5	5	4	5
Minnesota	4	4	4	5	4	4	4	4
Mississippi	1	1	1	1	1	1	1	1
Missouri	4	4	4	5	3	4	4	4
Montana	1	1	1	1	1	1	1	1
Nebraska	3	4	1	1	1	3	3	3
Nevada	1	1	1	1	1	1	1	1
New Hampshire	1	1	1	1	1	1	1	1
New Jersey	5	5	2	2	5	5	4	5
New Mexico	1	1	1	1	1	1	1	1
New York	2	3	1	1	2	3	1	2
North Carolina	1	1	1	1	1	1	1	1
North Dakota	1	1	1	1	1	1	1	1
Ohio	5	4	4	2	4	3	4	4
Oklahoma	1	1	1	1	1	1	1	1
Oregon	4	4	4	1	4	1	3	4
Pennsylvania	4	4	4	2	4	4	3	4
Rhode Island	4	3	4	3	3	3	3	4
South Carolina	1	1	1	1	1	1	1	1
South Dakota	1	1	1	1	1	1	1	1
Tennessee	4	4	5	2	3	1	4	3
Texas	4	4	5	4	3	1	4	4
Utah	2	1	1	1	1	1	2	2
Vermont	3	4	3	1	3	1	1	3
Virginia	4	4	1	1	3	4	2	3
Washington	5	5	4	1	4	1	4	4
West Virginia	4	3	1	1	3	3	3	3
Wisconsin	4	3	3	5	4	3	3	4
Wyoming	1	1	1	1	1	1	1	1

Note: 1 = nothing, 2 = pending, 3 = fair, 4 = good, 5 = excellent.

FIGURE 3.2

OVERALL EASE OF USING STATE VOLUNTARY CLEANUP PROGRAMS

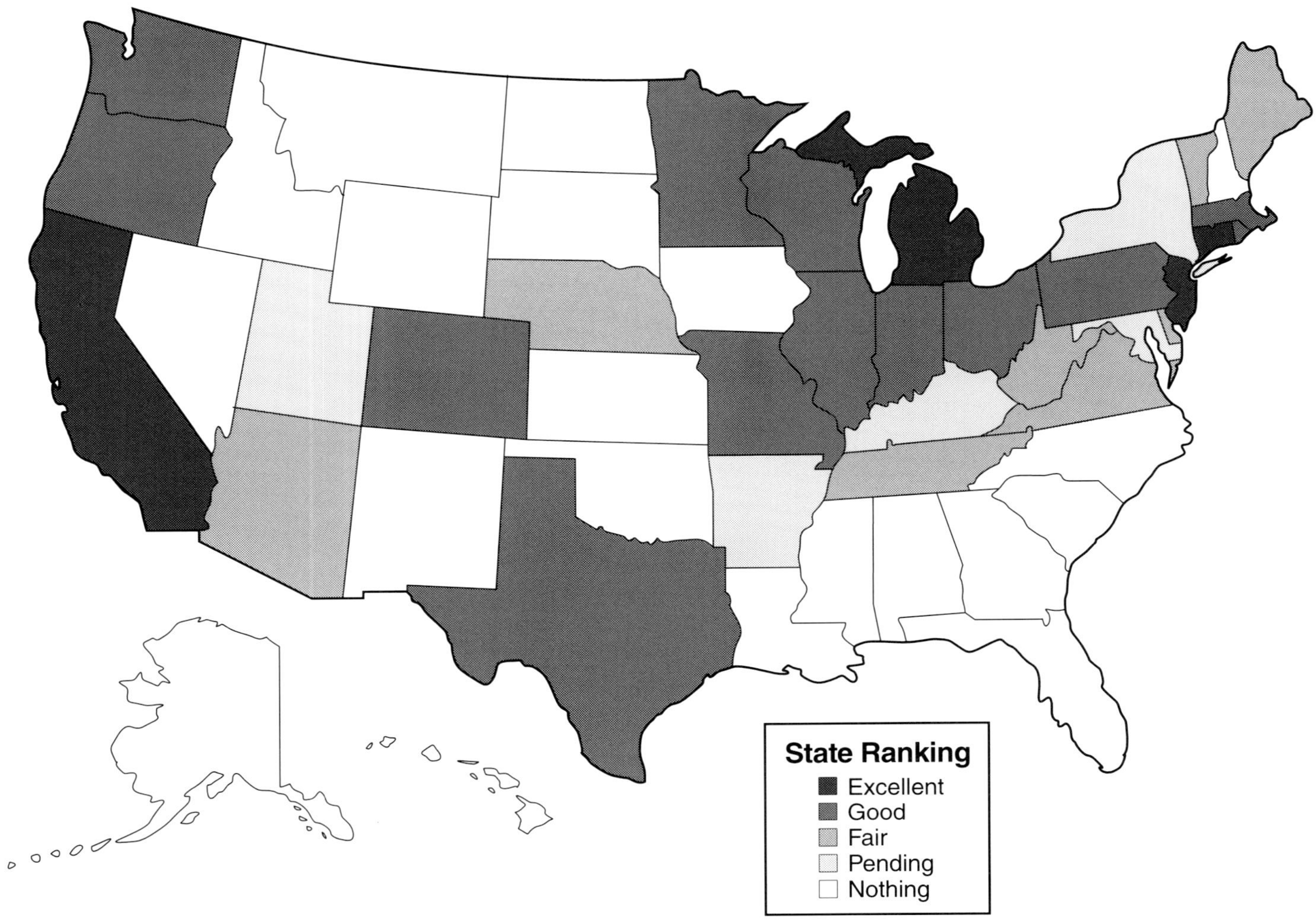

Prepared by Northern Ohio Data & Information Service, The Urban Center, Cleveland State University, Cleveland, Ohio.

dards allow for encapsulation (under parking areas, for example), the removal of contaminated hot spots, and, under certain conditions, no further remediation.

Of the 26 states with RBCAs, 14 have good or excellent standards already in place. Four more have proposed comprehensive RBCA standards but have not yet approved them. Nine have implemented standards that are less than comprehensive, and four states with programs have not addressed RBCAs. Overall, the adequacy of RBCA standards is encouraging.

State Closure Letters

Closure letters serve to notify developers and lenders that site remediation is complete. Two levels of assurance are possible: NFA and CNTS. All but two of the states with existing formal VCPs offer some form of closure letter.

NFA. The weaker form of closure letter is No Further Action, which states that no further action is required on the site *regarding the remedial action just completed*. It does not address any other contamination on site. This type of closure letter may also be called a Certificate of Completion, Letter of Completion, No Additional Action letter, or some other similar name. It is usually issued by the state agency running the VCP, but in some states (notably Ohio and Massachusetts), it may be issued by a certified private consultant.

Covenant Not to Sue. Stronger than NFA, the Covenant Not to Sue is usually issued by the lead state agency or state attorney general. The aim of the CNTS is to bind all other state agencies (and sometimes local jurisdictions within the state) not to sue in the future, subject to certain conditions, or "reopeners." These closure letters are closely related to liability exemptions (discussed later). Nearly twenty states offer a CNTS, and some NFA letters may also serve this function.

The fine print on a reopener can potentially reduce the value of a CNTS to a developer or lender. Most states allow reopeners for fraudulent activity or for a future change in land use. These provisions are reasonable because they are under the developer's control. If the site was remediated under an RBCA tied to a proposed use, a deed restriction must be recorded on the property in at least nine states. The reopener for land use is a lesser problem, because it does not come into play unless the site's use changes. It may, however, reduce the market value of the property and therefore affect the quality of the collateral for a lender.

Some reopeners, however, are more onerous. For example, seven states have CNTS reopeners for prior undiscovered contamination. A few states have reopeners for a change in the economics of remediation or for a future change in cleanup standards. A CNTS issued in these states has less value, because substantial uncertainty still exists about the closure of these sites.

Memorandum of Understanding with EPA

This important intergovernmental agreement addresses whether or not a state-issued CNTS or other closure letter is also binding on EPA. In actuality, each of the ten EPA regional offices makes its own arrangements with the administrators of the state VCPs. Generally, EPA's position has been not to issue a direct CNTS for each site managed by a state VCP, which would put the agency in the loop for each brownfield remediation project, swamp it with an excessive amount of paperwork, and delay final approval of remediation.[5] If EPA did issue these letters, then developers and lenders would want them for all sites. Therefore, EPA is never bound by a CNTS for a state VCP. In principle, it must leave itself a way back into the remediation process, through a reopener, if major undiscovered scientific evidence concerning, for example, new carcinogenic materials comes to light. Whether lenders can live with this uncertainty is the crux of the value of a CNTS.

In fact, some states (New Jersey, for example) have had a substantial number of brownfields developed without benefit of a CNTS or MOU. In the absence of these documents, however, developers and lenders require much greater knowledge about the science of remediation and other related matters. This expertise is hard to attain and time-consuming to produce, and so the lack of these terminal documents probably deters many players from entering the arena.

A negotiated Memorandum of Understanding, also sometimes called a Memorandum of Agreement (MOA), between EPA and the state that issued the CNTS allows the CNTS to stand, subject to certain narrowly defined conditions. The best language attained so far is in EPA Region 5, where EPA has signed MOUs with five of its six constituent states. The language conveys EPA's intention not to take further action unless an "imminent and substantial threat" to human health or the environment occurs or under "emergency or exceptional circumstances." A total of nine states have MOUs with a similar level of assurance from EPA. A few states will proactively argue the need for EPA to issue a "comfort letter" or prospective purchaser agreement with its EPA region on behalf of a successful remediator. Seven states are currently attempting to negotiate MOUs with their respective EPA regional offices. The remaining ten states are not actively pursuing an MOU or have not gotten to that stage yet. In any case, a successful remediator can always try to get a nonbinding comfort letter from EPA regarding its site.

The two states with a primarily private VCP, Massachusetts and Ohio, have not yet obtained an MOU from EPA, although both are attempting to do so. In the past, EPA has expressed some concern about quality control, the privately issued NFA letters, and the use of consultants for auditing in these programs. In other words, the lack of direct state control over their VCPs may be a problem for EPA. These states and others that use a private VCP may need to generate some statistics on quality control before EPA provides an MOU. In this regard, a recent audit of VCP consultants in Massachusetts showed that 81 to 92 percent performed adequately, but whether this percentage is sufficient for EPA remains to be seen. These issues, as well as challenges to industry standards of cleanliness, may affect the timing of the Ohio VCP's ability to obtain an MOU from EPA Region 5.

Exemptions from Liability

These exemptions are a key component of each state's VCP. Exemptions are usually available for potential lenders, new owners, and, in rare cases, from lawsuits by third parties. In many states, exemptions from liability are *not* available for potentially responsible parties or other known polluters. In others, PRPs who volunteer to remediate their properties can obtain the exemption.

Lenders have traditionally avoided new lending on brownfields because of concerns about strict, joint, and several liability under CERCLA. This fear was further exacerbated by the infamous *Fleet Factors* case, which caused substantial anxiety in the lending community and helped dry up debt capital for contaminated properties for several years in the early to mid-1990s. As recently as a few years ago, lenders with nonperforming loans were declining to foreclose, letting the defaulted borrowers keep the keys to the building and then writing off the loan as uncollectible. In states with no explicit exemptions from liability for lenders, CERCLA or a state equivalent defining lenders' liability generally applies.

The first line of defense for lenders is the quality of the NFA or CNTS issued to the owner or operator. In addition, the fewer reopeners and the better the MOU, the more likely that the owner or operator will be able to manage any future expense of cleaning up contamination while maintaining debt service coverage ratios at a comfortable level and avoiding foreclosure.

In the event of default on a mortgage and foreclosure by the lender, the new exemptions for lenders' liability under state laws should be a big help. The key, however, is language in the statutes concerning the management activities lenders may undertake after foreclosure. If the restrictions on lenders' behavior after foreclosure are too tight, lenders may not be able to minimize their losses (that is, maximize the sale price of foreclosed property) and still maintain the exemption from liability. Thus, the value of real estate (as collateral) going into the loan may be discounted, requiring more equity from the developer (and reducing the rate of return) or killing the deal. Eleven states have explicit exemptions from liability for lenders that should protect them if they have to foreclose on the property, manage it during a reasonably brief period for the purpose of selling the property, and do not cause additional contamination to be released. Another 11 states have such exemptions, but the definition of "management" during foreclosure appears to be somewhat narrow. A few others are just starting programs and developing exemptions. In all states, the new federal provisions protecting lenders and trustees from liability apply.

Also popular are exemptions from liability for new owners, tied to the quality of the NFA or CNTS and whether or not an MOU is in place. Thirteen states have very substantial exemptions available for new owners who successfully complete remediation. With very few exceptions, those owners who cannot complete remediation do not get an exemption from liability. Seven more states have exemptions for new owners, but sellers and future owners may not be covered to the same extent. And several states are still developing better liability exemptions for new owners.

Exemptions from third-party liability are rare. Only three states (California, Maine, and Virginia) provide any explicit protection from third-party suits. Sometimes liability protection is only partial. In Virginia, for example, one type of third party, neighboring property owners, must allow testing for contamination on their property or forgo the right to sue for losses resulting from environmental damage. Further, a number of state UST insurance funds may pay for remediation costs associated with off-site contamination caused by a UST, which is a form of third-party claim.

Financial Inducements

Such incentives may include direct loans and grants for site assessment and site remediation or indirect incentives, such as tax credits or tax abatement. These programs are not widely used—but they should be. Eight states fund site assessment, site remediation, or both, and a significant number of sites in those states have been involved in VCPs. Sometimes, as in California, Connecticut, and New Jersey, funding for remediation is reserved for the neediest blighted urban sites.

A few states offer tax incentives directly to end users to cover remediation expenses after cleanup. For instance, Ohio grants a 10 percent investment tax credit applicable to corporate income tax. Eight other states have some, but lower-caliber, financial assistance. Several of these programs involve low-interest loans for remediation. Considering developers' preference for grants (because brownfields usually cannot support more debt), loans may not be that helpful, especially for new developments. A few states also grant breaks on local property taxes for brownfields. Because enterprise zones, which provide similar tax abatement programs for property taxes, already exist all over the country, however, the relative impact of these programs for brownfields is likely to be small. Three states also have proposals for financial incentives pending. And as of July 1, 1997, several federal legislative proposals containing tax credits and other financial incentives for brownfields had been introduced.

Participants in VCPs

VCPs are oriented toward owners with no potential responsibility for the contamination. Except in one case (with a pending proposal), potentially responsible parties with enforcement actions pending are generally excluded from VCPs. Three states explicitly exclude sites on the NPL, and seven states exclude sites with USTs from VCPs (although ten states allow sites with USTs to participate if they contain other forms of contamination). West Virginia's program is for abandoned sites only, and one of Connecticut's two VCPs as well as Kentucky's pending plan are targeted at government agencies only.

Other Issues

Most states charge participants in a VCP for the cost of managing or reviewing the cleanup. Nineteen of the 30 states with VCPs have an explicit fee structure, with the typical cost being $2,000 to $5,000 at the beginning plus another few thousand during the process. Some states charge $50.00 to $80.00 per hour for staff time to review documents and guide remediation.

Five states have explicit guidelines for public participation, which typically allow public comments on remediation early in the process. This provision typically allows neighboring stakeholders, if any, to be brought in early, rather than appearing as a surprise later in the process, which could delay remediation and development of the project.

Summary of Federal and State Brownfield Development Programs

CERCLA and RCRA, with their EPA-led mandatory enforcement procedures for cleaning up contaminated properties, are still in effect for remediation of sites determined to be a substantial health risk. Many brownfield sites, however, are not contaminated enough to fall under their mandates. Until recently, however, no program was available that did not have strict provisions for liability, and as a result, few contaminated properties were developed.

In response, 30 states have enacted voluntary cleanup programs to facilitate the development of brownfields. A few states have several programs, some targeting urban sites requiring large subsidies and others facilitating development on well-located, lightly contaminated properties that can be readily developed without substantial public dollars. Such programs will help substantially in future brownfield development.

Notes

1. See Wendy Wagner, "Overview of Federal and State Law Governing Brownfield Cleanups," in *Brownfields: A Comprehensive Guide to Redeveloping Contaminated Property,* edited by Todd Davis and Kevin Margolis (Cleveland: Hemisphere Corp., 1997), for a comprehensive discussion of federal legislation.

2. See William G. Miller, *Managing Environmental Mandates for Multifamily Housing: 1997. A Compendium of Federal Laws and Regulations,* Chapter 2 (Washington, D.C.: ULI–the Urban Land Institute, 1996), for a succinct summary of laws and regulations concerning asbestos, especially friable asbestos.

3. Ibid., pp. 68–81.

4. See Davis and Margolis, *Brownfields: A Comprehensive Guide,* for a comprehensive and detailed analysis of individual state programs and how to use them; and Charles Bartsch and Elizabeth Collaton, *Coming Clean for Economic Development: A Resource Book on Environmental Cleanup and Economic Development* (Washington, D.C.: Northeast Midwest Institute, 1995), for a good background of the state programs and contacts from the perspective of economic development.

5. William Haubold, EPA Region 5, personal interview, July 1996.

4 How Many Brownfields Are Out There?

Just how many brownfield sites are in the United States? While several different groups have estimated parts of the problem, few have been able to sort out the big picture and come up with credible estimates of the number of sites, their total acreage, and the percent of urban area in brownfields. Part of the problem can be explained by a reluctance on the part of some to accumulate lists of brownfields because of the fear of stigmatizing contaminated properties. A second reason is the lack of a clear definition of "brownfield." And a third is the lack of data on unlisted sites and the extent to which sites overlap other listed sources. This chapter addresses these issues and provides an estimate of the number and acreage of brownfield sites by type and as a percentage of the land in selected large cities in the United States.

Two main categories of brownfields have been designated. The first includes those on publicly known lists of contaminated sites. The environmental consulting firm ERIIS, an industry leader in providing data for environmental Phase I studies, supplied a list of these sites for this study. According to its database, 384,400 different listed sites in the United States are perceived to be or are actually contaminated. Just under three-quarters of that number are confirmed sites of leaking underground storage tanks. Some of these sites, especially LUSTs, are of interest to real estate developers.

The second category of brownfields includes those underused sites that are not on any lists but, based on their past use, are perceived to be contaminated. A partial estimate of these sites was generated through the use of economic base analysis of structural changes in the economies of 31 large U.S. cities since 1963 (see Appendix A for the methodology used in this analysis). This approach recognizes that brownfields are the outcome of years of decline in manufacturing, trade, transportation, and residential uses of our center cities. Based on a moderately restrictive definition of brownfield, the analysis estimates that 75,000 formerly industrial brownfield sites are located in these central cities, on 93,000 acres, or about 5 percent of the land area in these communities. Another 20,000 acres are present in these same cities in the form of residential brownfields. A substantial number of these properties could be of interest to brownfield developers.

Depending on the overlap between the listed brownfields and the other vacant and contaminated sites, and assuming little development of these sites has occurred, the total number of nonresidential brownfield sites in the United States is at least 500,000, excluding commercial brownfields (where former retail gas stations are likely to include a high proportion of LUSTs) and residential brownfields.

Attempts to Look at the Big Picture

The most widely cited source of information about number of brownfield sites is a study by the U.S. General Accounting Office, which estimates that 130,000 to 450,000 contaminated commercial and industrial sites are located in this country.[1] A recent study by the U.S. Conference of Mayors reveals 43,000 acres of brownfields in 16,000 sites among the 39 cities surveyed, including about 20 larger cities with populations over 100,000.[2] The definition of brownfields varies somewhat among cities, however, and the study did not attempt to generalize findings to other cities.

EPA is required to keep lists of known contaminated sites under CERCLA. A total of 40,000 sites are or have been on one of these National Priorities Lists, which have now been divided into three groups. EPA also compiles information about leaking underground storage tanks: about 275,000 sites were known as of late 1994. Various other lists, including RCRA and toxic release inventories, enumerate sites, but the toxic release inventory includes many properties that probably cannot be considered brownfields because they are economically viable in their current use. A majority of states also keep their own lists of the most contaminated sites (e.g., hazardous wastes), but many of these lists overlap with federal lists. This overlap among sites may occur when sites have multiple sources of contamination, or lists are compiled at different times or by different agencies.

A Reluctance to Compile Lists

No comprehensive accounting exists of brownfield sites in the United States. Most states and cities do not keep their own comprehensive brownfield registries, and although EPA has its lists, it has been "delisting" some sites on the Comprehensive Environmental Response, Compensation, and Liability Information System (CERCLIS) list (discussed in more detail later). Moreover, the United States is not alone in its reluctance to inventory brownfield sites. In the U.K. in 1991, legislation was passed and a concerted movement begun to establish a national registry of brownfields. It met with so much resistance that it was withdrawn in 1993.[3] Part of the problem was that property owners did not want a list. British property owners are used to a much higher degree of confidentiality than in the United States, as property records in the U.K. are private, unlike property records in the United States, where they are a matter of public record.[4]

One important reason making lists unavailable is that U.S. property owners do not want their property stigmatized by being on a list or have the property reduced in value.[5] This approach appears shortsighted, however. With disclosure laws regarding transfers of property on the books in many states and with banks requiring environmental assessments before lending money, can anyone except an unsuspecting buyer really be fooled? Moreover, being on a brownfield list is not always bad, as the registries may qualify certain properties for participation in brownfield programs.

While virtually all states do track which U.S. Superfund and UST sites are present within their borders, most states do not attempt to keep comprehensive lists of brownfields, including other unlisted sites or other sites where environmental investigations have occurred but the level of contamination is well below that required to be on the NPL. A few states—California, Connecticut, and New Jersey, for example—have state registries of contaminated property.

Municipal developers and politicians often do not like lists for several reasons. First, it takes time, staff, and money to compile and keep the lists, diverting these resources from other more fiscally pressing uses, such as police protection. Moreover, publicizing the number of brownfields may make the city look worse than other areas that do not have the information, thus creating bad public relations and clarifying the extent of the problem so local groups can insist progress be measured against a clear baseline. Having an inventory and following through with subsidies based on a predetermined formula would depoliticize the allocation of funds for development, reducing the discretionary power of local politicians.

Some cities, on the other hand, *keep* lists of brownfields for their own reasons. Milwaukee has a "do not acquire" list so it can avoid walking into an environmental time bomb when considering whether or not to take title to parcels whose property taxes are delinquent. Minneapolis uses lists for strategic property acquisitions. Bridgeport, Connecticut, has a list to facilitate development, compiled in part using EPA pilot funds.

Defining Brownfields

In the most general sense, a brownfield is a previously used piece of land that cannot be redeveloped because of a combination of factors, including possible environmental contamination from prior use or uses and perhaps market forces. The opposite of a brownfield is a greenfield: a piece of virgin land, usually in the suburbs. Most established urban center cities have no greenfields, as all available parcels have been developed at least once, many more frequently.

EPA Region V defines brownfields as "abandoned, idled, or underused industrial and commercial sites where expansion or redevelopment is complicated by real or perceived contamination."[6] This definition has three important aspects—the limitation of past land uses to industrial and commercial, the implication of demand (underused with respect to development) as a condition, and perceived rather than actual contamination—but each aspect has its own limitations.

This widely accepted definition includes only uses that were formerly industrial and commercial, potentially limiting the number of brownfield sites by ignoring other intensive institutional uses, such as landfills and rural contamination from agriculture or military bases, and excluding formerly residential uses. What of residential brownfields? During the past several decades, some cities experienced a massive loss of housing units, and the fiscally stressed cities handled many units under duress after they fell into dangerous disrepair. Often the units were demolished quickly, the debris bulldozed into the units' basements, and the debris covered up with one or two feet of fill dirt. These "vacant" lots may have garbage, asbestos, and lead jumbled up with bricks and mortar. Some are privately held; others are publicly owned through foreclosures because of delinquent property taxes. The costs of cleaning up such properties are likely to be lower than for industrial sites, but they still reflect a substantial increase in development costs. Moreover, asbestos and lead in residential brownfields may increase costs tremendously and present marketing problems, especially in the Northeast and Midwest, where lead in center cities is a constant problem.

The definition is unclear with respect to demand: Does "industrial and commercial" refer to past or future use of the property? As a result of functional obsolescence and changes in the relative attractiveness of locations, no guarantee exists that because a property used to be industrial, its best use is still industrial. A more specific question is whether the property can be prevented from attaining its highest and best use. It is possible that for many contaminated sites, the highest and best use is a vacant lot. Are they brownfields? What of properties held speculatively for future development? Is payment or nonpayment of property taxes an indicator of brownfield status?

Third, using perceived rather than actual contamination as sufficient to qualify a site as a brownfield broadens the number of potential brownfields. Virginia Aveni, an early leader in issues involving brownfields, broadens the definition of brownfields further to include adjacent property that is perceived to have off-site effects.[7]

This book employs a broad, urban definition of brownfields oriented toward realistic development. It includes all sites in EPA's definition above and excludes rural and agricultural sites. All sites on EPA's list or other public lists are potential targets, although, as a practical matter, the most polluted sites (those on EPA's Superfund list) are not likely candidates for development because they are excessively expensive to clean, are primarily public health problems, and fall into CERCLA's strict, joint, and several liability arena if developed. Also included on the lists but probably precluded from development in the near future are active legal landfill sites, which are presumably at their highest and best use in the public interest. With the recent downsizing of the military, some surplus military bases have become available for development. Because of their size and (in the case of naval bases) location, some bases present excellent opportunities for development. The strategies discussed in this book also pertain to these properties, although federal ownership and unexploded ammunition present additional complexities that are not explicitly covered. Formerly residential lots that are held in the private sector and are current on their property taxes are also excluded, but lots taken in tax foreclosures are considered residential brownfields.

Listed Brownfield Sites

Numerous lists exist of brownfield sites in the United States. Environmental Resources Information and Imaging Services (ERIIS), an environmental consulting firm in Herndon, Virginia, has compiled a current list of all sites on the various government lists, by location (see Figure 4.1). Unless otherwise stated, the listed sites described in the following paragraphs are based on data for October 1996 (usually for March through September 1996, depending on when a particular list was updated).

EPA's National Database

EPA keeps track of contaminated land using a three-tiered database: 1) the National Priorities List; 2) the list of CERCLIS sites; and 3) the list of sites where no additional remedial action is planned.

The Superfund Sites. The highest tier in the database is the National Priorities List, which lists the 1,318 known most polluted sites in the United States. Three mechanisms are available for placing sites on the NPL. The primary mechanism is EPA's hazard ranking system (HRS), the second allows states or territories to designate one top-priority site regardless of score, and the third allows a site to be listed if it meets all three of the following requirements:

- The Agency for Toxic Substances and Disease Registry (ATSDR) of the U.S. Public Health Service has issued a health advisory that recommends removing people from the site;
- EPA determines the site poses a significant threat to public health; and
- EPA anticipates it will be more cost-effective to use its remedial authority (available only at NPL sites) than to use its emergency removal authority to respond to the site.

Realistically, very few, if any, of the sites are viable for development in the near term, because they entail perceived public health problems, excessive cleanup costs, long time frames, and strict, joint, and several liability to anyone in the chain of title. Cleanup of a few select sites has been completed, however.

CERCLIS Sites. The middle tier of EPA's database contains the 11,298 sites on the CERCLIS list. These sites are possible future candidates for the Superfund list, and EPA currently supervises them. Their status on the CERCLIS is transitional, however, depending on what investigations reveal. They could be upgraded to a Superfund site or delisted to the lower category, NFRAP (no further remedial action planned). Until they are further classified, most CERCLIS sites are of little interest to developers.

To determine whether a site goes from CERCLIS to NPL or to NFRAP, EPA evaluates each site individually based on certain criteria. EPA's hazardous ranking system, formally in place since 1990, evaluates the observed actual or potential negative effects of the contamination on groundwater, surface water, air, and soil. Typically, regional EPA offices conduct a preliminary site assessment and, if necessary, sampling to determine whether the sites could achieve a score of 28.5, the threshold that would make it a candidate for the NPL. If the site scores below 28.5, it is put on the NFRAP list and referred to the state environmental agency for further attention.[8]

NFRAP Sites. EPA generally removes sites from the CERCLIS list when there is no further interest in them as potential Superfund sites. These delisted sites, where no further remedial action is planned, numbered 27,183 as of October 1996. They are typically larger sites (the average size in Cuyahoga County, Ohio, for example, was eight acres), and their owners often have deep pockets. Some of these sites could be of interest to real estate developers.

RCRA Treatment, Storage, and Disposal Sites

The Resource Conservation and Recovery Act created the RCRIS tracking system, which tracks hazardous materials from cradle to grave. Businesses with sites in this system are in the Toxic Release Inventory. Many of the sites are not brownfields; they only use or handle regulated materials, and some may have released regulated materials into the air or water. A portion of them, however, the RCRA Treatment, Storage, and Disposal (TSD) sites, receive materials from other RCRA sites. Basically, these 3,665 sites are hazardous waste landfills. Of the TSD properties, 1,788 sites were undergoing some type of corrective action in mid-1996. These properties present few opportunities for development

Leaking Underground Storage Tanks

Part of RCRA requires states to track and improve the management of underground storage tanks. Virtually every state now keeps a list of these sites, which include many operating businesses with nonleaking USTs. In addition to the list of sites with tanks, another (overlapping) list contains only sites known to have leaked. EPA estimates that 275,000 confirmed leaking tank sites existed at the end of 1994, with new leaks discovered at the rate of 5,000 per month.[9] ERIS's estimate, culled from state lists with double counts from multiple leaks at any given site deleted, consistently puts the number of LUST sites in the United States at over 275,800.

This total figure does not include "orphan tank sites," that is, those sites where the regulating agency is unaware of the location or nature of an old tank system. According to a recent study in Cleveland, the estimate for orphan sites is higher in the center city, where at

FIGURE 4.1

Total Listed Brownfield Sites in the United States

	NPL	CERCLA	NFRAP	State HWS[a]	RCRA TSD	LUST	SWF[b]	Total	Final
Alabama	13	170	504	170	80	2,340	199	3,476	3,300
Alaska	8	87	230	2,883	17			3,225	2,900
Arizona	11	193	694	1,364	37	3,837	323	6,459	5,475
Arkansas	13	117	265	117	26	749	144	1,431	1,300
California	93	566	2,497	26,916	268	30,091	3,994	64,425	38,400
Colorado	17	208	359	208	50	3,291	1,666	5,799	5,600
Connecticut	16	457	280	710	197	2,594	145	4,399	3,700
Delaware	20	35	222	286	13	1,904	22	2,502	2,250
District of Columbia	0	26	8	26	1	644	0	705	675
Florida	59	485	508	600	111	20,679	1,755	24,197	23,600
Georgia	14	466	489	323	104	4,689	136	6,221	5,900
Hawaii	4	77	116	77	11	664	21	970	900
Idaho	9	51	187	51	13	969	268	1,548	1,500
Illinois	38	414	1,226	707	211	13,096	3,430	19,122	18,400
Indiana	35	279	1,316	91	126	4,056	160	6,063	5,975
Iowa	20	213	400	69	71	5,144	260	6,177	6,100
Kansas	14	226	322	226	49	7,619	145	8,601	8,375
Kentucky	20	137	452	137	143		940	1,829	1,700
Louisiana	14	122	490	670	66	1,621	34	3,017	2,400
Maine	11	107	91	418	10	5,547	4,648	10,832	10,625
Maryland	15	116	320	477	41	1,641	74	2,684	2,250
Massachusetts	31	629	347	10,348	36	11,226	1,097	23,714	19,625
Michigan	80	218	1,447	2,897	76	7,546	1,941	14,205	13,425
Minnesota	43	74	383	204	38	8,621	454	9,817	9,650
Mississippi	3	95	329	723	37	1,575	127	2,889	2,475
Missouri	23	415	877	52	99	960	103	2,529	2,475
Montana	8	61	172	279	11	2,462	492	3,485	3,250
Nebraska	9	170	231	170	45	6,028	53	6,706	6,525
Nevada	1	35	168	35	11	965	187	1,402	1,375
New Hampshire	17	129	51	129	4	1,548	40	1,918	1,800
New Jersey	114	745	863	6,749	136	11,605	1,203	21,415	19,800
New Mexico	11	97	268	97	22	2,034	263	2,792	2,700
New York	87	691	941	1,672	105	7,012	2,033	12,541	11,575
North Carolina	23	215	579	1,060	104	8,055	382	10,418	9,475
North Dakota	2	17	55	17	9	547		647	625
Ohio	35	312	988	1,448	199	19,739	169	22,890	21,775
Oklahoma	10	150	635	30	37	2,523	751	4,136	4,100
Oregon	12	101	313	1,724	22	7,682	346	10,200	9,700
Pennsylvania	109	504	2,375	104	238	7,322	1,108	11,760	11,650
Rhode Island	12	191	103	191	4	894	30	1,425	1,225
South Carolina	26	181	325	585	82	4,237	443	5,879	5,375
South Dakota	3	32	76	32	2		270	415	375
Tennessee	17	320	526	165	82		628	1,738	1,650
Texas	30	408	2,176	47	324	19,154	6,202	28,341	28,300
Utah	12	152	142	152	35	2,221	414	3,128	2,975
Vermont	8	78	61	1,044	8		221	1,420	1,300
Virginia	25	227	415	227	96	10,358	661	12,009	11,775
Washington	58	167	531	1,473	62	4,299	325	6,915	6,225
West Virginia	6	151	403	151	35	1,214	22	1,982	1,825
Wisconsin	41	138	312	142	44	13,468	4,106	18,251	18,125
Wyoming	3	43	115	43	17	1,349	391	1,961	1,925
Total	1,303	11,298	27,183	68,516	3,665	275,819	42,826	430,610	384,400

[a]HWS = Hazardous waste site.
[b]SWF = Solid waste facilities.

least one-third of actual sites were not known to the Ohio UST agency. In the suburbs, on the other hand, an estimated 90 percent of the sites were known.[10] Because of their corner locations, many LUST sites present excellent opportunities for development.

Solid Waste Facilities

Every state contains landfills for solid waste, hazardous waste, and construction and demolition debris. They also have resource-recovery sites for recycling. These facilities are typically fairly large, over ten acres. They are not generally on the RCRA TSD list, however, and some would be of interest to developers.

State Hazardous Waste Sites

According to ERIIS, individual states also keep lists of hazardous waste sites. In most cases, these sites are the same as the federal ones and those kept by the state UST regulator, and most sites are listed in more than one place. California's CALSITES list, for example, includes almost 27,000 sites. When sites listed elsewhere are excluded (those without an EPA identification number), however, all states combined have an estimated 22,300 on their state lists, or just over 5 percent of the national total.

Total Listed Sites in the United States

As shown on Figure 4.1, the total number of brownfield sites in the United States from the various lists exceeds 430,000. Some sites are counted twice, however, so ERIIS cross-checks all federal lists using a system called FINDS. This methodology results in a total estimate of 384,400 sites in the United States as of September/October 1996. These estimates are believed to be accurate to the nearest 25 sites for each state.

Figure 4.2 shows the breakdown of listed sites in the United States, by type and source. The pie chart is dominated by LUSTs, at 64 percent of all listed sites. State hazardous waste sites (16 percent) and solid waste facilities (10 percent) are also fairly common. The EPA group, including NPL, CERCLIS, NFRAP, and RCRA treatment, storage, and disposal sites, combined is about 10 percent.

Figure 4.3 shows the concentration of these listed sites, expressed in sites per 100 square miles, for each state. The states where brownfields are concentrated most intensely are smaller states in the Northeast; Massachusetts, Rhode Island, New Jersey, and Delaware all had more than 100 sites per 100 square miles. Connecticut, Ohio, Illinois, Wisconsin, Florida, and Maine had the next highest concentration, 30 to 100 sites per 100 square miles, and California, Texas, Kansas, Iowa, and all the Great

FIGURE 4.2

LISTED BROWNFIELDS IN THE UNITED STATES, BY TYPE (1996)

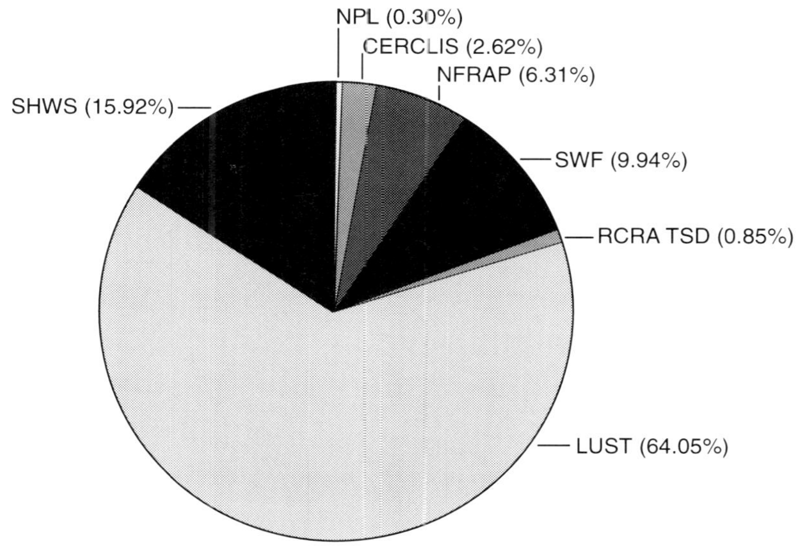

Source: ERIIS database.

Lake and Atlantic Coast states not already mentioned were in the third highest group, 10 to 30 listed sites per 100 square miles. The rest of the South and Midwest, the Rocky Mountain states, and the western states had the lowest concentration of listed sites per 100 acres, under ten.

Unlisted Brownfield Sites

No complete information exists on unlisted brownfields. Such sites may include industrial, commercial, and formerly residential lots that contain functionally obsolete, underused, or abandoned buildings. (Chapter 5 provides some information about some unlisted sites for a few midwestern cities.) The most recent study of unlisted sites was conducted by the U.S. Conference of Mayors in January 1996. The 39 cities that participated in the survey contained a total of 16,000 sites on 43,000 acres. These figures do not necessarily exclude listed sites, however, and each community defines "brownfields" its own way.

Because many brownfields are the result of sustained economic decline, another way to estimate brownfield sites and acreage is to examine structural changes in the economy, especially in the manufacturing, trade, and transportation sectors. Many center cities (especially older U.S. cities in the Rustbelt and Northeast) hit

FIGURE 4.3

CONCENTRATION OF LISTED BROWNFIELD SITES BY STATE

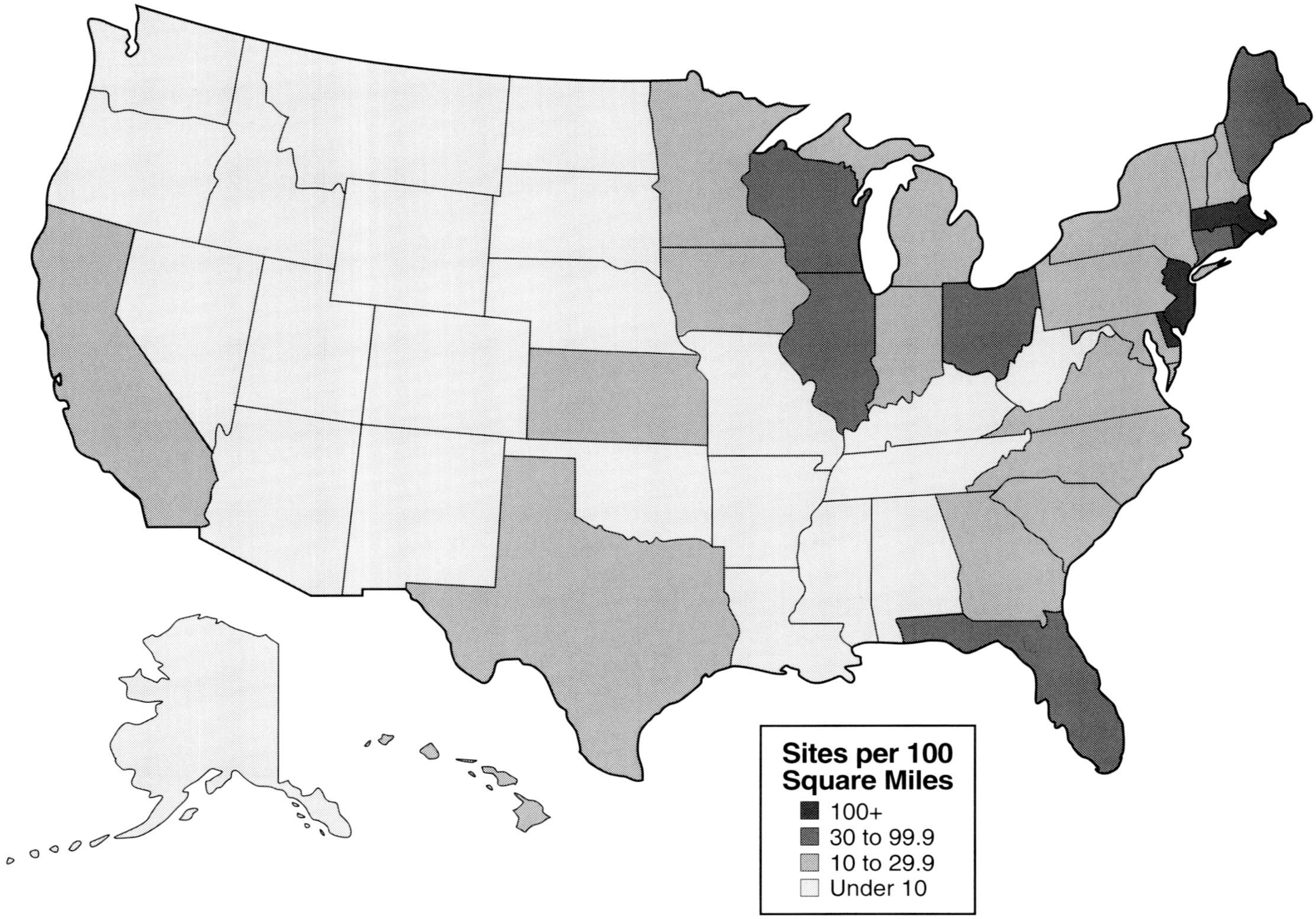

Source: Northern Ohio Data & Information Service, The Urban Center, Cleveland State University.

their economic peaks in the 1960s, and since then, many jobs have left the center cities and migrated to the suburbs or overseas. Some plants relocated, others closed down, and many of them were not recycled and became brownfields. Thus, a net loss in industrial, commercial, transportation, and trade firms and employment should be closely correlated with the generation of brownfields. Such properties may contain residue from industrial processes or other activities, which may be expensive to remediate. More important in the broad definition of brownfield, they are perceived to possibly be contaminated as a result of their past use or uses, because most would be considered a "hit" on a Phase I environmental analysis, which considers historical use of the property.

Over the same time, many commercial businesses in center cities also suffered. Shopping malls opened in the suburbs, and households moved out to follow jobs there. Urban streetcars were removed. In many cities, a large number of retail establishments became functionally obsolete properties and closed, and their buildings were abandoned. These sites are commercial brownfields. Fortunately, unless the stores were gas stations, auto service shops, dry cleaners, or other concerns that used chemicals, or were used as midnight dumps, these sites contain mostly construction and demolition debris, which is relatively inexpensive to dispose of unless asbestos and/or lead is mingled with it. These properties are also brownfields and, because no record exists of

FIGURE 4.4

ESTIMATES OF BROWNFIELD SITES AND ACREAGE IN 31 U.S. CITIES AS OF 1994

City	Industrial Brownfield Sites	Industrial and Commercial Brownfields (Acres)	City Land in Nonresidential Brownfields (Percent)	Residential Brownfields (Acres)	City Land in All Types of Brownfields (Acres)	Total City Land in Brownfields (Percent)
New York, NY	31,501	32,985	17	-6,294	26,691	13
Chicago, IL	9,098	13,377	9	5,058	18,435	13
Detroit, MI	4,939	6,849	8	6,737	13,587	15
Philadelphia, PA	4,527	6,961	8	486	7,447	9
Cleveland, OH	2,626	4,067	8	2,656	6,723	14
St. Louis, MO	2,098	2,853	7	2,587	5,440	14
Pittsburgh, PA	1,365	1,992	6	2,476	4,469	12
Newark, NJ	1,968	2,138	14	1,385	3,523	23
Boston, MA	3,310	3,532	11	-145	3,387	11
Buffalo, NY	1,417	1,833	7	988	2,821	11
Baltimore, MD	1,411	2,467	5	-34	2,432	5
Milwaukee, WI	1,194	1,912	3	259	2,171	4
New Orleans, LA	943	1,205	1	834	2,039	2
Minneapolis, MN	1,030	1,422	4	489	1,912	5
Rochester, NY	633	1,004	4	695	1,699	7
Norfolk, VA	17	-220	-1	1,857	1,637	5
Cincinnati, OH	866	984	2	491	1,475	3
Providence, RI	737	994	8	348	1,342	11
Washington, DC	833	1,194	3	96	1,289	3
Louisville, KY	293	439	1	760	1,199	3
Oakland, CA	368	529	1	305	833	2
Akron, OH	147	563	1	263	827	2
Atlanta, GA	975	365	0	439	805	1
New Haven, CT	474	741	6	8	749	6
Jersey City, NJ	440	386	4	237	623	6
Bridgeport, CT	312	641	6	-107	534	5
Seattle, WA	132	536	1	-312	224	0
San Francisco, CA	894	726	2	-517	210	1
Birmingham, AL	-91	-195	0	403	208	0
St. Paul, MN	210	320	1	-170	151	0
Kansas City, MO	897	957	0	-1,009	-52	0
Total	75,564	93,557	5	21,269	114,830	6

contamination, are unlikely to be on any lists (although some will overlap with LUST sites). In Milwaukee, for example, about one-third of the sites on the city's "do not acquire" list are former gas stations.[11] Because the perception of contamination may be substantial and actual cleanup costs modest, this type of property could represent a good opportunity for development if it is in a good location.

Finally, unlisted sites may include abandoned houses and buildings, and dump sites containing construction and demolition debris mixed with garbage. Residential sites may have asbestos, lead, or some other unknown lightly contaminated material. Vacant residential lots constitute lightly contaminated "minibrownfields." In the rush to the suburbs from center cities during the past few decades, many owners abandoned their houses. Fiscally stressed cities such as Cleveland and Detroit were overwhelmed by the number of boarded-up houses, and, rather than giving them a proper burial, they demolished houses wholesale, bulldozed the debris from the house into the basement or cistern, and covered it up with a foot or two of fill dirt. By now, some of these properties are publicly owned. Some cities, including St. Louis and Cleveland, have land banks to recycle these lots in the future, and New York City has a similar program for acquiring sites delinquent on property taxes. The number of residential brownfields is generated by the net loss of housing units that were demolished and abandoned after manufacturing jobs left the center cities since the 1960s. If well located, these lightly contaminated brownfields may represent an excellent opportunity to develop property at a cost moderately higher than developing greenfields (see Appendix A for the methodology used in the economic base analysis).

Results of the Economic Base Analysis

Figure 4.4 shows the results of the economic base analysis. It lists U.S. cities in declining order of total acreage in brownfields estimated by this "shrinkage" methodology. The leaders are New York, Chicago, and Detroit, each with over 10,000 total acres of brownfields. The next tier of cities, where total acreage in brownfields (including vacant residential sites) is at least 2,800 and brownfields as a percentage of overall city land area account for about 10 percent or more, includes Philadelphia, Cleveland, St. Louis, Pittsburgh, Newark, Boston, and Buffalo.

The total number of industrial brownfield sites (derived from contraction in the manufacturing, transportation, and wholesale trade sectors) for the 31 cities is just over 75,500. If smaller commercial brownfields are included, then the estimate of nonresidential brownfields in these cities is 93,500 acres. Over half this total can be found in the top three cities, and over three-fourths of the total is found in the top ten cities on the list. These nonresidential brownfields represent a large portion of the total city land area in the Northeast: New York, Newark, and Boston all have an estimated 10 percent or more of their overall land area in nonresidential brownfields, followed closely by Chicago, Detroit, Philadelphia, and Cleveland. In sum, about 5 percent of urban land in the 31 cites is estimated to be nonresidential brownfields.

Brownfields from the loss of housing, while less contaminated than industrial brownfields, are also an important part of the picture. Chicago, Detroit, Cleveland, St. Louis, and Pittsburgh all lost a large portion of their housing stock, much of it in single-family detached units, during the study period. These losses amount to at least 2,000 acres of residential brownfields in each of these communities. While housing losses were also great in other cities (Philadelphia, for example), much of this loss may have been conversions from single-family units to duplexes or the loss of more space-efficient multifamily structures or townhouses. Some cities, such as New York and to a lesser degree San Francisco and Boston, have had a substantial *increase* in housing stock, which consumed some of the available land left by the shrinking industrial base. Others, like Kansas City, annexed their way to an expansion of housing.

Overall, the 31 communities contain an estimated 114,800 acres of brownfields, an average of 6 percent of their land area. The city with the heaviest concentration of brownfields is Newark, at 23 percent, followed by the same other large cities mentioned earlier. Providence is also high on the list, with 11 percent in brownfields. Cities in the Northeast and Great Lakes area have the largest percentages of their land area in brownfields, but cities from all over the country are represented on the list.

Notes

1. U.S. General Accounting Office, "Community Development: Reuse of Urban Industrial Sites," GAO\RCED 95-172 (Washington, D.C.: Author, June 1995).

2. U.S. Conference of Mayors, "Impact of Brownfields on U.S. Cities: A 39-City Survey" (Washington, D.C.: Author, 1996).

3. In New Zealand and parts of Australia, in contrast, national and state legislation holds communities responsible for the completeness of local property records, including all available public information about past land use, remediation systems remaining on site, and past discharges of contaminated materials.

4. Paul Syms, "Effects of Industrial Contamination on Residential Land Values in the United Kingdom," *Land Contamination and Reclamation* 4(1), 1996, pp. 49–56.

5. Peter Patchin, "Contaminated Properties: Stigma Revisited," *Appraisal Journal,* April 1991, pp. 167–72.

6. William Haubold, EPA Region 5, personal interview, July 1996.

7. Virginia Aveni, Cuyahoga County Planning Commission, personal interview, April 1996.

8. Bob Myers, EPA Superfund Office, telephone interview, December 1996.

9. *Adair et al.* v. *Chevron et al.* 1995, pp. 32–33.

10. Robert A. Simons, "BUSTR Orphan Tank Analysis in Cuyahoga County (Cleveland: Cleveland State College of Urban Affairs, The Urban Center, 1995).

11. Rudy Salcedo, City of Milwaukee, telephone interview, July 1996.

5 The Supply of and Demand for Brownfields

One of the main questions with regard to brownfields is whether or not demand exists for them. Cleaning up the most severely contaminated sites is motivated by environmental rules, yet most brownfields are not "highly contaminated." This reality suggests that communities need to strengthen the rationale for economic development (cleanup and reuse) of less contaminated sites. An important component of such economic development strategies is generating market demand. The imbalance between the modest demand for the large supply of urban brownfields in inner cities and the resulting implications of this oversupply of contaminated land are the focus of this chapter.

The study presented in this chapter was prepared by the Great Lakes Environmental Finance Center (GLEFC) at Cleveland State University. Its central purpose is to determine the balance between demand for and supply of brownfields in four major Great Lakes cities: Chicago, Cleveland, Detroit, and Milwaukee. The results are designed to demonstrate the need for public and private players to account for market realities in approaching the cleanup and development of brownfields, and they can be helpful in devising future strategies to increase the demand for "clean" brownfields in these cities. These strategies are crucial in increasing the impetus for future cleanup and development.

The demand for nonresidential acreage in the four central cities over the next five years is generally small: 100 to 500 acres, depending on the market. Overall demand, including housing, ranges from 200 to 1,600 acres. The research shows a 10- to 160-year supply of brownfields relative to market demand, depending on how narrowly brownfields are defined and how effective recent state legislation could be in promoting demand. The most plausible estimate, assuming state initiatives are reasonably successful, is a 30- to 50-year supply of brownfields. This analysis has important implications for future land use planning, allocation of scarce resources for cleaning up brownfields, policies guiding real estate developers, local and national public and private capital markets, and regulatory actions by state and federal environmental agencies. Based on the inability to obtain accurate and detailed data from local authorities on contaminated lands within their jurisdictions, most cities appear to be operating in a vacuum when it comes to gathering market information about brownfields.

Overview of Methodology

This study examines both the demand for real estate and the supply of brownfields in the four urban markets. GLEFC's definition of brownfields includes both perceived and actual contamination that prevents development supporting the highest and best use of properties, and attracting future market demand. It excludes Superfund sites regarded as major health hazards rather than opportunities for economic development. The methodology is summarized in the following paragraphs and fully explained in Appendix B.

Demand for Brownfields

Real estate projections for industrial, office, and housing development for each metropolitan area studied focused on the ability of the central city to compete for the space within the metropolitan real estate market. Space needs, calculated in square feet, were converted to acres, which can thus be compared with the supply of brownfields as apples to apples. Demand was projected for the five years from 1996 to 2001 for all four metropolitan areas. Two demand scenarios were prepared for each market. The first assumes a continuation of recent past trends in absorption. The second, "best-case" scenario assumes the center city's share is increased substantially (as much as two to three times, depending on the market) based on better site and area marketing, more proactive planning for site assembly, and further improvements in state and federal legislation and regulations concerning brownfields.

The Supply of Brownfields

As noted previously, information on the supply of brownfields is very difficult to acquire. Communities tend to avoid land registers and locally generated lists of sites because of their perceived stigma, making compiling an inventory difficult. Although federal lists such as CERCLIS and NFRAP are available and states maintain data on LUSTs (whose sites are numerous but typically small and often already developed), listed brownfields reflect only a small portion of total brownfield sites. In Cleveland, for example, only an estimated 5 percent of the total number of sites and 30 percent of overall acreage are listed.

Thus, the vast majority of brownfield sites are unlisted. An accounting of known sites by postal zip code was developed for Cleveland and the rest of Cuyahoga County to analyze the supply by small geographic area. The following analysis details the relationship between supply of and demand for brownfields. Estimates of total brownfield acreage have been prepared for the center cities of Detroit and Milwaukee to enable broad policy analysis.

Summary of Real Estate Demand In the Four Study Cities

A summary of demand for land in the center cities through 2001, by type, is presented in Figure 5.1. Demand for industrial and office land, assuming a continuation of past trends, indicates a need of 170 to 300 acres of land in each city through 2001. If residential demand is included, overall demand for land in the center cities ranges from 220 acres in Detroit to 1,650 acres in Chicago, with Cleveland (430 acres) and Milwaukee (505 acres) in the middle.

Assuming an optimistic scenario with successful state voluntary cleanup programs, demand for nonresidential land in the center cities would increase to 330 to 510 acres. If residential demand is included, overall demand for land in the center cities ranges from 490 acres in Detroit to 4,770 acres in Chicago, with Cleveland and Milwaukee (both with 940 acres) again in the middle.

The Supply of Brownfields

Determining the supply of brownfields is a vital component in analyzing demand and developing effective public policy for dealing with these properties. The determination directly affects state and local fiscal policy, and local land use planning. Although managers in the larger cities (in economic development or planning, for example) have expended substantial efforts on assembling and financing brownfield sites, they also appear hesitant to publicly acknowledge the magnitude of the problem. Thus, citywide planning for the development of brownfields becomes very difficult. And according to British brownfield development expert Paul Syms, these attitudes are consistent with those in the U.K., where an ambitious brownfield registry was envisioned in the

FIGURE 5.1

FIVE-YEAR DEMAND FOR CENTER-CITY REAL ESTATE BY TYPE (ACRES)

	Industrial, Manufacturing	Industrial, Distribution	Industrial, Office/ High Tech	Industrial Total	Office	Industrial + Office Subtotal	Housing	Total
CONTINUED-TRENDS SCENARIO								
Chicago	–18	238	4	224	5	229	1,420	1,649
Cleveland	85	173	22	280	4	284	146	430
Detroit	111	69	–5	175	–3	172	46	218
Milwaukee	–	–	–	281	21	302	204	506
Total				960	27	987	1,816	2,803
OPTIMISTIC SCENARIO								
Chicago	195	267	45	507	5	512	4,260	4,772
Cleveland	151	307	40	498	4	502	438	940
Detroit	111	185	61	357	–3	354	138	492
Milwaukee	–	–	–	307	21	328	612	940
Total				1,669	27	1,696	5,448	7,144

Note: Chicago's, Cleveland's, and Detroit's analyses are comparable and complete. Milwaukee has no data on industrial submarkets.

FIGURE 5.2

ESTIMATED ACREAGE OF BROWNFIELD SITES IN FOUR GREAT LAKES CITIES

	NFRAP and CERCLIS	LUST	Nonresidential Unlisted	Subtotal Nonresidential	Residential, Publicly Owned	Grand Total
Chicago	1,712	131	3,373	5,216	–	–
Cleveland	1,072	36	1,664	2,772	793	3,565
Detroit	664	177	4,573	5,414	–	–
Milwaukee	352	87	156*	595	–	–

*Milwaukee's do-not-acquire list uses a more conservative definition of brownfields, and it excludes residential sites and industrial and commercial parcels where property taxes are current.

Source: GLEFC, Levin College of Urban Affairs, Cleveland State University.

FIGURE 5.3

REAL ESTATE DEMAND RATIOS FOR BROWNFIELD SUPPLY IN FOUR GREAT LAKES CITIES (ACRES)

	Supply of Nonresidential Brownfields (Acres)	Five-Year Demand for Industrial/Office Development: Past Trends	Five-Year Demand for Industrial/Office Development: Optimistic	Supply/Demand Ratio (Years of Supply): Past Trends	Supply/Demand Ratio (Years of Supply): Optimistic
Chicago	5,200	229	512	22.8 (113.9)	10.2 (50.9)
Cleveland	2,772	284	502	9.7 (48.8)	5.5 (27.6)
Detroit	5,400	172	354	31.5 (157.4)	15.3 (76.5)
Milwaukee	595	302	328	2.0 (9.9)	1.8 (9.1)

Note: These estimates, especially for Chicago and Detroit, are approximate and likely to be modified with more detailed analysis. Milwaukee's definition of brownfields is more focused than that for the other communities.

Source: GLEFC, Levin College of Urban Affairs, Cleveland State University.

early 1990s, then abandoned within several years because of widespread local resistance.

This analysis of the acreage of brownfields in the four study cities used the best available data, including the NFRAP and CERCLIS lists, state lists of LUST sites, GLEFC's estimate of unlisted brownfield sites in Cleveland and Cuyahoga County, and other published surveys. It provides a rough estimate of the total supply of brownfields in the four Great Lakes center cities. The main policy measure used was the ratio of industrial demand to supply, expressed in years. These estimates, from mid-1996, are not comprehensive, and they may not reflect the opinions of local administrators. Documentation of brownfields in Chicago, Cleveland, Detroit, and Milwaukee is included as Appendix C.

Summary of Brownfield Supply in Central Cities

Figure 5.2 shows the total estimated brownfield acreage for the four communities. The estimates for Chicago and Detroit are preliminary, based on a compilation of outside sources. The figures for Cleveland are internally consistent and more accurate. Milwaukee's numbers are internally consistent but more narrowly defined.

The estimated acreage of nonresidential brownfield sites (all publicly listed sites plus formerly industrial and commercial sites) in the four center cities ranges from 600 in Milwaukee to more than 5,000 acres in Detroit and Chicago. Cleveland's nonresidential brownfield acreage is an estimated 2,800. These estimates should be considered the minimum for each city for 1995 and 1996.

Analysis of Brownfield Supply and Demand

This section includes a general assessment of the balance between supply and demand for the four center cities as well as a more detailed analysis for Cleveland to provide insights into the dynamics of location and market. Of primary concern is the magnitude of the oversupply of brownfields.

Nonresidential Demand across Center Cities

Figure 5.3 compares the supply of nonresidential brownfields with demand for nonresidential (industrial and office) center-city real estate for both past trends and optimistic (best-case) scenarios. This supply/demand ratio reveals the extent of oversupply. For example, the ratio of the nonresidential brownfield acreage in Detroit to the five-year demand for industrial and office land in the city, assuming past trends for market demand continue, is 31.5, implying that it would take more than 150 years to absorb all the brownfields in the city of Detroit. The optimistic demand scenario, which assumes a strengthening of the demand for brownfields based on new state laws, still leaves a 77-year supply of brownfields. Neither of these figures addresses residential brownfields converted to industrial use or the location or suitability of the sites (in terms of minimum viable acreage) with respect to demand. Overall, in the four cities, the oversupply is very large, from over 150 years for Detroit to ten years in Milwaukee using its narrow definition of brownfields. The central findings indicate a minimum of 30 to 70 years of supply of nonresidential brownfields relative to market demand, under the best case.

A Closer Look at Cleveland

This subsection extends the supply/demand analysis of nonresidential brownfields to address the overall demand for brownfields, including housing, competition between suburbs and center cities, and the location of businesses. The analysis, using a geographic information system with a small-area database in the greater Cleveland market, compares the demand for various types of real estate in the center city (in acres) with the supply of brownfields in Cuyahoga County.[1] If it is assumed that recent past trends in demand continue, a total of 284 acres of nonresidential land would be needed. An additional 146 acres of mostly smaller, scattered sites would be needed for housing in the city. Thus, housing represents an important component of the demand for brownfields. The best overall case would more than double this demand, to a total of 940 acres over five years.

The overall supply of brownfields is much greater than overall demand. The center city appears to have a 42-year overall supply of brownfields, assuming a continuation of past trends of overall market demand, including that for housing. The best-case scenario, implying a successful Ohio voluntary cleanup program, would reduce this amount to just under a 20-year supply of brownfields. This outcome is more favorable than the analysis of nonresidential supply and demand in the city, which had almost a 50-year supply of brownfields available to meet demand (a 28-year supply under the best case).

Geographic Breakdown of the Supply of Brownfields

Where are the pockets with many brownfields and little demand? Figure 5.4 answers this question, showing Cuyahoga County sites with historically low demand superimposed over zip code areas. The larger circles (supply) in areas of lightly shaded demand demonstrate the oversupply of brownfield sites with respect to demand. Slices of the pies reflect listed and unlisted sites by acreage. The larger pies, dominated by dark slices representing unlisted sites, superimposed on a light background where industrial demand is low indicate that some locales within the county have a very substantial imbalance between supply and demand. Outlying suburban areas appear to have very few brownfields and plenty of market demand, shown by the darker background shading.

FIGURE 5.4

SUPPLY OF AND DEMAND FOR BROWNFIELDS IN CUYAHOGA COUNTY, OHIO (ACRES, 1996 TO 2000)

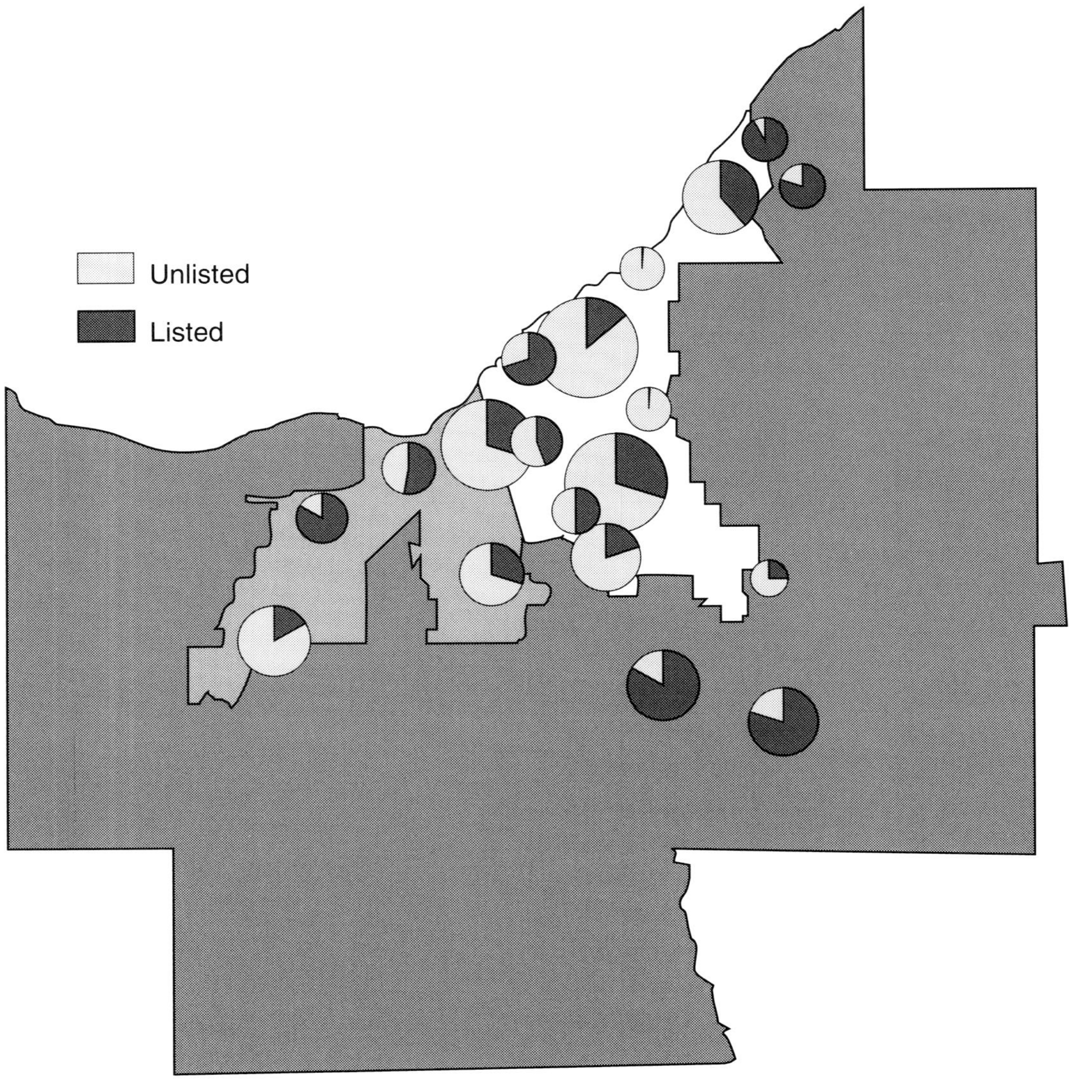

Prepared by Northern Ohio Data & Information Service, The Urban Center, Cleveland State University, Cleveland, Ohio, July 1997.
Source: Great Lakes Environmental Finance Center database.

For industrial development, proximity to highways is a critical factor. This factor is also shown in Figure 5.4, which identifies highway routes and 3/4-mile buffers around interchanges. While the brownfield properties on the city's near west side have competitive access to highways, large pockets on the city's east side are less convenient and may not be competitive for development. If one considers only those properties larger than one acre as suitable for demand, the implication is that several thousand acres, mostly in smaller parcels with less desirable locations that are perceived to be more expensive to develop, may not be needed for development in our lifetimes. Only 60 percent of unlisted vacant formerly industrial or commercial land and 40 percent of unlisted brownfield sites in the county are already larger than one acre. In general, the industrial land market is strongest for sites of at least three acres. Thus, unless these smaller properties are combined with other properties (whether brownfields or not) and made suitable for industrial development through site assembly, they would not be competitive for industrial development.

Implications of the Imbalanced Market for Real Estate Developers

The main implication of this imbalance for brownfield development and finance is the recognition that the supply of brownfields is vastly larger than demand for real estate. Most large markets probably contain many decades' worth of brownfields compared with demand for nonresidential real estate. Once cities realize that the supply of brownfields substantially exceeds demand for them, some would likely attempt to rectify the situation. Cities with foresight could plan for this surplus land to be held in an interim yet beneficial use, such as parkland or a golf course, requiring federal and state environmental regulators to enact standards of cleanliness for the uses.

Real estate investors, lenders, and developers are interested primarily in economically viable brownfield sites. The presence of surplus brownfields is likely to depress the price of potentially viable sites and make their development more difficult, because greater public subsidies would be required to bring the net cost of development closer to that for uncontaminated sites. Further, because the demand for such sites is relatively low and the supply so large, the market for brownfields is a buyers' market. Owners of potentially viable industrial brownfields would probably prefer to have nonviable sites designated as other land uses, as it could only have a positive effect on the sale price of developed industrial lots after remediation. Developers who plan to acquire a brownfield should make certain it is large enough to satisfy an end user and is in a superior location. Savvy communities would likely beef up funding for infrastructure in promising areas to stimulate industrial demand and rezone properties to their highest and best use to stabilize land prices.

A poorly located brownfield may be suited only for parkland or as a buffer between low-density land uses. It may be hard to determine how to properly and cheaply remediate these less desirable brownfields, because state cleanup programs are focused on economic development. Cities will likely end up owning much of the excess supply.

Note

1. Robert A. Simons and D. Iannone, "Brownfields: Supply and Demand," *Urban Land*, June 1997, pp. 36–38+.

6 The Brownfield Developer's Toolbox

This chapter provides brownfield developers with a toolbox of potential real estate, environmental remediation, and financing strategies for successfully moving a brownfield into the marketplace. The tools are grouped by type, roughly along chronological lines in the development process for a brownfield. These steps are as follows:

1. Determining whether the brownfield can be excluded from the development project;
2. Becoming familiar with the state VCP and range of possible outcomes;
3. Preparing a preliminary financing plan and a financing plan for remediation;
4. Controlling the site;
5. Remediating the site;
6. Obtaining permanent financing;
7. Monitoring contamination and preserving the CNTS.

Because development of the tools is evolving, new tools must be explored frequently.

This chapter identifies the categories of tools and potential tools in each category for every major step in the brownfield development process. The figures in this chapter provide more information about each tool, including the tool's name, a description, and potential problems and opportunities. The categories of tools include government regulatory issues in the VCP, remediation finance (grants, loans, equity, and tax incentives), real estate strategies, remediation strategies, permanent financing (grants, loans, equity, and tax incentives), loan guarantees and insurance, and government-led coordination.

This chapter assumes that a developer wants to undertake a real estate deal and that the need to acquire a piece of property is part of site assembly or a previously purchased brownfield is under consideration for development. If the site has already been acquired, skip the section "controlling the site." If the brownfield in question has little value or is most highly valued as open space, this chapter may not be directly applicable. Moreover, the chapter does not address brownfields owned by government agencies. A private developer in negotiation with a government agency will find this chapter useful, however.

Determining Whether the Brownfield Can Be Excluded

The first step in the development process for any real estate deal, including one with a brownfield, is to undertake a market analysis for the property. Can end users be identified? If the property has some value in economic development, this chapter can help the developer identify tools needed during development. Given the nature of the concept for the property, what is needed for development? Can the project be completed without developing the brownfield? Could the brownfield be left as an outparcel?

To proceed:

1. Conduct a market study.
2. Prepare a site plan with and without the brownfield.
3. Determine whether the concept excluding the brownfield is feasible.

Becoming Familiar with the State VCP

Familiarize yourself with the applicable state laws covering VCPs (see Chapter 3 for details). Fewer options exist in situations involving strict, joint, and several liability; Superfund, NPL, or CERCLIS sites; or states without VCPs, because there is probably little or no exemption from liability for new owners. After becoming familiar with the situation, you must decide whether to remediate the brownfield or abandon the project.

If the project is located in a state with a voluntary cleanup program, then consider the local cleanup process. Is it flexible and accessible? Ask an environmental consultant whether working through risk-based corrective action would keep costs down. If remediation is successful, can you obtain a CNTS? Does the state have a memorandum of understanding with EPA and other agencies keeping the state from future actions, assuming no change in proposed land use? Are other situations onerous?

If a brownfield contains a LUST, what will remediation be like? Are the state's actions regarding USTs coordinated with the state EPA? Is a voluntary cleanup program feasible, or would it be easier to just get an NFA letter from the agency that regulates USTs? Are there multiple sources of contamination? If so, would cleanup require one regulatory process or two? Find out which agency will take the lead in guiding the project through remediation and approval.

Prepare a preliminary estimate for the cost of remediation (within the nearest 20 to 30 percent, based on experience with similar properties). Then conduct a back-of-the-envelope financial analysis. From the standpoint of the real estate deal, is remediation so expensive that the deal would not turn a profit (or at least minimize losses)? If you still have doubts about the project, it might be advisable to get permission from the owner or seller to test the soil during preparation of the preliminary estimate to ascertain the extent of contamination, if it has not already been tested. Knowing the proposed use of the parcel (down to the exact location of parking lots, which can double as caps to contain contamination) and local guidelines for RBCA is advisable.

Will a local lender advance funds for development of the brownfield? Under the most likely scenario for remediation, will bankers accept assurances resulting from the VCP? Have they done so in the past? Does the state exempt lenders from liability? What recourse will they require?

Once these issues have been sorted out, determine whether the project is still feasible. Infeasibility could be based on diminished market demand, high costs of remediation, bad timing and missing a window of opportunity, lenders' uncertainty, or general confusion about brownfields in states where legislation covering VCPs is not sufficiently developed to be useful.

Figure 6.1 includes brief definitions of the most important terminology used in discussing voluntary cleanup programs.

Preparing Preliminary And Remediation Financing Plans

After you decide to proceed with the project, the next step is to look for some funding for site assessment and remediation. In most cases, the developer funds site assessment, and in relatively rare cases where land values are high, the developer may be able to finance remediation without public assistance. Outside money comes in the form of grants, loans, and tax incentives. Michigan and New Jersey, for example, award grants for site investigation and remediation. Some cities provide funds, especially through community development block grants or empowerment zones. Remember that if you accept government money for site assessment, any findings in-

FIGURE 6.1

VOLUNTARY CLEANUP PROGRAMS

Tools	Description	Comments
Coordinated hierarchy of state agencies Formal site assessment/cleanup procedures	Established hierarchy for state agencies with one designated the lead agency. Definition of who qualifies as a volunteer. Clear process for undertaking the VCP. Clear steps leading to the closure document.	First step is a baseline analysis of condition, which may involve an agreement between the volunteer and the state about which documents will be reviewed. Next step is remedial action plan, followed by approval of remediation just completed. Clear procedures in case of multiple contaminants.
No further action letter	Closure letter for projects that have complied with voluntary cleanup procedures. Sometimes called a "certificate of completion."	Pertains only to issuing agency and the remediation just completed. Does not cover other actions by other regulatory bodies.
Covenant not to sue	A stronger version of an NFA letter, in which the issuing agency promises that no further legal action or remediation is needed once the approved remediation plan for a site has been satisfactorily completed.	CNTS typically binds other state and often local agencies, but state CNTS does not guarantee that other federal agencies (such as EPA) will not pursue future action.
State memo of understanding regarding CNTS with U.S. EPA	Allows state CNTS to bind U.S. EPA's future actions, subject to certain conditions.	If no MOU is in place, EPA may offer "comfort letters" to interested parties instead. EPA Region 5 has the most advanced MOU arrangement with its states.
Liability exemption for lenders	Such an exemption may indicate that lenders who do not participate in management of the property, who complete a baseline assessment, and who do not generate contamination are not liable for existing contamination.	Definition of management and length of time lenders can hold a property after foreclosure and before sale of the asset varies.
Liability exemption for new owners	CNTS is a form of protection in this case. Usually volunteers not responsible for prior contamination are exempt after a successful cleanup.	Typically, CNTS can be transferred to new owners.
Risk-based corrective action Explicit standards for cleanliness	Defines standards of cleanliness based on land use for different proposed uses. Typically, standards are different for residential, commercial, industrial, or parking uses. Also considers local soil conditions and groundwater, and specifies concentration thresholds for each toxic substance.	Standards less than pristine theoretically increase chance of public health problems. Combined effects of multiple toxic compounds are underspecified. Deed restrictions limiting future changes in land use may be required. Understanding of health risks may change over time. RBCA first introduced as a formal risk-based system established under RCRA for underground storage tanks.
Reopener for change in land use and other reasons	Certain use-based cleanup restrictions may be placed on the CNTS if land use in the future is changed. If land use is changed, the assurance found in the CNTS may be "reopened" or invalidated. Fraud is also grounds to reopen the covenant.	Other reopeners may include a change in cleanup technology, economics, or cleanup standards.
Groundwater containment zone	The quality of groundwater in a designated (urban) area cannot reasonably be improved to the quality of drinking water. Criteria for contaminated groundwater in a brownfield may allow for containment rather than improvement of the quality.	Under development or recently enacted in several states. May take the form of urban designated zones, groundwater nonattainment zones, and/or groundwater risk management. Potentially could reduce costs and risks of cleaning up brownfields but could have major impacts on local land use and infrastructure planning.

FIGURE 6.2

REMEDIATION FINANCE

Tools	Description	Comments
State site assessment and site remediation grants	State grants for site assessment and remediation.	A few states, including Michigan and New Jersey, have substantial funds available for grants, and similar programs are pending in several other states. Funds may come from the environmental agency or through the economic development agency for industrial or commercial projects.
State remediation loans	Loans at below-market interest rates for cleaning up brownfield sites in VCPs.	Several states have loan pools for remediation of brownfields, and more programs are pending.
Industrial development bonds	Industrial development bonds, which are tax-exempt municipal revenue bonds, are used for site assessment and cleanup.	Limited supply of public funds because bond pools are linked to specific projects. IDBs, limited to $50.00 per capita or $200 million statewide, compete with other public uses for funds.
Community development block grants	CDBGs are municipal discretionary funds available for investigation and remediation of sites.	CDBGs are generally for center cities. They must create opportunities for low- to moderate-income persons and reduce slums and blight.
Local/in-kind grants	Municipal land banks can donate lightly contaminated residential lots with clear titles to brownfield projects for site assembly.	Several U.S. cities have banked land; many communities own properties obtained through foreclosures resulting from delinquent property taxes.
Local public loan pools	Loans available for community development, often at the discretion of the municipal community development department.	Not available in all cities or use is restricted.
Empowerment zone loans	Section 108 loan funds can be used for acquisition and development of brownfields. Below-market interest rates.	Available only in federally designated empowerment zones. Can also be used in conjunction with CDBG funds to reduce project debt, forgive principal.
Philanthropic foundations	Some development-oriented foundations provide seed money for feasibility analyses and gap financing.	NPI in Cleveland has started strategic site assembly for industrial brownfields.
Tax increment financing	A local government initiative, TIF provides a stream of funds to pay back bonds used to fund cleanup costs. Additional property taxes are dedicated to repayment of municipal revenue bonds.	Used for brownfields in Connecticut. Cannot be used with property tax abatement.
Brownfield development company	Brownfield development companies can use their expertise to manage cleanup and finance it for shared ownership in your property.	Out-of-town brownfield development companies generally are interested only in large properties at a deep discount.
Equity	Developer provides cash or bond in transaction.	The old-fashioned way.
Equity in a REIT	Brownfield investment funds. As a result of deep discounts in acquiring potentially stigmatized properties, investment opportunities may be available.	Further research is needed—untested so far.
State remediation tax credits	Some brownfield cleanup expenses eligible for a 10 to 15 percent tax credit, up to $750,000.	Recently enacted in Ohio. Only solvent firms with projects can benefit in the short term.
Federal brownfield tax credits	Proposed but not yet enacted. Up to $2 billion could be available.	Would be very useful if tax credits could be used in conjunction with other programs and if they could be transferred to other parties.
Brownfield industrial remediation accounts	Proposed legislation would permit sizable companies to set aside funds for remediation and reuse of land.	No program for small businesses. Untested so far.
Tax breaks for banks	Incentives for banks to lend cleanup funds to small businesses, and to publicly owned and orphan sites. Tax credits based on the interest on the loan available directly to banks.	Unknown issues concerning lenders' liability.

FIGURE 6.3

REAL ESTATE STRATEGIES

Tools	Description	Comments
Delisting	Contaminated portions of the property are split or sectioned off from the total property. Clean portions are used or sold to finance remediation of the contaminated property. A strategic plan is necessary that should include an environmental assessment.	Good for enhancing cash flow and funding the cost of chemical analysis and property assessment. Loss of use of part of the property. Possible nonsale of property. Market acceptance an issue.
Mineral rights	Contaminated subsurface material is recognized as having mineral value and sold to a third party. Surface and air rights can be used for development.	Possible legal problems, as contaminated materials have negative present value. Probably ineligible for secondary mortgage market because ownership is not fee simple. Mining states may be the first to try this option.
Land lease	Public, nonprofit, or private owner leases land to developer, retaining ownership and environmental liability.	Probably ineligible for secondary mortgage market because ownership is not fee simple.
Flexible strike price purchase option	Buyer and seller agree on an unimpaired market price, but final funds due to seller are contingent on actual expense of cleanup. Buyer and seller equally responsible for uncertain expenses of cleanup.	Requires fairly accurate estimate of cleanup costs before remediation begins. Used in the U.K.

volving the site are likely to be public information forever. Some venture capital may be available, but because of the risk involved, the cost is often prohibitively expensive.

Finding funds for remediation requires considering prospects for longer-term financing—perhaps public loans and grants, the construction loan for real estate improvements after remediation, the permanent real estate loan, developer equity, leverage, debt service coverage, tax breaks, loan guarantees or insurance, recourse, and an indemnification letter. Identify end users. Find out which parties require which documents to participate, and get letters of intent from them, subject to explicit conditions. Does the paperwork include any impossible conditions or deal killers? Some local governments have proactive brownfield programs (Michigan's REUS–A Team, for example), which can concurrently help with site assessment, remediation grants, the VCP, and regulatory stumbling blocks along the way. Minneapolis, Milwaukee, and other communities have prepared inventories of brownfield sites, which could be helpful with site assembly. Eventually, coordinated public funding may be available.

At the end of this phase, funds for remediation will be in place, sources of public money ascertained, and expectations of lenders and equity partners specified.

Figure 6.2, "Remediation Finance," addresses possible grants for site assessment and remediation, including state and local government and philanthropic sources, state and local loan pools, community development block grants, sources of equity, and federal and state tax incentives.

Controlling the Site

If you as developer already own the site, skip this section and go to the next. Consider acquiring the privately owned property through normal real estate channels by writing a purchase option. To do so, you must have an estimate of the property value in a remediated (unimpaired) condition so you can arrive at a sale price and a potential loan-to-value ratio. It will not be easy to get. A new approach is required, such as the flexible strike price option, used in the U.K.[1] If you know the unimpaired value and a range for preliminary remediation costs, then write a contract with an agreed-upon gross sale price and a clause specifying that the seller's net proceeds will be determined after remediation is complete. Thus, the buyer and seller split uncertainty over the expense of remediation, with incentives to the buyer to keep costs down. The transaction is complete after remediation is officially over. Allow extra time to get the state's sign-off on remediation. And allow even more time in states with a new VCP and few successful graduates. Is the cost-minimizing remediation plan consistent with the option period? If the deal falls apart, where is the liability?

For a site where the previous owner is an acknowledged responsible party, such as an oil company that operated a gas station on the site for a number of years, the seller may sell the property and agree to pay all remediation costs. Doing so could benefit the project greatly, because it would take a lot of uncertainty out of financing. The seller might also offer a letter indemnifying the purchaser against future costs of remediation.

If the potential buyer is uncomfortable with remediating it, allow a brownfield specialist to remediate it, then buy the property with a clean bill of health. This option is much more costly, of course.

Figure 6.3 lists real estate strategies for controlling the site, including the flexible strike price. For acquisition of a property owned by a local public agency, see the in-kind grant on Figure 6.2. Sources of equity listed in Figure 6.2 could be helpful for a risk-averse buyer. And if an acknowledged polluter is the seller, see "indemnification letter from seller" on Figure 6.6.

Remediating the Site

Minimizing costs subject to state approval, market acceptance, and bankers' comfort is the overall strategy for brownfield remediation. To meet this end, a risk-based corrective action or comparable site- and use-oriented approach to remediation should guide the plan. Draft several possible approaches to remediating the property—which should go well beyond just hauling away any suspected contamination to a landfill at an exorbitant cost (probably enough to kill the deal).

The environmental consulting industry—including large and small vertically integrated firms, and firms that specialize in one type of contamination (e.g., USTs)—eagerly awaits the opportunity to help you remediate your site, usually for a fee. (Many states require official licenses to remediate sites and issue documents.) The ideal firm is experienced in the type of remediation problems you may encounter with your brownfield site. The firm should have already obtained closure documents from your state VCP and should have active staff (and political) connections to the regulators. Because remediation and site design should be closely integrated to minimize costs, you should have a land planner on your development team.

Regardless of which environmental consultant you select, a mixed approach to remediation could be most effective. Find the "hot spots," where contamination is well above state-mandated limits. Remove these hot spots, take them to a landfill, or remediate them on or off site, whichever is less costly. Take all other moderately contaminated soil and treat it on site, where possible, to avoid excessive costs for hauling and burying it. One of many soil remediation processes may be used. Larger amounts of soil to be treated mean economies of scale, and the unit prices of treatment may come down substantially in the future as new technologies become feasible.

Clay and some other dense, impermeable soils are usually associated with lower remediation costs, because they can be contained on site. Contaminated groundwater, on the other hand, implies off-site soil tests, pumping, extraction wells, angry neighbors, potential third-party lawsuits, and lengthy delays. If groundwater is substantially contaminated, allow one or two years to remediate the problem to a satisfactory level, which could have a major impact on the timing of remediation relative to your project's marketing window. If the site is optioned, groundwater is a factor in setting the option period. Check to see whether your property is in a groundwater containment zone or urban groundwater area, which could change the ground rules substantially.

Once the problem has been confined to on-site soils and the soil remediated to acceptable levels, move or confine the soil to parts of the site with little anticipated use or exposure to future users (under parking lots or roadways, buried and isolated with a barrier underneath foundations, for example) and encapsulate it where feasible. For example, lightly contaminated soil could be collected and left under local streets, which could then be deeded over to the local government. Thus, coordinating remediation strategies and real estate strategies to reduce liability is key.

You must also consider the effect remediation could have on neighbors of the property. Neighbors who are concerned about on-site treatment or less costly methods of remediation such as incineration could cause delays. If this problem seems likely, consider hiring a planner who specializes in working with neighborhood groups. Above all, avoid the NIMBY syndrome (not in my back yard), which can produce costly delays and reduce support for the project in seeking public money. Figure 6.4 lists 15 techniques for remediation of a site.[2] Development of remediation techniques is evolving, and you should check to see whether new tools are available or unit prices have come down substantially.

FIGURE 6.4

REMEDIATION STRATEGIES

Tools	Description	Comments
Haul/bury	When legally permitted, contaminated soil and demolition debris are hauled to and buried in construction material dumps and low-level waste dumps so property can be reused. Widely practiced.	Hauling and burial costs are very high. Expensive to sort out previously buried material.
No treatment	In many cases, limited contamination should be left alone. If contamination has been tested, levels are below state-mandated limits, and contaminants are nonvolatile, they may be left in place.	Useful for very low to moderate contamination. Acceptance by lenders an issue. The limited amount of contamination, if removed, could disrupt ecosystems more than if the property were left undisturbed.
Removal of hot spots	After systematic site testing, material well above state-mandated limits can be removed off site; other material can be treated on site.	Good strategy for minimizing costs.
Selective on-site burial	Highly contaminated but nonmobile and inert contaminated material can be concentrated on site and buried. Areas where contamination was removed are then available for use. Areas used to store contaminated material could be used for roadways and landscaped sites.	Low cost—saves expense of hauling and burying material. Market acceptance an issue. May be appropriate for nonvolatile substances. Deed restrictions may apply.
Encapsulation	Encapsulation methods for completely covering hazardous asbestos in buildings can be used for contaminated property when soil below is clay or prevents groundwater contamination. Property surface is paved and made available for limited use (such as parking lots). Method should not be considered when soil is contaminated by a volatile substance. Extensive assessment necessary. Accepted practice in several states.	Low to moderate cost. Moderate risk with proper assessment, analysis, and planning. Bank acceptance an issue. May require deed restrictions.
Partial encapsulation (capping)	Most undesirable contamination removed, while less contaminated soil is contained under clay, building structures, or plastic barrier covered with soil. Users of surface soil protected, but lower soils may be affected.	State regulators and lenders may not accept this solution in all cases. Barriers may have finite effective life. Groundwater may be affected. May require deed restrictions.
Absorption	The addition of absorbent materials (such as hay, sawdust, cement, kiln dust, fly ash, furnace slag, and clay minerals like zeolite, bentonite, and kaolinite) to the soil promotes the absorption of contamination like a sponge. Mixtures of soil and absorption materials must be combined carefully so soil's integrity is not destroyed.	Low to moderate cost (although absorbent materials may be expensive). Volatile materials must be removed.
Biological treatment	To promote cleanup without removing the soil, biodegradation breaks down contamination through the application of specific microbes or communities of microbes to the soil. The application of microbes is tested on the property before full treatment. Field conditions such as oxygen levels, pH, and temperature must be extensively monitored to sustain growth of the microbes. Good alternative for large tracts of land.	Moderate to high cost, including costs for laboratory modeling, field testing, sampling and monitoring, and the microbes themselves. Appropriate for petroleum products.

FIGURE 6.4 (continued)

REMEDIATION STRATEGIES

Tools	Description	Comments
Soil washing/steam stripping	Many volatile and semivolatile organic compounds found in low concentrations can be removed by the application of steam. This technique requires flushing or injecting water into contaminated areas; water is then drawn off into a vacuum steam stripper, which removes the organic contaminants. Note that this process can treat only contaminants that are highly soluble in water.	Low to moderate cost, including sampling costs. Availability of equipment a factor. Generally works best on petroleum contamination.
Soil vapor extraction	Process removes volatile organic compounds from soils that are undisturbed or have been excavated in large piles (only to the water table). Air is injected into the ground, transferring volatile materials from the soil to the air. Air stream removes contaminants from the soil or water for further processing.	Moderate cost, including sampling and monitoring costs. Difficulty removing all volatile organic compounds. Collected contamination must be treated or disposed of properly.
Air stripping	Used for remediation of groundwater contaminated with volatile organic compounds, such as solvents. Passes air through the water to improve the transfer between the air and water in its gaseous and liquid phases. Water from contaminated area pumped into the top of a tower packed with plastic objects as air is blown through the bottom. Volatile material adheres to surface of plastic objects. Technology suited for lower concentrations of volatile organic compounds. Spray systems, tray towers, diffused aeration, or mechanical aeration can substitute for packed towers.	High costs of designing specific solution for contaminated property. Design and assessment must be done case by case. Appropriate for petroleum products.
Pump and treat	Solution involves pumping fluids into a containment area and collecting them and contaminated groundwater for future treatment. Wells are used for pumping, drainage tile collection systems or waste ponds for recovering fluids. Water is usually pumped in, but a variety of solvents can be added to the system, depending on the contaminants. Solvents used bind with the contaminants for easier transport with water for off-site disposal.	High cost. Uncertain length of treatment. Frequent monitoring required.
Land treatment/land farming	Treatment involves applying uncontaminated soil to a contaminated area at a controlled rate and then mixing the soils in the subsurface area. Uses biological, physical, and chemical processes that naturally degrade and immobilize contaminated wastes. Agriculture principles are used to hasten bacterial growth, such as adding nutrients, aerating the soil, adjusting pH, and controlling moisture. Wastes removed may include volatile and semivolatile organic compounds and heavy metals. Heavy metals absorbed by soil particles.	Moderate cost, including the cost of new soil, and sampling and monitoring costs.
Laser separation	Separates chemical and radioactive contaminants from metals in bulk and surface sources. A pulsed laser beam precisely removes the contaminated layer of a metal while high-efficiency particulate air filters capture the removed particles and prevent them from resettling on the cleaned area.	Very-high-cost method currently being tested. When operational, will improve safety, create less secondary waste and no hazardous chemicals, reduce volume of waste, reduce costs of decontamination, and allow valuable metals to be reused.
Incineration	Burning substances on site or off site.	Unpopular with neighbors.

FIGURE 6.5

PERMANENT FINANCING

Tools	Description	Comments
Community development block grants	CDBGs are also available for funding permanent loans for remediated sites. They can be used in conjunction with empowerment zones to reduce project debt and forgive principal.	Flexible, discretionary funds. Heavy competition from other potential recipients.
Local nonprofit foundations	Can provide gap financing for real estate projects. Subordinated debt at favorable rates.	
Bank loans	Private lending institutions provide debt service. Community Reinvestment Act motivates participation in center cities.	Lenders concerned about liability. Greater scrutiny of the value of real estate collateral.
State economic development authority	Most states have below-market-interest-rate loans available for businesses. Brownfields are eligible, especially if jobs are created.	Quality of contaminated real estate as collateral is an issue.
State revolving loan fund	Same as above but designated for brownfield projects.	
Local public loan pools	Loan pool for community development. Loans at discretion of city development agency.	Restricted and not available in all cities. Cleveland has a $40 million Neighborhood Development Investment Fund.
Loans for empowerment zones	Section 108 funds in Cleveland earmarked for below-market-rate acquisition and development loans. Completed projects on brownfields may be eligible.	May also be available for permanent loans.
Tax breaks for empowerment zones	Employers in empowerment zones are allowed faster equipment depreciation for hiring residents of the zone.	
Property tax abatement	Can be used for residential and industrial properties.	Cannot be used with tax increment financing. Popular in Ohio, Connecticut, and some other states.
Industrial development bonds	Permanent financing at below-market rates.	Cap on funds means heavy competition for money in each state.
State housing finance authority	For worthy residential brownfield projects, some state housing finance authorities provide construction and permanent financing if guidelines for low- to moderate-income housing are met.	Michigan and possibly other states are active in this arena.
Real estate investment trusts	REITs can benefit from lending funds for urban projects.	Untested at this point.

To keep liability manageable after remediation is complete, several real estate strategies may be helpful. Delisting a portion of the property (which isolates residual contamination on site but outside the property used for the bank's collateral), using mineral rights, or leasing part of the land to a third party may help concentrate the minimal amount of residual contamination and make bankers more comfortable. Delisting uses the proceeds from the sale of clean parts of a larger project to finance cleanup of contaminated parts, an excellent way to enhance cash flow. This approach generally creates a separate legal entity (parcel or lot) for the contaminated part of the site by splitting the site horizontally into clean and contaminated portions. Selling off subsurface contamination as mineral rights is a similar (as yet untested) approach, which splits the bundle of real estate rights vertically. Leasing land to a surface user rather than selling it fee simple is another way to reduce the environmental liability for future site occupants. The latter two strategies leave liability as the seller's concern.

FIGURE 6.6

FINANCIAL GUARANTEES

Tools	Description	Comments
Insurance	Some private insurance policies will insure new buyers against known problems for a limited period of time.	Little actuarial evidence available. Terms of policy usually shorter than financing term. Not comprehensive. Expensive because not yet available for a portfolio of loans.
Creditworthy tenant	Major creditworthy tenants with a signed lease make lenders more comfortable.	
Personal recourse	Developer required to pledge personal assets to pay back loan in event of default.	Not popular with developers.
Indemnification letter from seller	Seller or responsible party with deep pockets agrees to reimburse current or future owners against future environmental problems.	Popular with lenders.
Municipal groundwater mitigation fund	Used in groundwater management zones involving a property-based or polluter-based tax assessed over a designated area. Funds used to offset any future costs of groundwater cleanup. Municipality absorbs liability for future cleanup.	Under development in San Francisco Bay Area. May represent a substantial contingent liability for the municipality or its development agency.
Higher debt service coverage ratio	Lenders may require cash flow cushion to cover additional expenses for project.	May be reasonable if additional environmental monitoring is required.

When remediation is complete, obtain the CNTS and other assurances from the state, and any indemnification letters from the previous owner. Negotiate the conditions under which reopening the CNTS can occur. Finally, try to obtain a memorandum of understanding that binds other agencies to the VCP agency's CNTS.

The next step is obtaining the construction loan, bringing in the clean fill and the bulldozers, and finishing site preparation.

Real estate strategies to minimize liability are shown in Figure 6.3, remediation strategies pertaining to both soil and water contamination are described in Figure 6.4, and Figure 6.7 lists local government activities that could be used to coordinate remediation and accelerate approval.

Obtaining Permanent Financing

When remediation is complete, prospects for long-term financing are now the primary concern, which could include the construction loan and permanent financing. Grants and tax breaks are usually more desirable than debt for the permanent real estate loan, because site preparation costs are substantially higher for brownfields than for comparable greenfields on virgin land in the suburbs.[3] While many loan programs are available to provide financing below prevailing interest rates, too much long-term debt from several sources involves a more complex deal, requirements for several programs, loan subordination, debt service coverage, and adequate collateral. Consider needs for equity, leverage, and rate of return, and available debt service coverage when structuring the deal.

With a compelling public purpose for the property, property tax abatements, other tax breaks, and public gap financing to cover the excess site development costs of brownfields may be feasible. Most central cities have community development block grants available, and a few have empowerment zones, which may provide low-interest loans or even grants to reduce principal. Gap financing or other public funds are tempting, but they involve complications. For example, if you fail to perform certain requirements (say, create a certain number of jobs in a set period of time), some public agencies seek to have some of the money refunded or to shorten the abatement period.

Tax incentives for brownfields are new, but they have a lot of potential. Some states (Ohio, for example) allow an income tax credit for the eligible costs of brownfield remediation. Although it is a step in the right direction because it allows remediation without additional debt, this program appears not to benefit derelict properties.

FIGURE 6.7

GOVERNMENT-LED COORDINATION

Tools	Description	Comments
Coordinated implementation team	City/state team consisting of a wide variety of professionals (city planners, state environmental regulators, attorneys, environmental scientists, real estate and project managers) who meet regularly to consider projects case by case, smooth over differences, organize the next activity, and consider financial options. This proactive process reduces the number of players who do not possess enough information to make decisions.	Groups can grow too large for effective decision making. Detroit's REUS–A Team is an excellent example of an effective team.
Coordinated funding source	In Britain, a single fund exists to coordinate allocation of development funding, request competitive bids, analyze costs and budgets, and set goals for financial leverage.	Not tested in the United States, which has distinct federal, state, and local sources of funding.
Inventory of brownfield sites	Detailed list of potential brownfield sites, including known and suspected contamination, site characteristics, legal issues, market demand, and priority for receiving funding. Needed for efficient allocation of funds.	Resistance from property owners. Potential for stigmatizing listed sites.
Local government as lead environmental coordinating and permitting agency	Local government obtains sign-offs from state agencies and becomes the coordinating environmental permitting authority. As long as brownfield developers stay within prescribed guidelines, can approve a project quickly.	Under development in EPA pilot project in Emeryville, California. Consistent with approaches used in U.K., Australia, and New Zealand.
Brownfields "look-up" database	Local government maintains a record of approved cleanups, required remediation practices, and soil conditions. Property owners nearby who can show their property has very similar conditions can "look up" past practices and use those approaches to remediate their own sites.	Under development in Oakland, California.
Interim site for soil remediation	Where overall demand for sites has been determined and no land use–based soil cleanliness standards exist, soil from residential development sites can be taken to a future industrial site, cleaned there to industrial standards, and be used as fill dirt. Saves costs of burying soil.	Requires planning for contaminated multisite activities.

Moreover, the short-term benefits to an operator at a single location (for example, a gas station) experiencing a large loss as a result of site remediation are slim: The firm might not be able to take advantage of the tax credit until state corporate income taxes are due several years later. If the Ohio tax credits were transferable, however, or if a federal initiative created a national tax credit for cleanup, a secondary market could be developed, comprising corporations that could take advantage of the tax breaks (much like the federal low-income housing tax credit program).

A lender might still require additional assurances about the contamination, especially if a state does not have a meaningful exemption from liability for lenders. Some other methods of assurance are environmental insurance, personal recourse, or a creditworthy tenant with a very strong balance sheet. Some lenders will not touch a brownfield deal without an indemnification letter from the seller (an oil company, for example) or a creditworthy tenant. Lenders may also want a higher debt service coverage ratio. And not yet explored are the effects of reopeners on the real estate's value if the bank has to foreclose on the property.

Figure 6.5 lists several loan programs, a few sources of outside equity, and some interesting local tax incentives available for brownfield development. Local governments might have pools of capital available or otherwise provide the funds needed, perhaps through tax increment financing.

Figure 6.6 shows six "guarantees" to satisfy lenders who are nervous about liability. Some communities are developing ways to separate contamination of groundwater from contamination of the soil.

Monitoring Contamination and Preserving the CNTS

Once the project is up and running, the issue remains of maintaining the integrity of any CNTS or NFA letter received from the state. For example, periodic monitoring of groundwater quality may be required to keep the state and your lender satisfied. Any change in land use (from a parking lot to industrial use, or from commercial to residential use, for example), especially if it is more intense and requires a different standard of cleanliness under the prevailing RBCA, would probably necessitate "reopening" the CNTS agreement with the state. The developer of a brownfield project with this problem should include an environmental consultant in the budget.

Figure 6.7 identifies some emerging practices that local governments can engage in to facilitate development.

Notes

1. Paul Syms, "Effects of Industrial Contamination on Residential Land Values in the United Kingdom," *Land Contamination and Reclamation* 4(1), 1996, pp. 49–56.

2. See also Peter Lederman and William Librizzi, "Brownfields Remediation: Available Technologies," *Journal of Urban Technology* 2(2), Spring 1996, pp. 21–30.

3. Charles Bartsch, "Financing Brownfields Cleanup and Redevelopment," *Northeast Midwest Economic Review* 8(5), July 1995, p. 5.

7 Lessons from Thirteen Brownfield Development Projects

This chapter summarizes 13 successful brownfield development projects to derive lessons applicable to future development, covering many aspects of the projects related to remediation, subsidies, profitability, financing, and development strategies, and noting similarities and differences between international cases and U.S. cases. It also identifies the strategic tricks or features that made each case work.

Some interesting patterns have emerged. For example, public subsidies for the projects depended on local land values. Where land prices were high, subsidies were low. The average public subsidy was about 20 percent of the land value. Remediation costs typically represented about 10 percent of the project's total value, but some projects with innovative remediation techniques kept the remediation costs below 5 percent. Private sector financing was available for most projects but typically required indemnification and loan-to-value ratios of 0.5 to 0.6.

The Cases

Regional Mall in Waterbury, Connecticut

Connecticut has several VCPs, including one oriented toward urban sites needing very large subsidies. This 1.2 million-square-foot regional mall on 90 acres received over $40 million in public funds. GGP/Brass Mill, Inc., the developer, has finished construction of this project on the site of a former brass-rolling mill, and the property opened in fall 1997 (see Chapter 10).

Winchester Factory in New Haven, Connecticut

The U.S. Repeating Arms Corp. (which manufactures Winchester rifles) is the beneficiary of a new 225,000-square-foot state-of-the-art manufacturing building on 15 acres. Olin Corp., the former owner, voluntarily remediated the extensively developed former armaments site with help from the state of Connecticut and a local not-for-profit corporation. The factory, one of the largest new inner-city factories built in New England in decades, was occupied in 1993. Strong local financing helped keep Winchester in New Haven (see Chapter 10).

Low-Income Housing Project in Detroit, Michigan

Michigan's government is very strong in terms of leadership, regulatory issues, and financial support of brownfields. The city of Detroit played a very strong role in site assembly and remediation of this modestly sized, lightly contaminated project (see Chapter 11). The Helen Butler Odean apartments contain 96 low-income rental housing units on an $8^{1}/_{2}$-acre former urban renewal site. V.I.S.I.O.N.S., the not-for-profit developer and apartment manager, has fully leased and occupied the project, and is currently moving on to the second phase. The project was financed by the Michigan State Housing Development Authority.

Health Clinic in Detroit, Michigan

The Detroit Community Health Connection (DCHC), a not-for-profit entity, recently opened a 13,000-square-foot building on a one-acre site that formerly contained a gas station (see Chapter 11). The city of Detroit had a major role in organizing remediation and assisting in assembling the site. DCHC opened its doors to patients in late 1996. Federal grants guaranteed the bank loan.

EastRock Shopping Center near Cleveland, Ohio

Ohio's new privately oriented VCP takes an untraditional approach, and its permanent environmental regulations just took effect (see Chapter 12). EastRock is a 19-acre mall expansion project in a suburb of Cleveland. It is one of the first to be remediated and go through the state's new VCP; it received a CNTS in early 1997. The case features bank financing, local property tax abatements, state income tax credits, state remediation loans, and a specialized brownfield remediation expert. Demand for the project was known, because it is an expansion of a successful suburban community shopping center. The established developer has a strong balance sheet. Land is under remediation and in the leasing phase.

West New York, New Jersey, Housing Complex

New Jersey has advanced brownfield laws with very flexible standards for cleanup. This 158-acre master-planned housing complex overlooks midtown Manhattan across the Hudson River (see Chapter 13). The former railyard and transfer station was mildly contaminated with nonvolatile hydrocarbons, which are to be contained on site. The developer, Roseland Property Company, has begun remediating the property and has lined up partners and builders for the first three neighborhoods, which will contain a total of 1,100 housing units. Construction is expected to begin soon.

Chiron Life Sciences Center in Emeryville, California

California is an innovator in the field of brownfield development, with two state agencies offering programs. The state encourages local initiatives, so the small, commercial Oakland suburb of Emeryville has emerged as a leader in local brownfield development by acting as facilitator. Chiron's 2.2 million-square-foot research and development facility on 25 acres is one example of how the risk in brownfield transactions can be spread around so all parties are satisfied (see Chapter 14). Washington Advisors, a California-based consulting firm, facilitated the offshore financing for the deal.

Three Cases in Auckland, New Zealand

New Zealand is known for its clean and green environment, but it also has its share of formerly contaminated property. Almost all authority for environmental regulation of contaminated property lies with the local political jurisdiction or the regional government. Private consultants have a large role. Chapter 15 covers remediation and data about land sales for a 13-acre shopping center on the site of a former paint factory, a 40-unit, four-story condominium project on a coal gasometer storage facility, and a 26+-unit residential project on a former bus garage. High density and robust land prices drove the finances on these projects, which were developed without government subsidy.

Three Cases in Manchester, England

Manchester's approach may represent the future for brownfield development in the United States. The British are several years ahead of even the most progressive states in the United States, having already grappled with brownfields by the early 1990s. They have several important features we do not, such as higher land prices, stronger local government planning that prevents greenfields from emerging, a real estate industry that encourages appraisal of contaminated property both before and after remediation, and coordinated government funding and regulation. Greater Manchester, which is very similar to many U.S. Rustbelt cities, has seen more than ten large (over 100 units) brownfield housing projects and a 250-acre, internationally competitive industrial and business park. Chapter 16 summarizes the successful development of two housing projects (one with for-sale units and one with rental units) and the industrial park.

Research Design and Sampling For the Case Studies

Generally, knowledge about successful brownfield projects is in the early discovery stage, and very limited detailed public information is available.[1] Therefore, this chapter's primary objective is to describe the situation. By selecting only successful cases, this study employs a retrospective, not random, research design. The main analytical tools used are pattern matching and explanation building.[2] While much can also be learned from unsuccessful projects, analysis of failed cases is left for future work.

The successful cases represent diverse conditions and provide models for development of brownfields. Only projects with favorable outcomes (under construction or already developed) are included. A spectrum of real estate uses is represented, including retailing, for-sale and rental housing, industrial and R&D space, and a health clinic. Regulatory environments range from state-led, tightly controlled environments with substantial subsidy (Michigan and Connecticut) to privately led projects with state concurrence (Ohio). The U.K. and New Zealand cases feature mostly city-led environmental permitting. Various types of soil and groundwater were contaminated. The international cases in the U.K. rely heavily on the government's support, while New Zealand has stronger land markets and virtually no government role.

Data Analyzed in Each Case Study

To ensure consistent analysis, the same data were requested for each case, although in some situations, the information (especially that pertaining to profit and other financial outcomes) was not available or was proprietary. Moreover, the amount and extent of publicly available property data in the U.K. and New Zealand is much less than in the United States.

The case material is broken down into three groups, summarized in Figures 7.1, 7.2, and 7.3. Figure 7.1 pertains to the first part of site development, including the background of the site, the final use of the real estate, the development team, and the remediation process. Figure 7.2 pertains to the project's financial aspects, including financing, risk allocation, subsidy, and outcomes. Figure 7.3 concerns the strategic features that made the project work.

Development Background, Site Preparation, and Remediation

Real Estate Use after Development

The 13 cases represent a cross section of retail types in seven jurisdictions. Real estate uses after development include three retail centers (two community shopping centers of 220,000 square feet and one super regional mall of 1.2 million square feet), six housing projects (two low-income, low-rise rental projects of about 100 units, two market-rate for-sale housing projects, one high-density building with 40 condominium units, and one high-rise project with over 1,000 units at completion), two industrial manufacturing facilities, one small health clinic (13,000 square feet), and one very large (2.2 million square feet) research and development facility. Project costs range from $2 million to $700 million in value of buildings at completion. Typically, projects ranged from $8 million to $20 million.

Type of Developer

Seven projects were led solely by a private sector, for-profit real estate developer, including one national player, three experienced regional developers, an industrial firm remediating its underused sites, and a small international player in the Pacific Rim. One brownfield was being developed by a private firm for its own use. Two deals used a combination of private developer and community development corporation (CDC), where in both cases the CDC was used as a remediation contractor and to reduce liability. One of these projects was codeveloped by a national REIT. Three projects were developed only by CDCs, two of them relatively small and the third a large, established quasi-autonomous nongovernmental organization (QUANGO).

Type of Contamination and Groundwater Monitoring

Prior uses for the cases included manufacturing (seven sites), public service facilities such as a bus garage (two projects) or utility storage, a rail yard, residential use, and a gas station, which dictated the type of contamination to be found on site. Types of contamination could be broken down into petroleum based (roughly in order of severity, polynuclear aromatic hydrocarbons; volatile organic compounds; and benzene, toluene, ethylene, and xylene from USTs), and heavy metals (copper, nickel, lead, and arsenic, and PCBs from transformers). Most sites also contained construction and demolition debris from former structures on site. Five sites contained petroleum-type contamination, and two had heavy met-

FIGURE 7.1

REMEDIATION AND BACKGROUND OF THE BROWNFIELD CASE STUDIES

Case	Location	Real Estate End Use	Type of Developer	Type of Contamination[a]	Groundwater Monitoring Required?	Feature of Remediation	Type of Closure Document[b]	Deed Restrictions?
Regional Mall	Waterbury, CT	1,200,000 square feet, retail	For-profit CDC	Multiple types, including groundwater	No	Dig and dump	CNTS	No
Winchester Factory	New Haven, CT	225,000 square feet, industrial	For-profit CDC	Petroleum, heavy metals, groundwater	Yes	CDC contractor cap	NFA letter	Yes
Low-Income Housing	Detroit, MI	96 apartments	CDC	Lead	No	Very light contamination	NFA letter	On any removed soil
Health Clinic	Detroit, MI	13,000 square feet, clinic	CDC	Petroleum	No	City organized	CNTS	No
Shopping Center	Cleveland, OH	220,000 square feet, retail	For profit	Groundwater, petroleum, heavy metals	Yes	Flexible CNTS, cap	CNTS	Yes
Housing Complex	West New York, NJ	1,100 units	For profit	Light hydro-carbons	Yes	Cap	NFA letter	Yes
Life Sciences Center	Emeryville, CA	2,200,000 square feet, R&D facility	Owner-occupied	Petroleum, heavy metals, groundwater	Yes	Cap, separate approvals for soil and groundwater, groundwater risk management	Groundwater management plan, NFA letter	Yes
Shopping Center	Auckland, NZ	220,000 square feet, retail	For profit	Petroleum, heavy metals	No	On-site remediation	None	No
Condominiums	Auckland, NZ	40 units	For profit	Hydrocarbons	Yes	Vapor barrier used to remove hot spots	None	Vapor barrier
Residential Project	Auckland, NZ	26+ housing lots	For profit	Heavy metals	No	Remediation to background levels	None	No
Residential Project	Manchester, U.K.	135 townhouses	For profit	Heavy metals	No	Hot spots, cap	None	No
Residential Project	Manchester, U.K.	119 apartments	For profit	Petroleum	No	Phased remediation, soil placed under roadways	None	No
Industrial Park	Manchester, U.K.	250 acres, industrial	CDC	Various	No	Community development corporation organized	None	NA

[a]Petroleum includes volatile organic compounds and BTEX. Heavy metals may include lead, PCBs, nickel, and arsenic.
[b]Closure type for overseas markets are in generic U.S. equivalents.

FIGURE 7.2

Financial Data and Outcomes of the Brownfield Case Studies

Case	Real Estate End Use	Value per Square Foot of Land Area	Remediation: Amount[a]	Remediation: Cost per Square Foot of Land Area	Remediation: Percent of Total Project Cost	Public Funds: Amount	Public Funds: Percent	Profit as Percent of Total Project Cost	Indemnification	Mortgage/ Loan-to-Value Ratio
Regional Mall	1,200,000 square feet, retail	$7.00–10.00	$28 million	$5.64	13%	$41 million	19%	11%	City/TIF	0.7 LTV construction loan
Winchester Factory	225,000 square feet, industrial	$1.00–2.00	$3.4 million	$5.67	15%	$5.3 million	24%	24%	Parent company was previous site user	0.77 LTV on industrial revenue bonds
Low-Income Housing	96 apartments	$1.00	$200,000	$0.58	3%	$3.1 million	48%	3–10%	No	0.8 LTV public, first
Health Clinic	13,000 square feet, clinic	$1.00	$110,000	$3.22	6%	$200,000	8%	5%	Federal loan guarantee	0.5 LTV private, first
Shopping Center	220,000 square feet, retail	$6.00–10.00	$5.6 million	$6.77	19%	$5.5 million	17%	NA	Considering insurance	0.6 LTV private, first; public, second
Housing Complex	1,100 units	$6.00–8.00	$4 million	$0.58	3%	0	0	Very large	None	Joint venture
Life Sciences Center	2,200,000 square feet, R&D facility	$25.00–30.00	$10 million	$10.90	1%	$20 million	3%	7%	Parent company	LTV greater than one "credit deal"
Shopping Center	220,000 square feet, retail	$13.00–17.00	$3 million[b]	$5.30	10–15%	0	0	NA	No	NA
Condominiums	40 units	$40.00	$400,000[b]	$4.17	4%	0	0	NA	Partial from prior owner	Construction loan
Residential Project	26+ housing lots	$40.00	$300,000[b]	$1.06	3%	0	0	NA	No	NA
Residential Project	135 townhouses	$2.00–3.00	$900,000[b]	$3.01	11%	$2 million[b]	21%	14%	No	Internal financing
Residential Project	119 apartments	$2.00–3.00	$900,000[b]	$5.20	11%	$1.2 million[b]	15%	NA	No	Yes
Industrial Park	250 acres, industrial	$1.00–3.00	$16.5 million[b]	$1.52	15%	$41 million[b]	39%	NA	No	Yes

[a] Including some construction costs.
[b] Equivalent in U.S. dollars.
NA = Not available.

als in the soil only. The remaining six sites contained both types of contamination, generally affecting both soil and groundwater.

Six sites had some problems with groundwater. After remediation, five of the projects required ongoing groundwater monitoring.

Remediation

The type of remediation depended on the contamination. All but one project elected to clean to less than pristine standards. Typical money-saving devices included capping or encapsulating the contamination (six projects) and digging out hot spots (six projects). Several projects used multiple, compatible remediation strategies. Diluting contamination or relegating it to parts of the site with limited risk to users (such as parking lots) was also common. At several sites, remediation was phased to work around regulatory constraints and market conditions. One project used extensive on-site remediation. In several cases, developers took over partially remediated projects, thus saving on costs.

State Closure Documents and Deed Restrictions

The kind of closure document varied widely. Three deals received a CNTS, the strongest form of closure, and four received NFA letters. One received a combination of an NFA letter and approval of the remediation plan.

None of the six cases in the U.K. and New Zealand received any real closure letters, although they did receive local approvals to proceed, and some New Zealand cases received "opinions" from regional water quality planners. In New Zealand, environmental contamination is treated similarly to a nonconforming use, requiring a variance or special use permit. All 13 projects received opinions or statements of completion from environmental consultants, although their importance (with respect to closure of remediation) varied widely, depending on regulatory venue.

Of those properties with contamination remaining on site, six had deed restrictions filed with the appropriate local authority. The presence of a deed restriction is consistent with the use of caps, and it is often consistent with remediating the site to a nonresidential use, although three of the housing projects had some form of deed restriction.

Financial Ratios, Liability Reduction, And Deal Structure

Land Values

Land markets in some areas are quite depressed (Detroit, Manchester, and New Haven, for example), ranging from $1.00 to $3.00 per square foot (in equivalent U.S. currency). Well-located retail sites in Ohio and Connecticut and the 158-acre housing site in New Jersey were valued at $6.00 to $10.00 per square foot.

The highest land values were in New Zealand, from $13.00 to $17.00 per square foot for a retail site to $40.00 and up per square foot for land in well-located infill sites. In the San Francisco Bay Area, land values for research and development property were likewise high, $25.00 to $30.00 per square foot.

Cost of Remediation

Remediation costs, in U.S. dollars, are expressed in dollars per square foot of land area and as a percentage of the project's total cost if known. Remediation expenses generally include only those known to have been paid by the current or most recent owner; some sites were partially remediated earlier by others who went bankrupt.

Remediation costs varied widely, from about $100,000 for a one-acre site to $28 million for 90 acres. A more meaningful figure is dollars per square foot of land, which ranged from less than $1.00 to a projected $11.00. The average figure was $4.12 per square foot of land, and four projects cost less than $2.00 per square foot of land.

Remediation costs as a percentage of the completed project's value averaged 9 percent. Five projects had very low remediation costs, under 5 percent. At two of the U.S. sites where the groundwater was acknowledged to be undrinkable, the owners were permitted to encapsulate contamination on site so as to minimize the risk to occupants.

Two New Zealand sites had low percentages because the value of the built improvements was so high. All but one of the remaining projects had remediation costs of 10 to 15 percent of total project costs. This outcome was the most typical. One project incurred expenses of about 19 percent of cost, but this outcome is expected to come down because some of the costs of remediation (a parking lot doubling as a cap on contamination, for example) are actually legitimate construction costs.

Public Subsidies

Because brownfield development projects are not well accepted on the market, public funds were an important part of most projects. Only the three projects in New

FIGURE 7.3

STRATEGIC FEATURES OF THE BROWNFIELD CASE STUDIES

Case	Real Estate End Use	Site Acquisition	Remediation	Financing and Cash Flow	Lenders' Comfort	Marketing
Regional Mall	1,200,000 square feet, retail	Strong state role: money and site assembly	Remediation by CDC		Tax increment financing/ city indemnification	Great location
Winchester Factory	225,000 square feet, industrial	Teamwork of former owner and local nonprofit development	Strong state financing, remediation by CDC	Industrial revenue bond	Olin Corp. land lease, indemnification	Loan guaranteed by parent company
Low-Income Housing	96 apartments	Very light contamination, prior remediation		1% permanent public loan, low-income housing tax credits		Strong demand
Health Clinic	13,000 square feet, clinic	City-guided remediation		Assistance of well-financed medical entity	Federal loan guarantee	
Shopping Center	220,000 square feet, retail	Prior remediation	Multifaceted consultant, first CNTS	4% public remediation loan, remediation income tax credit		Very good visibility
Housing Complex	1,100 units	Bought at $0.30 on the dollar	Handshake approval of remedial action plan, rolling NFA letter	Joint venture partners with deep pockets		Outstanding views and location
Life Sciences Center	2,200,000 square feet, R&D facility	Prior remediation, city in chain of title	Responsibility for groundwater and soil split, groundwater risk management zone	5% lease	Hybrid consultant convinced offshore banks project involved managable risk in land lease, project design	Indemnification from parent company for loan guarantee
Shopping Center	220,000 square feet, retail	Free demolition	On-site remediation	Company's remediation expertise		Property marketed as cleaner than clean
Condominiums	40 units	High land prices	Vapor barrier	Split off parcel for sale		Offshore marketing, park view
Residential Project	26+ housing lots	Free demolition, high land prices	Remediation to background levels			Very nice neighborhood
Residential Project	135 townhouses	Prior developer		Vertically integrated company, coodinated public funding		
Residential Project	119 apartments		Phased remediation	Coordinated funding policy		Strong demand, competitive prices
Industrial Park	250 acres, industrial	Proactive infrastructure investment and site assembly	Remediation by QUANGO	Subsidy from QUANGO		Strong demand

Zealand and the housing project in New Jersey received no public subsidy. The amount of public money, which is generally the present value of federal, state, and local subsidies, depended on what type of remediation was required. It often took the form of grants for remediation, mortgage loan subsidies, and property tax abatements. Two projects received minimal subsidies, ranging from 3 to 8 percent, four projects received public subsidies of 15 to 21 percent, and three received subsidies of 24 percent or more, up to almost 50 percent. Of the projects receiving the most subsidy, two were industrial and one was low-income housing. Not surprisingly, the projects with the lowest land values often received the highest subsidies, and the projects with high land values received little or no subsidy. This pattern is significant, because it may be subject to municipal policy. Both Connecticut cases and the California case are using some form of tax increment financing.

Profit

Estimates of the developers' profit were available for only six of the projects. It can be inferred, however, that, because the projects were built, the rate of return for all of them was above the break-even point. (The rate of return is generally applied to the real estate project, rather than to the developer, after debt service and before income taxes in a future "stable year.") The not-for-profit developers received a return of 5 to 10 percent, which also applied to the owner-occupied R&D facility (7 percent). For-profit developers of housing and retail space obtained 11 to 14 percent profit, and the industrial firm with a large public subsidy achieved a return of over 20 percent. And the developers of one project acquired the land at such a discount and incurred remediation costs so low that the rate of return is likely to be very high. In short, the developers of these brownfield projects were able to achieve adequate rates of return on their investments.

Indemnification and Loan Terms

Five of the brownfield projects had some type of loan guarantee or indemnification against potential future environmental problems. A typical case in the United States that had received private sector financing also received some form of indemnification or loan guarantee. For the projects without private sector financing, however, the loan-to-value ratios and terms were generally lower than for typical uncontaminated real estate projects (i.e., a loan-to-value ratio of 0.7 to 0.8 on a private sector first mortgage, no public second mortgage, and no indemnification).

Of the six projects that were under construction or at earlier stages, four had obtained construction loans and two were financing the project out of their own funds. One of them received loan guarantees. Four have obtained first mortgages from the private sector (one has a contingent agreement subject to approval of the site plan). The two U.S. loans had loan-to-value ratios of 0.50 and 0.60, and one of them has received a loan guarantee. Two projects have public sector first mortgages (one is an industrial revenue bond), and one has a loan guarantee. One project has a commitment for a subordinated public second mortgage at a 0.2 loan-to-value ratio. Financing data were unavailable for several of the foreign projects, but it is known that they did receive financing.

Strategic Features of the Real Estate Deals

Features that make a brownfield project work often involve a combination of strategies that work together to get the project over an early hurdle or allow it to spread the risk among all the parties. Figure 7.3 describes strategies that, in general, reduced liability for future participants, kept costs down by using creative remediation techniques, or both, and strategies that linked several parts of the process.

Site Acquisition

Two cases involved community development corporations that proactively prepared industrial sites for development, providing a steady supply of land for the market with minimal delay. A variation of this approach was to have local government acquire and remediate all or part of the sites. The state often provided funds to support local efforts.

Several projects were able to benefit from prior, partial remediation on the site, which kept remediation costs down and allowed developers with expertise to acquire the properties at fire-sale prices.

Remediation

Not only did the use of caps reduce costs by overlapping remediation and construction expenses, but it also enabled a link between remediation and site design. In several cases, encapsulated soil was used for parking lots, and lightly contaminated soils were placed under roadways, allowing access to future utilities. Other cases obtained regulatory approval for remediation, then remediated the site in phases, compatible with construction and market conditions. Nine projects enjoyed direct government grants for remediation, or reimbursement after remediation to offset costs.

Financing and Lenders' Comfort

Financing and convincing lenders of a project's feasibility is still the hardest part of a brownfield deal to overcome. Without the credit of a substantial company behind the deal, most banks appear unwilling to provide permanent financing for brownfield projects. Even with loan guarantees, brownfield deals in this country still have lower loan-to-value ratios than conventional real estate projects. Land leases, partitioning sites to third parties, regulatory closure letters, and indemnification against expenses for future environmental problems help some, but these strategies in and of themselves have not been sufficient to entice banks to finance projects.

It is hard for most nonscientists to understand the potential future risks involved in brownfield deals. Several cases moved forward because multidisciplinary consultants were involved who were familiar with both environmental risk management and real estate valuation, banking, or law. When risks can be quantified, banks can render a business decision on the request for a loan.

Public lending and loan guarantees is also a familiar pattern. Four cases involved a strong public role, although the form of the loan was not consistent.

Marketing

Four projects were in excellent locations, which in turn permitted aggressive marketing based on views, visibility, or access. Two of these projects encapsulated contaminated soil and received an environmental statement or deed restriction. The high-rise housing project will be marketed to segments not overly concerned with potential contamination, such as empty nesters. One developer is marketing the project, sight unseen, in Pacific Rim countries.

Two projects target low-income housing residents who depend on public assistance. These tenants are attracted to the newness of the projects, and both projects have long waiting lists.

Keeping good records can also pay off in marketing. One project in the Pacific Rim was able to achieve very close to market price for its brownfield retail parcel by marketing the site as "cleaner than clean" compared with similar properties with no record of environmental conditions.

A Typical Brownfield Development Project

Typically, a brownfield developer should buy a well-located brownfield site at a significant discount where demand is substantial, then remediate the site using a combination of risk-based criteria (to keep costs down) and real estate strategies that design the site around the remaining contamination to reduce risk to future occupants. Remediation can be expected to cost about 10 percent of the project's value. At the same time, the developer should obtain the highest-quality closure document available from state regulators.

State or local governments can be expected to subsidize up to 20 percent of the project's costs. Lenders are unlikely to finance remediation or provide a mortgage until the appropriate closure document is in place. Even then, a lower loan-to-value ratio can be expected. The developer should also seek indemnification against future environmental contamination and/or loan guarantees from prior users or a government or other entity.

International Cases Compared With U.S. Cases

The U.S. and international case studies are different in several areas—and materially different in some cases.

Similarities

All the cases occurred in English-speaking countries with fairly robust private sector economies. Basic remediation techniques and scientific procedures were the same. In fact, many of the environmental consulting firms involved maintain offices in several countries.

Location of the property was always a factor of prime importance, especially for retail sites. Spectacular views were also very important. Basic demographic trends in the three countries were also fairly similar. Developers sought to minimize the costs of cleanup to leverage the financing deal.

Differences

Government roles in the three countries were quite different. In the United States, the federal government's substantial role in setting standards is on the wane with the advent of state voluntary cleanup programs. At present, the U.S. government has no financial role in encouraging the development of brownfields. In New Zealand, the national role is limited to enacting key legislation. In the U.K., the major federal roles include enacting key legislation, establishing procedural guidelines, taking a very strong role in financing brownfield development, and setting explicit funding guidelines. New Zealand has no brownfield subsidy programs.

In the United States, every state has its own approach to brownfield development, and the states have the power to guide innovative brownfield development. New Zealand and the U.K. have no state level of government, although in New Zealand, regional governments are analogous to state governments in the United States.

Local roles are strongest in New Zealand and the U.K. In all cases, the local government was required to keep good property records on all matters, including environmental issues. It provided leadership and granted consent for planning and for closure of environmental cleanup. Thus, local government is the key player in the other countries, something that has been attempted only on a pilot basis in the United States (in Emeryville, California).

The availability of information is very different. Virtually all property records in the United States are freely available to all. In New Zealand, many records about a property's past are available, but data about transactions and loans are harder to obtain. In the U.K., records of transactions are generally not available, and real estate information is scarce.

Registers of contaminated property are being developed in New Zealand as a result of laws requiring local governments to be responsible for the correctness and completeness of land records. In the U.K , registers were suggested but never implemented. Experience with registers is mixed in the United States.

Because only the United States has closure letters and liability exemptions issued by government bodies, the role of environmental consultants was great in the U.K. and New Zealand. The provider of closure in those countries is the environmental consultant, who works for either the private or public sector as a reviewer.

Notes

1. See Charles Bartsch and Elizabeth Collaton, "Industrial Site Reuse and Urban Development: An Overview," *Cityscape* 2(3), September 1996, pp. 17–61, which focuses on economic development projects, excluding housing.

2. Robert Yin, *Case Study Research: Design and Methods* (Thousand Oaks, Calif.: Sage, 1994).

8 Allocating the Costs and Risks of Developing Brownfields

Progress has been rapid toward lowering the costs of remediation and financing site assessment and remediation. Many states have made it much easier to clean and develop contaminated sites. Some offer financial inducements for remediation. And as more sites are cleaned, technology for remediation is likely to become cheaper. Thus, the next real stumbling block for brownfield development is on the real estate side rather than cleanup side of the problem. Because real estate is usually leveraged, lenders and outside equity investors need to become more comfortable with construction and permanent financing for brownfield properties, especially with the risk involved.

This chapter focuses on the activities, abilities, and niches of private and not-for-profit equity players in the brownfield arena; the role of private and public lenders and their relative preferences concerning risk; and the potential role in quantifying environmental risk of hybrid consultants, and public and private insurers.

Equity Players

Brownfield equity players generally are risk takers, in the market to earn big profits by buying low, remediating the property, and selling it quickly. They can pass along exemptions from liability in the form of an NFA letter or CNTS to subsequent owners. Such equity players generally have a market niche and range of expertise that covers several parts of the brownfield problem. They often have an exit strategy planned in advance. Some are vertically integrated players with large holdings. They often shoot for large projects with the potential to attract institutional investment, leaving smaller projects to local developers or to property owners who stumble across a brownfield while seeking to develop another real estate project. In addition to the firms profiled in the following subsections, several others operate in other parts of the United States.

Mars Equities

Mars Equities, a Chicago-based real estate investment company, specializes in acquiring and remediating well-located brownfield properties for the institutional-grade commercial and industrial markets. The firm grew out of an environmental contracting business. According to the company's acquisitions director, the firm began buying brownfields in 1989 and has invested over $90 million in 22 sites. Although Mars owns property in numerous states, the bulk of its acquisitions have been in Minnesota, Illinois, California, and, more recently, Texas and Florida. Mars buys properties for cash at 30 to 60 cents on the dollar (or less), requiring a before-tax internal rate of return of 18 to 23 percent. The average holding period is two to three years and the exit requirement no longer than five to six years. The company's strategy is to "fully" remediate the property, using on-site methods or the dig-and-dump approach if needed, and seek the highest level of closure document possible. Hence, it generally avoids containing contamination on site and risk-based cleanup.

Catellus Corporation

Catellus is a publicly held, full-service real estate development firm active in California, with holdings in several other western and midwestern states. It grew out of a division set up to manage and dispose of land assets from the Santa Fe Railroad. Catellus has grown into a major player in the brownfield arena, acquiring, remediating, and developing medium to large sites for various types of industrial, commercial, mixed-use, and residential property. Its holdings include over 830,000 acres of land (much of it from the old railroad portfolio) and about 16 million square feet of income-producing property with a current value over $1 billion. Its development record includes more than ten projects of considerable scale, several of which are former industrial facilities in prime locations with excellent views. Catellus has also participated in joint ventures with other responsible parties and brownfield companies. According to the director of environmental services in Catellus's San Francisco office, the company is able to obtain financing from U.S. lenders for some of its projects with residual contamination and active remediation on site.

LandBank, Inc.

Located in Denver, San Francisco, and Washington, D.C., LandBank has specialized in land restoration since its creation in 1994. Several of the company's principals were formerly environmental consultants. The firm is now 20 percent owned by International Technology, a large environmental consulting firm. The firm is vertically integrated, with functions including real estate investment, environmental law, site remediation, and environmental insurance. It also enters occasional joint ventures with firms such as Catellus. According to one of LandBank's principals, the firm has acquired three properties to date at a cost of $20 million. It is also investing remediation and legal expenses in these holdings. All three are close to sale to developers and investors, who are already lined up. LandBank also has 15 other properties under signed contracts at a total acquisition price of $150 million.

The firm seeks to buy properties cheaply and has a target of at least 20 percent for internal rate of return, although it has considered strategic acquisitions with a projected IRR below 20 percent to maintain existing relationships with developers. The final use of its real estate is flexible, and LandBank considers residential conversions and projects where market demand exists.

One sought-after function is environmental insurance in which coverage, language, cost, and term are often tailored for participants in a specific deal. This vertically integrated firm can obtain financing for its remediated properties from debt venture funds because of its insurance expertise, and its ability to prepare risk profiles for environmental engineering and then provide insurance with a term equal to or longer than the debt instrument.

Hemisphere Corporation

Based in Cleveland, Ohio, Hemisphere was formed in 1995. Both of its principals are attorneys who understand the legal and remediation sides of the brownfield equation. Their knowledge is particularly strong in Ohio, where they were key in drafting the state's VCP, and understand involving the private sector. The firm's services include guiding site remediation and producing closure documents for sites using a risk-based approach (see Chapter 12). Hemisphere also recently began acquiring sites with commercial and industrial potential, including sites with underground storage tanks, for its own portfolio.

Not-for-Profit Corporations

Several models exist for not-for-profit entities in the brownfield arena. For the most part, they seek to revitalize properties with some market potential that are too small or troubled for private players to consider. Not-for-profit companies might focus on a geographic area or specific product or service, depending on their mission. Some are created specifically for the remediation of a particular site. Most, but not all, take title to contaminated property.

Phoenix Land Recycling Company

This new not-for-profit company was established by Clean Sites, Inc., a national brownfield player, to operate in Pennsylvania. It has received substantial funding from philanthropic organizations, including Heinz Endowments. Phoenix plans to select sites with a high potential for reuse, conduct the environmental investigation, and have remediation plans approved by state regulators. Once remediation costs have been quantified, Phoenix plans to market the properties to private parties, seeking to recoup its investment upon sale or through joint ventures. Hence, its niche is to provide information about the costs of environmental remediation.

CCLR

The California Center for Land Recycling, supported by a major grant from the James Ervine Foundation, was formed in 1996. It provides technical assistance to community-based organizations and to developers and other parties to develop specific sites. According to its director, CCLR hopes to undertake brownfield projects that meet criteria for environmental responsibility, economic feasibility, and community support. CCLR is developing a series of outreach programs and plans to have demonstration sites soon.

Neighborhood Progress, Inc.

This Cleveland-based organization has been actively rebuilding sites in the city of Cleveland. It conducts development for its own account, delivers technical assistance to smaller community-based organizations, and provides gap financing, such as below-market-rate second mortgages, for other worthy projects. Having completed several hundred units of market-rate housing since 1993, NPI is a large player in this market segment. Funded by local philanthropic foundations and industry, NPI recently moved into the field of strategic assembly of brownfield sites for industrial and commercial development. According to a project director, NPI has acquired several acres of brownfields to supplement the holdings of a notorious five-acre factory site that burned two years ago and plans other acquisitions. Its niche is sites with marginal economic potential, leaving prime development sites to the large players.

Science Park Development Corporation

SPDC was established to receive brownfield property from Olin Corp., which acknowledged responsibility for an industrial complex in New Haven, Connecticut (see Chapter 10). SPDC receives partly remediated buildings, conducts some additional remediation and renovation, and then markets and manages the properties. By actively remediating property and holding land leases under former brownfields occupied by others, SPDC also acts as a shallow-pocket liability shield for other players in the deal.

Lenders

Generally, lenders are amenable to participating in brownfield projects if risks can be quantified. Construction lenders, where repayment of principal takes months or a few years, are mostly concerned about the borrower's collateral relative to contingencies in the construction budget for unknown site costs and whether or not the project has or can readily obtain takeout financing. Permanent lenders, whose capital is tied down for a decade or more, are much more concerned about the borrower's defaulting and potentially owning a stigmatized asset of questionable value. Many conventional private lenders still appear to be reluctant to lend funds on formerly contaminated lands with some contamination remaining on site without a loan guarantee or strong indemnification letter. Thus, brownfields are still credit deals rather than real estate deals.

According to a spokesman from Aegon USA Realty Management:

> In today's environment, if lenders can be comfortable with risk, given the fierce competition to sell money, then lenders will lend. If lenders lend, then developers will develop. Lenders control the developer's risk because they recognize that substantially all the developer's risk is shared by the lenders. Legislation and regulations that protect lenders from liability do not protect the lender's exposure in the project itself.

The rest of this section presents the views of lenders regarding their relative comfort with certain recent key developments. Comments about construction and permanent financing are based on interviews with a few experienced brownfield lenders in the United States.

Surveys of Lenders' Attitudes

Studies have been conducted of lenders' and investors' attitudes toward contaminated sites. For example, William Kinnard and Elaine Worzala's survey of 135 lenders and investors in 1995 found that many would consider financing or investing in potentially contaminated property.[1] Sites with nuclear contamination were understandably least popular among lenders, while about one-quarter of lenders surveyed would consider sites with nonleaking underground storage tanks acceptable. Only 10 percent would extend financing for sites with contaminated groundwater. These results were published before many state VCPs went into effect, however.

Another survey, reported in the premier issue of *Brownfield News,* found that just under one-quarter of lenders surveyed still have concerns about environmentally impaired real estate.[2] While "fully" remediated properties can readily be financed, opinions differ about which agency's definition of "clean" is reliable. The overall trend appears to be for banks to feel more comfortable with EPA's or the states' flexible standards for cleanliness, but the group of banks requiring *no* residual contamination grew substantially, to about one-quarter of the lenders surveyed. Banks are also looking more carefully at the effects of nearby contaminated property on borrowers' loan applications.

Construction Lenders

PNC Bank is typical of a progressive commercial lender active in New Jersey and Pennsylvania. It provides construction loans, provided takeout financing is in place. Although lending decisions are driven primarily by the potential borrower's credit history, PNC is also concerned about the value of its collateral if troubles arise.

PNC has financed properties where the outcomes of remediation varied, but in general, if a site is totally clean or if the state has deemed remediation complete, the outcome of remediation in and of itself would not hinder financing. The bank is flexible about working around encapsulated contamination left on site, so long as the land under buildings is clean. It is seriously concerned, however, about ongoing groundwater monitoring and third-party lawsuits.

The quality of a state closure document offers some comfort, but it is not an ironclad guarantee of lenders' comfort. A memorandum of understanding with EPA is potentially quite valuable, but PNC has made loans without one, based on "good science." Reopeners for changes in land use are considered routine. And liability for lenders appears to be acceptable in states where liability exemptions are codified and where no restrictions have been placed on lenders' holding periods in the event of default. Lenders tend to be very concerned about providing financing in a state with no brownfield program, and the federal liability exemption does not cover all applicable statutes, only CERCLA.

On the critical issue of collateral, indemnification by a company with deep pockets and very creditworthy anchor tenants offer the most security. The presence of insurance would be a valuable component of a bank's decision to lend funds (with comprehensive environmental insurance preferable to stop-loss), especially if the premium is reasonable and the term matches the life of the loan and runs with the property. Stocks in escrow and letters of credit also provide real comfort, and cross-collateralized property provides some value.

Construction loans for brownfield deals at or close to industry interest rates, and loan-to-value and debt service coverage ratios are available if the deal has the right kind of collateral. For example, a developer might be required to reserve and maintain a 20 percent contingency fund for a construction loan.

State Public Housing Lenders

One public lender in the Great Lakes region provides subsidized permanent loans exclusively for housing projects and some construction financing. Similar to other permanent lenders whose capital is tied down for a decade or more, it is concerned about default, the quality of collateral, and the safety of the property for residential occupants.

The agency has provided financing for sites where the outcomes of remediation varied, but in general, if a site is totally clean or if the state environmental agency has deemed remediation complete, the outcome of remediation in and of itself would not hinder financing. The agency is flexible about working around encapsulated contamination left on site, so long as the land under buildings is clean and contamination is below "action" limits. The removal of hot spots is a moderate concern because of the potential for exposure to residents. Ongoing groundwater monitoring and third-party lawsuits are very serious concerns, however.

Because this state has very strong closure documents, the agency expects a CNTS to be available and considers the matter closed if one is attained. Reopeners for changes in remediation technology are not an issue, mostly because sites are generally already cleaned to residential standards. Further, lenders' liability appears to be fully accepted in this state, where liability exemptions are codified. Restrictions on holding periods for lenders in the event of default would be problematic, however.

The public lender is used to operating with borrowers who have limited collateral and normally requires indemnification from the borrower or owner, regardless of how deep its pockets are. Deals would involve a standard loan-to-value ratio for the industry, but debt service coverage ratios and interest rates are much more favorable to borrowers than in the private sector.

The case studies indicate lower loan-to-value ratios than for greenfield loans and a requirement for indemnification or loan guarantees to put permanent financing in place. Outcomes of the case studies appear to be more conservative than survey results. The effects are even more pronounced for institutional lenders.

Responsible Parties

Responsible parties, both willing prior owners and those required to participate through court action, can play important roles as site remediators and indemnifiers. Because they presumably have derived profits from the land for a number of years, it seems only fair that they should be part of the solution to the problem of brownfields. The courts may not let players with deep pockets off the financial hook, even if the land were sold long ago and several later property owners are involved. The depth of corporate pockets is an issue in how vigorously the courts pursue them and whether or not development could affect their bottom lines. Thus, solvent responsible parties have different approaches to the issue. Three of them are described in the following subsections.

ICI/Dulux

This offshore paint manufacturing company has many plants in several countries. Because the nature of the contamination (lead and hydrocarbons) is very similar in many locations, the firm has developed a site remediation and marketing team whose learning curve is virtually flat. The in-house team assesses the problem, conducts on-site remediation where feasible, operates the public input process, and has been able to market and sell several sites at close to market value. Its role is that of remediator and in some cases joint venture partner.

Olin Corp.

Olin's role is that of the responsible corporate citizen, having partially remediated several buildings and sites in one of its older industrial complexes and then turned them over to a not-for-profit corporation it helped create. Olin also provides indemnification to new occupants against future environmental liability. The company is comfortable with the latter role in part because the firm's research function allows it to understand the environmental risks of its actions. It also maintains some control over the generation of any new contamination by maintaining veto power over new tenants on remediated properties. The firm receives tax relief and good publicity for its efforts, which were key in revitalizing a depressed section of New Haven.

General Electric

This consumer products giant has numerous surplus properties in the United States and abroad. Several of the properties are large, strategic holdings in or near the downtown cores of moderately sized cities in the Northeast. GE also has a financial statement larger than most state or local governments and some foreign countries. Because of its size, any revenues from development of brownfields would be insignificant, so the financial incentive for development is not present. On the other hand, GE's pockets are very deep. Partly as the result of a recent court case, in which it was held responsible for contamination of an industrial property developed as residential that it had not owned for several decades (and that also involved several intervening owners), GE has become very averse to undertaking the risks of developing its brownfields, and decisions about disposing of sites are very closely held at the highest corporate levels. Other top-level firms may be in the same no-win situation with their corporate brownfield inventories. The very large opportunity cost to host communities is not internalized into the corporate giants' business functions, leaving an unfortunate situation of market failure needing new policies to address it. Other large firms, notably some oil companies that also have retail operations, have indemnified new owners when their gas station properties are shut down, remediated, and sold for development. These smaller sites, however, lack the strategic importance of downtown core properties that could form the nucleus of urban revitalization.

Hybrid Consultants

Many environmental consulting firms are available to help steer a site through the process. It is the hybrid consultants, however, who can add real value to brownfield development because they can speak several languages—environmental science and finance, the law and remediation, and property appraisal and remediation. The case studies discuss the important roles of these players in specific development projects. What is missing in this country are appraisers who can place a value on contaminated property "as is." Nearly all appraisers instead provide a value "as if clean." Without the valuation as is, which would provide value net of remediation cost and stigma, banks cannot ascertain a property's value for consideration in the loan-to-value ratio, and loans become even more difficult to obtain. According to a principal of the Real Estate Counseling Group of Connecticut, only a handful of appraisers in the United States are willing and able to perform this key function in appraising brownfields. He attributes this shortfall to fear of losing the appraiser's professional insurance and to lack of knowledge. Although the main appraisal bodies in the United States, the Appraisal Institute and the American Society of Appraisers, offer periodic seminars and some guidance about the valuation of contaminated property, they do not require appraisers to take specific steps in the case of environmental contamination. The official believes that in the future, a team approach will be more common, in which the appraiser would be one of several players, including those able to conduct scientific measurement of environmental issues and a person familiar with the site's environmental regulation process.

Great Britain uses a model that rectifies this situation. An appraiser in Manchester covers three key areas of a brownfield project, valuing the contaminated property, guiding remediation using a risk-based approach, and connecting projects with public funding and sometimes private financing (see Chapter 16).

Environmental Insurance and Indemnification

Insurance and indemnification by outside parties, including government bodies, are generally substitutes that reduce the uncertainty about which party is absorbing the environmental risk in a brownfield project. Neither is a loan guarantee that can assure a lender that debt service will be paid, but they do offer protection against a borrower's longer-term cash flow problems regarding unexpected expenses for environmental contamination. State VCPs that offer a CNTS absorb some of the future risk (subject to reopeners) by locking in regulatory statutes and procedures, assuring the other players that the rules of the brownfield game will not change.

Insurance

Environmental remediation insurance is still in the early stages, with little actuarial data available for complex problems. Only a handful of major carriers (including Zurich-America, Reliance-ECS, and AIG) have provided or currently provide environmental insurance for brownfield properties. Another potentially major player is Kemper Insurance, which has announced plans to enter the field. Other participants include reinsurers such as the Underwriters Reinsurance Group's URC environmental specialty group. Environmental insurance brokers, who work primarily for property developers, are also active; major brokers include ERIC, Neace Lukens (based in Columbus, Ohio), and Willis Carron. Such brokers search for the best products for the specific needs of a project from among the major insurance carriers.

Insurance against environmental problems is more readily available for properties with USTs through both public state insurance funds and private sources. In general, however, insurance for many other brownfield problems is often too expensive because it is available only for troubled properties. The language, term, coverage, and cost of a policy are often problematic in terms of the project's value and lenders' comfort. Above all, environmental insurance is not a substitute for loan guarantees.

At least two forms of environmental insurance are available. One form, stop-loss (also known as "cost cap coverage"), operates like a major medical policy. The property owner agrees to pay for present or future remediation, up to a predetermined dollar amount, and then insurance takes over up to the insured amount (typically double the cost of remediation). Hence, the owner's loss is stopped at a certain point. The cost is substantial but less than the comprehensive environmental risk policy described in the following paragraph. Stop-loss insurance is usually taken during site remediation. According to an official with Neace Lukens, lenders like stop-loss insurance because it helps eliminate fears of cost overruns that could render the developer incapable of finishing the project. Provided the developer has funds to cover costs up to the predetermined stop-loss amount, the bank's concerns about default on the loan are minimized. Typically, the cost of stop-loss insurance ranges from 3 to 6 percent of the limits purchased, which are typically equal to the remediation amount, depending on the developer's participation. Overall, this insurance reflects less than 1 percent of total project cost.

The other form of insurance is much more comprehensive and protects the property owner (and presumably the cash flow that supports any debt service on the property) against future environmental problems. This insurance is typically taken in addition to stop-loss coverage, either concurrently or after cleanup is completed. This type of insurance, referred to as "pollution legal liability," usually requires environmental engineering research case by case, which can make it very expensive. Fortunately, if an owner has purchased cost cap insurance and already remediated the site, then the cost of site investigation has already been allocated.

FIGURE 8.1

ALLOCATING EXPERTISE AND DIVIDING UP THE RISKS AMONG BROWNFIELD PLAYERS

	Reducing Costs	Communicating	Assuming Risk
Real Estate Developers	□	■	■
Brownfield Equity Companies	□	■	□
Not-for-Profit Companies	□		□
Lenders			■
Hybrid Consultants	□	□	
Appraisers			■
Insurance Companies	■		□■
Local Governments	□	■	□■
Responsible Parties	□		□
State VCPs	□	■	□

□ = Some in this category are making this effort now.

■ = This action needs to be greatly increased in the near future.

According to an official with LandBank, however, the needs of the insurer, property owner, and lender diverge somewhat in the critical areas of coverage, language, term, and cost. Owners want coverage against unexpected contamination; insurers generally want to cover only what is already known. Insurers want a shorter term to protect against long-term changes in regulation and the potential for discovery of additional contamination; lenders want the insurance term to coincide with the length of the loan. Cost has been the main impediment, because insurance is pegged to environmental risks, not to real estate values. Thus, for many smaller deals with complex environmental problems, a real mismatch can exist between insurance costs and value to the parties, and insurance may not be feasible. The cost for comprehensive environmental insurance can vary widely, from under $10,000 for a multiyear term to $250,000 or more for a longer term. For a larger property, multiyear policy discounts could make this option more affordable. Pollution legal liability insurance represents an increase of several percent in the cost of the deal and a large increase in transaction expenses. Moreover, this product pertains only to those deals where risks can be quantified. In sum, several equity players have indicated their dissatisfaction with available environmental insurance and do not see it as of value at this point.

Nevertheless, the field is becoming more competitive, and prices are dropping substantially. For a $5 million real estate deal with a $4 million loan and $1 million in cleanup costs, the typical cost for pollution legal liability coverage for a seven-year term, paid at inception, would be about $100,000, or 2 percent of project costs. This figure is about 20 percent lower than it was one year earlier. While this coverage is probably for a shorter time than the loan term, it should cover virtually all concerns of the lender. Even coupled with stop-loss coverage, brownfield remediation insurance should be available for about 3 percent of total project cost (or less) within one year.

What is needed, according to Bank of America's environmental service manager, is environmental insurance for a portfolio of loans, which would spread the risk and keep the cost down to a reasonable level (say, under $1,000 per loan). This type of insurance product recently became available.

Indemnification by Private Parties

Responsible parties have been forced, or in some cases have volunteered (e.g., Olin), to provide indemnification against future environmental problems. If the entity is well financed, this indemnification is very valuable to other parties in the deal, because it is clear where the risk is being absorbed. Having a not-for-profit corporation with shallow pockets created to remediate a site and then kept alive to indemnify site owners and lenders against future actions has some value in limiting owners' liability, but it does not necessarily assure that the problem will be fixed.

Government Bodies to Reduce Risks

This approach may be a trend of the future, in which market failure can justify government intervention to absorb some of the risks by indemnifying parties against future environmental problems. This indemnification would go beyond direct prior property ownership and responsibility for remediation. The municipal groundwater management zone being developed by Emeryville, California, is a good example of a local government's absorbing potential liability for future environmental problems (the financing mechanism has not yet been worked out). The community of Waterbury, Connecticut, offered more project-specific indemnification, agreeing to provide this assurance funded by tax increment financing.

The Players' Abilities

Figure 8.1 identifies current and future actions that each major group of players could take to close the gap between brownfields and greenfields: reducing the cost of development, communicating with others, and absorbing more of the risk of environmental uncertainty. With the exception of insurance products (which are on the brink of being available), virtually all players participate to some extent in reducing costs. What is lacking is developers', brownfield equity companies', local governments', and state VCP administrators' knowledge of the needs of other players, and they must improve communications, in part by providing information about specific projects. The main shortfall, however, is in the risks involved. Lenders and appraisers need to take on a larger share of the risk. The risk for lenders could be partially offset by more responsive indemnification and insurance products, and services from both public and private sector entities. The next chapter provides more recommendations on these and other matters.

Notes

1. William Kinnard and Elaine Worzala, "Attitudes and Policies of Institutional Investors and Lenders toward On-Site and Nearby Transactions," paper presented at the annual meeting of the American Real Estate Society, April 1996, Lake Tahoe, California.

2. Bill Mundy, "Intermediaries Influence Buyer Behavior: The Role of Banks and Environmental Firms," *Brownfield News* 1(1), 1997, pp. 29–30.

9 Recommendations for Brownfield Developers And Policy Makers

This final chapter in Part I contains recommendations for both brownfield developers and federal, state, and local public policy makers. The strategies for developers are intended to provide guidance on how best to deal with constraints at each stage of development. The chapter also includes suggestions for the real estate industry, including appraisers, lenders, and insurers.

Recommendations for Developers

The following recommendations have been gleaned from the successful case studies and from other research on brownfields from players who were not directly involved in the cases. The recommendations are presented roughly in chronological order in the development process. Many of these suggestions are from the strategic features presented in Figure 7.3 (p. 62). The recommendations cover site selection and design, environmental regulators, remediation, marketing and remediation tradeoffs, access to public funds, private financing, lowering risk, and guarantees. Perhaps the most important recommendation is to hire a consultant if your brownfield problem is particularly difficult.

Site Selection and Design

- *Select a site with high demand and great views that is heavily trafficked and in the path of future public investment.* While all real estate projects should be sensitive to this issue, brownfield sites with low demand will face more competition, probably delaying a project by requiring larger public subsidies, all else being equal.
- *Buy low.* Offer a heavily discounted price for the property, obtain the property at foreclosure, or buy the mortgage. If you buy it before remediation, you can get a very substantial discount.
- *Rezone the property before development.* This basic development and planning strategy can be risky, but

many brownfields are incorrectly zoned, and the potential to add value here is great. If you attempt this tactic, do not forget to consider impact on the neighbors and the need to manage public participation.

- *Build at a high density to amortize extra environmental costs.* This important principle simply dilutes expenses over a larger project. Public subsidies are also likely to be larger for a larger project.
- *Generally avoid single-family detached housing, unless the site is very lightly contaminated.* Marketing the project to families with children is probably a hard sell if play areas contain any residual contamination, even if they are capped. Moreover, cleanup standards (and therefore costs) for risk-based corrective actions are often substantially higher for residential properties. Unless you can put any remaining contamination under public roadways, it could be a tough project to market.
- *Design the site to minimize costs.* You can save costs and avoid delay by placing remediated soil under parking lots, keeping land under buildings relatively clean, and avoiding basements and other underground digging in some cases. To avoid any future excavation, you might also want to consider putting utilities aboveground. Sometimes cost savings can be substantial and may not negatively affect marketing the property.
- *Buy a larger site, clean all of it, and sell off part of it.* This strategy for enhancing cash flow is a good one, but make sure you will not be competing with yourself.
- *Save money by buying a previously remediated site.* Consider a site that another party has already partly remediated. The seller might be having financial difficulties, and you could get the property at a low price. But be aware that, although it will probably save you substantial amounts in remediation expense, you might also inherit environmental problems or liabilities that go with a poorly remediated site.

Dealing with Regulators

These recommendations depend greatly on what state your project is in, although many states are watching closely what other states are doing in similar situations. Eventually, most effective innovations will be more widely accepted.

- *Ask for a regulatory lead agency.* If your site involves multiple contamination, or if your state is crowded with regulatory players, ask all the state and local regulatory agencies to organize the regulatory hierarchy for you and designate one lead agency to coordinate requests from and needs of the other regulatory players. You would thus have only one primary point of contact whose word would be final
- *Ask for accelerated or local coordination.* Overseas and in some U.S. regions, municipalities are taking a larger role in coordinating and issuing environmental compliance permits, especially for brownfield sites with a common type of problem. Thus, the municipality can act as the coordinating agency and, in some cases, may have procedures for compliance predetermined and already cleared with the appropriate state agencies. Such a system can save time.
- *Negotiate the remediation process up front and obtain a verbal guarantee.* Depending on the state and your political connections, you may be able to obtain verbal guarantees from senior regulators regarding alternative remediation strategies and likely outcomes if you are successful.
- *Get the highest form of closure letter available from regulators.* This suggestion refers to the best form of closure available at each step of remediation, including approval of the plan, the certificate of completion, an NFA letter, CNTS, and a memorandum of understanding from EPA, if available. Your lender is likely to ask for a closure document if it is available, and if liability protection can be extended to future owners, the document should be capitalized into a higher sale price.
- *Separate regulation of soil and groundwater contamination.* Your state or municipality's support of this concept can have a major impact on which lead agency you select and how much closure you can expect for groundwater cleanups. If groundwater management is a viable public regulatory strategy for you, you should explore the possibility You should coordinate this decision with any cost-recovery procedures you might pursue, however.
- *Be prepared to accept monitoring to preserve the closure document.* Monitoring could be required to preserve the CNTS or other closure document. Budget for it and incorporate it into your marketing if needed.
- *Obtain closure in phases.* Obtain a closure letter for each phase of construction or for each project so you can go to the next phase without waiting. Doing so will help save on financing and carrying costs and may prevent you from missing a marketing window. You can also break off a troublesome part of the project from the rest and move on.
- *Use information from other projects.* Some communities have tables available so you can compare your

site with a recently remediated one close by. Doing so could save time and simplify the procedures you need to perform.

Site Remediation

The following suggestions are broad strategies that could apply to your project regardless of which technologies are used, but they pertain mostly to managing residual contamination left on site. Overall, remediation costs can be expected to average about 10 percent of project costs, or $4.00 to $5.00 per square foot of land. Remember to choose an experienced consultant, which may require certification in some states. And if your remediation project is highly visible, keep the neighbors informed.

- *Remove only hot spots.* There is usually no good reason to excavate an entire site. Spend some money on a well-designed report from a consultant, and develop a plan to remove only hot spots of contamination, thus saving transportation and disposal costs.
- *Use risk-based corrective action.* You can save a large amount of money by remediating a nonresidential site to the appropriate standard for an industrial or commercial end use rather than to the standard for near-pristine low-density residential use. A deed restriction is often required in such cases, however.
- *Use on-site remediation.* On-site remediation may include a variety of physical, chemical, or biological techniques, or a combination thereof. The physical approach may require a substantial investment in equipment. Thus, the numbers may work only for larger sites or for companies with several sites or for environmental or public remediators with portable remediation equipment. In any event, this approach may save the exorbitant costs of dig-and-dump excavation.
- *Cap or encapsulate contamination.* Encapsulation is fairly common where risk-based corrective actions are used. It can save large amounts of money, especially where construction costs overlap greatly with remediation costs. A deed restriction must usually be filed with local authorities, however, implying a tradeoff with marketing the property.
- *Remediate to surrounding levels.* Sometimes the area around your site will have a high level of some heavy metal or other substance, where the stated standard is much lower. In this case, it might be advantageous to argue that your site need be remediated only to concentrations consistent with this surrounding level, thus saving funds.
- *Encapsulate residual contamination under public space.* It could be effective to put any remaining contamination on site but capped under roadways. Doing so should have the added advantage of making the project easier to market and finance.
- *Maintain internal documentation and soil sampling.* This approach can reduce delays during construction when dealing with landfills. Often the quality of the remediated soil is an issue and you will still need to undertake independent sampling, but knowing what you have will help you make better decisions and may enable you to negotiate a better price with the landfill operator. Moreover, the records can help you document how clean your site is.
- *Consider litigation to recover your costs.* You may be able to recover some costs from previous owners, neighbors, or other responsible parties, even after the fact. Be aware, however, that certain protocols exist for site cleanup and cost recovery and that some procedures may preclude later efforts to recover costs. If you plan to pursue this route, make sure you follow the appropriate guidelines.
- *Keep the public informed.* Do not neglect to keep your neighbors informed of your activities, especially if on-site remediation is visible and prolonged. Use mail and public meetings to keep neighbors in the information loop and avoid delay.

Marketing/Remediation Tradeoffs

- *Market your property as cleaner than clean.* If you have kept comprehensive records of soil samples, you may be able to market your remediated site as "cleaner than clean," which would minimize the stigma when you market the property. The idea is to document how clean your property is, perhaps contrasting it with other parcels offered for sale in the market that may have undiscovered contamination. This strategy would also work well in conjunction with a solid closure document.
- *Consider the tradeoff between environmental restrictions and marketing.* A deed restriction in conjunction with RBCAs and/or caps may present a marketing challenge. Consider the cost savings and whether or not your project can absorb a longer time on the market. You might be able to avoid this problem by targeting market segments not likely to be concerned with any remaining contamination, such as high-rise housing for empty nesters.

Public Subsidies

Public subsidies can be worked into a brownfield package in a number of ways. The projects in the case studies typically received subsidies ranging from 15 to 20 percent of total project costs. Regardless of which form of public assistance you request, it would be a good idea to prepare a fiscal and economic impact analysis of reuse of the land before and after remediation. The amount of detail should reflect the amount of money you ask for. For example, before remediation and development, a brownfield may generate little or no tax revenue or jobs. After an appropriate public investment, however, the project could then be shown to generate annual revenue from property taxes, sales tax, and income taxes, which could justify paying back the public investment. The project might also provide jobs and other nonfiscal benefits. Most subsidies are made available through state programs, though some are locally available.

- *Ask for the land to be donated.* Get the city to donate any parcels it owns to your project. Some cities have land banks of tax-foreclosed properties set up for this purpose.
- *Get site investigation or remediation grants, if available.* Remember, however, that if public funds are used, information should be assumed to be public knowledge.
- *Have the city remediate the property directly.* The city can remediate the property (and step into the chain of title) and transfer it to you, legally and physically clean, with a closure document. Then, the city can later pursue cost recovery without holding up the project.
- *Apply for remediation tax credits, if available.* If they are not available, ask the local government to reimburse you for some expenses of remediation.
- *Get state permanent financing based on use of the land for economic development and housing.* Some states offer permanent financing for worthy projects, such as low-income housing, that can be built on brownfields. Such projects could be deeply subsidized.
- *Ask the local government for loan guarantees or indemnification.* This approach may be an emerging area over the next few years, especially if the local government can figure out how to secure this contingent liability exposure through insurance, self-insurance, or a taxing district. Loan guarantees would probably be more valuable in acquiring financing than indemnification against future environmental problems.
- *Obtain status as an empowerment zone, CDBGs, or other inducements, if available.* Shop around for available grants and loans through the usual political channels. Some cities require involvement of a not-for-profit entity to gain access to these funds.
- *Obtain local property tax abatements, if available.* This standard operating procedure all over the country does not necessarily work with some other inducements (e.g., TIF).
- *Get tax increment financing, if available.* TIF is a form of local improvement district that has substantial potential to provide a stream of funds to capitalize loan guarantees, groundwater remediation, or remediation expenses.
- *Ask for industrial development bonds, if available.* These public-purpose revenue bonds are generally tax exempt, but the competition for them is very intense because they are typically rationed at the state level. Hence, they are usually reserved for projects that propose to generate a high number of jobs.
- *Ask about a public/local groundwater mitigation fund.* A few cities are looking to pool funds through tax increment financing or other means to set funds aside for groundwater management. This approach could put the liability for groundwater cleanup on the city.

Lowering the Risk for Lenders

This group of strategies should help you with lenders. While not all are widely accepted, they should all work toward making lenders more comfortable and, in combination with other sensible strategies, may bring that private sector loan within reach. The approach is to work within the framework of a real estate deal rather than a credit deal. Hybrid consultants facile in both environmental and lending cultures are a definite plus.

- *Do not ask for a private sector remediation loan in the near future.* Some public loans may be available, however. Most banks will not touch such a plan, so do not bother asking unless it is a credit deal.
- *Split the sale of lots from contamination under an adjacent parcel.* The lender will probably be more comfortable if the loan pertains only to the cleaned part of the site. The remainder of the site could be used for parking, and held by a separate entity and leased to the owner as a parking lot for a long term.
- *Investigate a land lease.* A land lease from the remediator, seller, or developer provides a substantial measure of insulation for keeping past contamination problems separate from the property securing the mortgage. Use of the building and the lease's effect on cash flow may also be issues.
- *Employ good science to show how low the risk of harm is to inhabitants.* Environmental studies documenting potential effects of contamination on future site users and the real estate should be clear and allow lenders to quantify their business risk.

- *Expect to provide extra collateral, especially for a construction loan.* Plan to have more collateral set aside, a stronger balance sheet, and/or a lower loan-to-value ratio than for a conventional greenfield real estate deal.
- *Offer debt service coverage over normal industry levels.* For permanent loans, extra debt service coverage and lower loan-to-value ratios can make lenders more comfortable.

Loan Guarantees

- *Obtain insurance.* Stop-loss, pollution legal liability, or other types of insurance are most useful if they run for the same time as the loan.
- *Obtain indemnification letters from a deep-pocket polluter or other responsible party.* Indemnification would cover any future environmental problems and allow the deal to proceed based on the merits of the real estate transaction. The deeper the pockets, the more secure the lender will feel. Municipalities might also play this role.
- *Obtain indemnification from a not-for-profit remediator.* This approach is useful if no willing or able responsible party can indemnify the lender or future owner against expenses related to future environmental problems. Having a not-for-profit CDC remediate the property (especially if it steps into the chain of title and is still in existence) can afford some comfort for the lender.
- *Obtain a loan guarantee from a responsible party or parent company.* In a sense, this loan guarantee transforms the brownfield project into a credit deal, but it provides the most comfort for lenders. An outside party as guarantor can also be expensive.

Implications for Public Policy

This section includes recommendations for federal, state, and local governments. It considers policy in light of the evidence and trends suggested by the limited demand for brownfield sites, progress in state VCPs, and the successful brownfield case studies. For example, typical environmental remediation costs for successful projects (about 10 percent of total costs) are really not that large a portion of overall costs, especially for projects with only one type of soil contamination.

Public subsidies appear to exceed expenses purely for remediation, indicating that other presumably market-related costs are being supported. Subsidies should be made available in whatever form is most useful to the developer but should not inadvertently exceed a predetermined amount, say 15 to 20 percent of project costs. Industrial projects and low-income housing projects, because of their lower end value, require larger subsidies. Amortizing remediation costs that accrue to the site (such as for contaminated soil) as opposed to the regional or local environment (such as groundwater), and regulating and financing them separately may become more popular in the future.

The availability of equitable and efficient mechanisms for public financing to deal with nonpotable groundwater is an evolving concern, and big changes are likely in this arena over the next few years.

Federal Government

The federal government's role should be to deal with the overall regulatory environment, letting local governments deal with implementation of brownfield development programs. Hence, EPA should move toward more memorandums of understanding with the states. The federal government should act as a central observer of national trends in brownfield development, leaving the development and updating of a register to state or local governments. The federal government should consider supporting state and local governments with more EPA pilot projects and planning funds. Other specific recommendations follow.

- *Develop legislation with an automatic memorandum of understanding for states meeting a minimum standard.* A way should be available for EPA to systematically alleviate the pressure for memorandums of understanding for states meeting a certain level of voluntary cleanup program. This legislation should be developed by the federal government. If EPA is reluctant to give up the right to reopen projects "forever," one option would be to have a memorandum of understanding last for a certain number of years, say a decade or two, which would approximate the life of a typical mortgage loan yet still allow EPA to reconsider substantial changes in scientific knowledge that may occur in the future.
- *Create a location for brownfields with transportation monies.* Many inner-city brownfields are poorly located, far from interstate highways, truck routes, rail and water ports, and other important transportation links. This disadvantage could be substantially reduced and the competitive position of brownfields enhanced by coordinated federal transportation financing through highway and ISTEA (Intermodal Surface Transportation Efficiency Act) funds to develop inner-city locations.
- *Offer remediation tax credits.* Very few states have programs that reward the private sector with grants to offset costs of remediation, and federal income

tax credits should be made available for this purpose. The tax credits would be available through filing tax returns and require little bureaucratic infrastructure. Only projects where property was actually remediated would be eligible, and the credits should be transferable to others.

- *Establish a database for monitoring outcomes of voluntary cleanup programs and sites affected.* Bankers are reluctant to lend funds because certain risks cannot be quantified. A database to compile evidence is necessary so risks can be quantified. State VCPs should be systematically monitored so innovations can be quickly applied elsewhere. And a database of properties should be established so that research can quantify the risks still poorly understood in the brownfield arena, such as the incidence of reopeners, the portion of remediated sites developed, appreciation of brownfields, the effect of deed restrictions on value, and the proportion of brownfields foreclosed.

State Government

The supply of brownfields is large and the demand for most brownfields relatively small. Hence, many surplus brownfields may sit for decades or longer before they are developed, if ever. Although many states have implemented voluntary cleanup programs oriented toward development of potentially economically viable brownfield sites, environmental standards should also be established for other long-term interim uses, such as active and passive parkland, buffers, and community gardens. States also need to plan for the orderly handoff of permitting responsibility to willing municipalities and enable them to perform these tasks. States can also support developing markets, and they can examine their tax and landfill policies as they affect brownfield development. Other specific recommendations follow.

- *Separate regulatory tracks for soil and groundwater contamination.* Some northern California and East Coast regions have already implemented this approach. Doing so can save time and money, and you can devote funds to mitigation rather than to excessive studies. Groundwater contamination is an areawide rather than site-specific problem. Soil contamination, on the other hand, must be addressed site by site.
- *Encourage more local control.* States should support local governments' attempts to take the lead in proactive measures like environmental permitting, development of information about comparable sites, and compilation of brownfield inventories. And states should train local regulators to accomplish these difficult and complicated tasks. While local control can alleviate regulatory bottlenecks, the state could deal with difficult cases.
- *Deal with the needs of large risk-averse firms with huge properties in strategic locations.* Some large, financially powerful companies own large portfolios of huge sites assembled in older northeastern and midwestern communities that are critical to reinvigorating their central cities. These responsible parties, however, are not risk takers and are more inclined simply to hold the properties to avoid future aggravation and bad press because disposition of the properties would have little or no impact on their bottom lines. States should investigate a financial mechanism that would encourage polluters to pay for cleanup while offering the communities an equitable outcome.
- *Support the market for demolition materials.* States could encourage the development of local markets for demolition materials, such as bricks and fixtures. In Sydney, Australia, and Auckland, New Zealand, for example, developers can contract out the demolition at a small profit rather than paying large fees to dump the material. If states do not directly support the market by buying materials, they should encourage local governments to do so.
- *Enact legislation covering landfills.* States that do not do so already should support stronger legislation that takes into account the actual costs and environmental implications of burying debris at a landfill. The responsibility for hazardous waste should follow its originator, even to a landfill. The absence of the apparent anonymity provided by some landfills would encourage more on-site remediation. And establishing higher charges to use a landfill would encourage on-site cleanup. In the long run, techniques for on-site remediation should be less expensive and create fewer problems for future generations.
- *Improve intergovernmental coordination.* More state and local governments should coordinate cleanup more closely to reduce the time required for development.
- *Develop targeted brownfield programs.* States should target development programs for specific problems—contaminated groundwater, urban sites requiring extensive subsidies, simple projects that could be addressed by the private sector or CDCs wanting to develop community gardens, parks, buffers, or other public spaces. One size program does not fit all.
- *Revise the tax structure.* State tax policy should be reviewed to take into account the development of

remediated brownfields. The state's tax structure may unintentionally work against the development of a property's highest and best use. While most communities receive revenue from income, property, and sales taxes, an emphasis on income tax and little on sales tax could discourage rezoning remediated brownfields for retail projects, even if it is the highest and best use for the property.

Local Government

Local government can play an important role by supporting realistic land prices, developing information about brownfields, taking a larger role in regulating contaminated sites, and reducing risk. In many ways, local governments are best qualified to guide subsidies toward their most effective use.

Doing nothing about brownfields is not a viable option, partly because it is politically untenable but also for fiscal reasons. Although county property tax assessors have generally been slow to recognize the effect of contamination on unsold properties, this situation is changing. According to a lawyer with the American Land Recycling Company in Pennsylvania, many companies with brownfield properties are asking for and receiving relief from property taxes. Governments cannot just stand still and expect property tax revenues from contaminated lands to remain stable.

- *Rezone the property to support realistic land prices.* Local planners and development entities, including designated brownfield coordinators, play a major role in developing brownfields. They should realize that many brownfields formerly used for industrial purposes will not be developed in our lifetimes. Thus, zoning and the designation of future land use for these properties should be realistic. Failure to do so could result in lower prices for well-located and potentially viable brownfields, making their development more difficult. Nevertheless, such a program will be politically difficult in many communities.
- *Develop a register of brownfield properties.* Local governments should collect all public data about contaminated properties as they exist (studies, listed sites, past use, and so on) and make the information available to interested parties. Such a register will guide development faster than the current approach of ad hoc deal chasing. At the same time it establishes a register, the local government should make development funds available. The registers must be made available so as to minimize threats to the tax base, because having public information available may lead to a large number of challenges to the property tax rate.
- *Rank brownfields in the order they need assistance.* Concurrent with the development of a register, local governments could designate brownfields needing immediate attention based on danger to the public health and economic development potential. Land banking or long-term interim uses are the lowest priority, with properties intended for open space somewhat higher. The probability that a brownfield can be assembled into an economically viable size is of prime importance when considering whether the parcel can be developed. Without proactive management of brownfields, the potential is diminished for larger cities to efficiently allocate scarce brownfield resources and stem the flow of industrial relocation to greenfield sites in the suburbs.
- *Develop programs to reduce blighted properties with little economic value.* More attention needs to be paid to reducing the negative effects of blighted brownfields on the local community. Because market demand is not sufficient to support most brownfields, a more modest goal is to turn them into neutral uses, such as buffers between incompatible land uses, active and passive recreation, or community gardens. Such properties could have indirect positive effects on neighborhoods, enhancing property values by removing a negative influence.
- *Control of brownfield permitting.* Local governments can play a bigger role in permitting, with the state's approval. This situation is common in the U.K., in New South Wales, Australia, and in Auckland, New Zealand, and California is experimenting with it. Having coordinated sources of local funding and a brownfield register would be part of this effort.
- *Finance groundwater management districts.* This suggestion applies to areas where groundwater is too contaminated to drink and municipal water is available from elsewhere. The local government could use tax increment financing.
- *Offer contingent liability and loan guarantees.* Financially able municipalities should consider offering loan guarantees for brownfield development to help the properties succeed in the market. One way to handle the contingent liability on the municipal books is to act as self-insurer or to securitize potential losses through revenue bonds.
- *Encourage mediation.* Local governments have an opportunity to guide brownfield development by encouraging mediation rather than litigation of special problems encountered by several players. The municipality may be able to shoulder some of the risk,

especially when development had already been approved and contamination was discovered later.

Private Sector Players

Real estate investors, lenders, and developers are interested primarily in economically viable brownfield sites. The presence of surplus brownfield sites is likely to depress the price of potentially viable sites, making their development more difficult. Because the demand for development sites is relatively low and the supply so large, brownfields are a buyer's market. This section addresses the roles of real estate players in developing economically viable sites. Appraisers, lenders, insurers, and capital markets can all play a role in the development of brownfields.

Appraisers

Property appraisers in the United States have generally been reluctant to provide valuations of unremediated brownfields, making transfers of unremediated brownfields very difficult because cleanup costs are not known with enough certainty. Without appraisals, lenders are unable to determine the property's value for the loan-to-value ratio; thus, any loans are usually based on a very low value, requiring more equity from the developer. Appraisers need to become more familiar with appraising contaminated property "as is," and they need professional insurance and more knowledge about brownfields. Innovations are needed in the transaction process. One option could be a flexible strike price, in which both buyer and seller share the variation in the cost of remediation.

Lenders

Lenders are reluctant to lend money for brownfield deals and appear to be hesitant about revealing their concerns to nonlenders. With bank regulations that discourage taking risks, lenders in particular need information for quantifying the risks involved in brownfield deals. Research needs to be conducted on the effects of RBCAs, caps, and other remediation techniques on the future use of the real estate and its value in the event of foreclosure. Information about the incidence and financial magnitude of reopeners would also be useful.

To satisfy requirements of the Community Reinvestment Act for lending funds in inner cities, banks that have not already done so could consider establishing a development bank subsidiary that is more willing to take risks to specialize in brownfield properties. The subsidiary would still be liable to the extent of its own portfolio. Profit would be expected to be lower than for the parent company. At some point, banks need to treat brownfields as real estate deals rather than credit deals or face more competition from public sector lenders.

Insurers

Comprehensive environmental insurance should be made available for an entire loan portfolio, not just presumably contaminated properties, to keep costs down. Insurance should run with the loan term. More data are needed so reserves for losses can be estimated and products brought to the market at reasonable prices. Insurers should continue to develop these products and make them available. If not, the public sector should provide them.

Capital Markets

When risks can be properly quantified, one or more brownfield REITs will likely be formed: Some brownfield equity players are already marketing themselves this way. Debt brownfield REITs may also be developed. It may be necessary for visionary not-for-profit entities to take the first step. For example, according to a spokeswoman for the Development Fund, based in San Francisco, the fund is launching a "financing initiative for environmental restoration" fund, essentially a brownfield debt vehicle. Regardless of the nature of the REIT, however, research focusing on diversification should be undertaken, because a portfolio may benefit from diversifying assets and picking up some sites in inner cities.

In Summary

Much progress has been made in understanding issues and problems involving brownfields, and moving the field beyond cleanup to real estate development. In many states, the stage is set for a substantial increase in the development of large numbers of brownfield sites when demand is present. From the developer's perspective, the terms of private sector financing are often problematic, and a strong public role is still needed to encourage and support development. The rest of the dilemma boils down to the lack of public information about the potential of brownfield development and the need to redistribute risk among the parties. A partnership between the public and private sectors could help achieve these goals. Then a developer could revitalize the brownfields that prevent urban areas from achieving their full potential.

Part II
Case Studies

10 Two Brownfield Development Projects in Connecticut

Since it first initiated voluntary cleanup programs several years ago, Connecticut has been at the forefront of encouraging development of contaminated property. Its New England location close to both New York City and Boston means that many parts of the state are within commuting distance of these two cities. The recent legislative change instituting a state income tax removed Connecticut residents' tax advantage and dampened residential growth in the state. Faced with the national recession of the early 1990s, Connecticut opted to take a proactive role in encouraging development through close coordination between the state's environmental and economic development branches. Projects that create new jobs are targeted for subsidies, and the state can and does take title to selected properties to create markets.

The two cases discussed in this chapter, after an overview of Connecticut's regulatory environment, are a regional shopping mall on the site of the former Scovill Brass Works in Waterbury, and Science Park in New Haven.

Connecticut's Regulatory Environment

Connecticut was among the first states to develop a voluntary cleanup program. It now has three programs. The major program, the Urban Sites Remedial Action Program (USRAP), began as a pilot in 1992. Two more programs were added in 1995: the Voluntary Remediation Program (VRP) and the 1995 amendments to the Connecticut Transfer Act (CTA). The lead agency for remediation is the Connecticut Department of Environmental Protection (DEP), closely coordinated with the Connecticut Department of Economic and Community Development (DECD). Connecticut's approach features a tight CNTS and a prominent role in funding and absorbing liability for projects that create jobs. It also uses new and flexible risk-based corrective actions. Brownfield projects in Connecticut have been completed without a formal agreement from

EPA's Region 1. Over 100 sites have received an NFA letter through the VRP or USRAP programs, and four covenants not to sue have been issued to date.

The VRP and CTA Programs

Intended for brownfield sites without major state subsidies, the VRP and CTA programs date from only 1995. The VRP is for sites on the state's list of contaminated (eligible) sites and includes financial inducements. For example, the 1995 program offered loans for assessment and site remediation at the state's cost of capital. DEP and DECD provide technical assistance and expedited environmental review for some projects rather than funds. For projects volunteered for the program, the VRP offers a CNTS for successful site assessments on contaminated property where the work is done by licensed professionals.

The CTA program applies to properties sold whose past uses include industrial or selected commercial activities associated with contamination. The CTA requires a statement about the site's status of contamination and which entity will be responsible for future cleanup. Some properties achieve a Form 1 closure status (clean site, with no release of contaminants). Properties transferred through Connecticut's cleanup programs receive Form 2 closure status (no further environmental action) through Form 4 closure status (remediated site with ongoing monitoring). These documents become part of the property's permanent record and are filed with the county.

Urban Sites Remedial Action Program

USRAP is the strongest and most popular of Connecticut's three programs. For the right projects, the state can step in to help remediate the site, absorb liability, and finance remediation through bonds issued by the Connecticut Development Authority, which has a $30 million environmental cleanup fund. Other USRAP projects are privately funded and receive expedited approval and technical assistance from DEP. According to DEP, "Connecticut has made a conscious decision to promote cleanup by developing urban sites through the USRAP initiative." Adds a spokesman from DECD, "Urban sites are more efficient to develop because infrastructure is already present." DECD gives priority to industrial projects that create basic employment and to certain large retail developments. In addition to financing cleanup, DECD has also offered abatement of property taxes to selected projects. Housing projects are not considered for USRAP, and the program is not intended for potentially responsible parties.

The first milestone in USRAP is DEP's approval of the remedial action plan. After the plan has been implemented, DEP signs off, noting that the work is completed. For sites with no ongoing monitoring, an NFA letter accompanies this step. The program offers a CNTS from DEP for parcels successfully remediated by an entity that is not a potentially responsible party and requiring no additional monitoring. When ongoing monitoring is needed, the state may still issue a CNTS, subject to monitoring; an NFA letter is issued as a last step when monitoring is completed. A licensed environmental professional must be involved. The program involves no reopeners, even for prior undiscovered contamination. If the state conducts the remediation, new owners are exempt from liability. The state may also fund site remediation, but the work is usually performed by a local development corporation.

USRAP is successful. According to DEP, a total of 33 projects had entered the program as of year-end 1996. Of the 12 receiving state funding, two are complete and three are under construction. Thirteen of the 21 privately funded projects are complete. Many of the privately funded cleanups are being conducted by responsible parties.

Cleanup Standards

The state's new approach to remediation involves risk-based corrective actions. Regulations promulgated in January 1996 established different standards for residential and commercial/industrial land. Impermeable caps, encapsulation using structural slabs, or other techniques are permitted in appropriate cases, such as nonresidential use. Sealing off contamination on site, however, requires DEP to issue a declaration of environmental land use restriction for the property. This declaration and other conditions of transfer under the CTA program become part of the property's permanent record and are recorded with the county.

Other Issues

Exemptions from liability for Connecticut lenders date back to 1985. Consistent with new federal legislation, lenders who foreclose on a property are not liable for damages in excess of the real estate's value.

Some communities in the state also offer tax increment financing to assist in financing infrastructure and other improvements. Other communities offer property tax abatement for new projects that generate a significant number of jobs.

Pending Actions

Legislation is pending that would set aside 3 percent of a property's value upon sale to offset the cost of orphan brownfields for properties receiving a CNTS. The fund has been stocked with $5 million. DEP is continuing

The Brass Mill Center has three strong real estate characteristics: excellent access from I-84, good visibility, and a large assembled parcel.

FIGURE 10.1

WATERBURY AND GGP REGIONAL MALL SITE

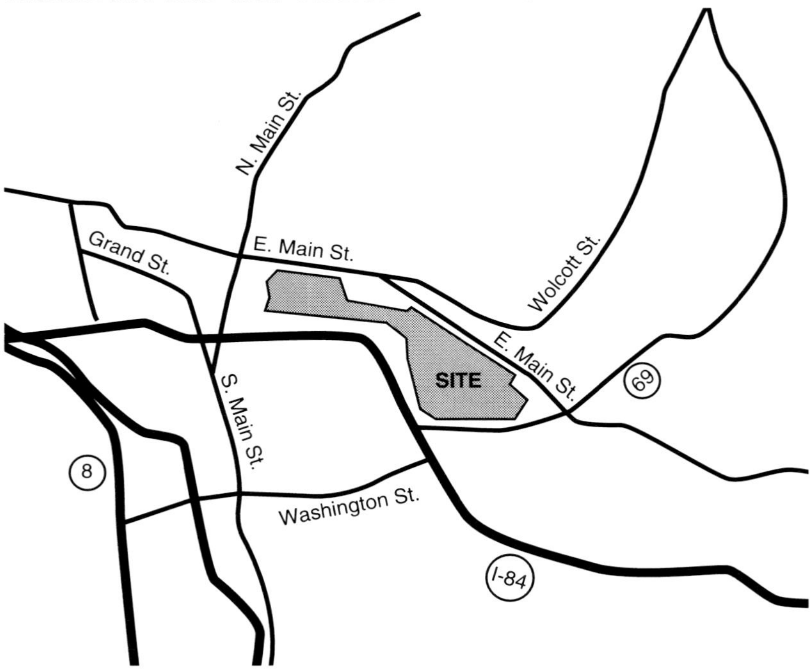

discussions with EPA Region 1 to obtain a formal memorandum of understanding for its CNTS (in place of the current "comfort letter" from EPA).

The GGP–Brass Mill Regional Shopping Center

Background

The Scovill Brass Works, on an 87-acre site adjacent to downtown Waterbury, Connecticut, and about 40 minutes west of Hartford on I-84 just east of its intersection with Route 8, had a workforce of about 12,000 employees at its peak in the 1940s. The Mad River runs through much of the northern part of the site.

With its giant rolling mill, the site was used as a brass factory, first by Scovill then by Century Brass, through 1986. When Century declared bankruptcy, however, no other responsible party with deep pockets entered the picture. In the late 1980s, a developer (New Waterbury, Inc.) bought the site and its unsecured buildings, intending to develop it into an industrial park. Though it started the project, progress was slow because of poor economic conditions in the late 1980s and the extent of contamination. The site was encumbered with at least $5 million in back taxes.

The site, accessible from three interchanges, extends along the north side of I-84. It has excellent highway access and visibility, and the location is suitable for a regional shopping mall. Land prices in central Waterbury for ten-plus-acre assembled parcels with negligible contamination (if available) are $7.00 to $10.00 per square foot. In reality, however, few parcels are clean, and many have negative value because of liens or other encum-

FIGURE 10.2

GGP REGIONAL MALL SITE PLAN

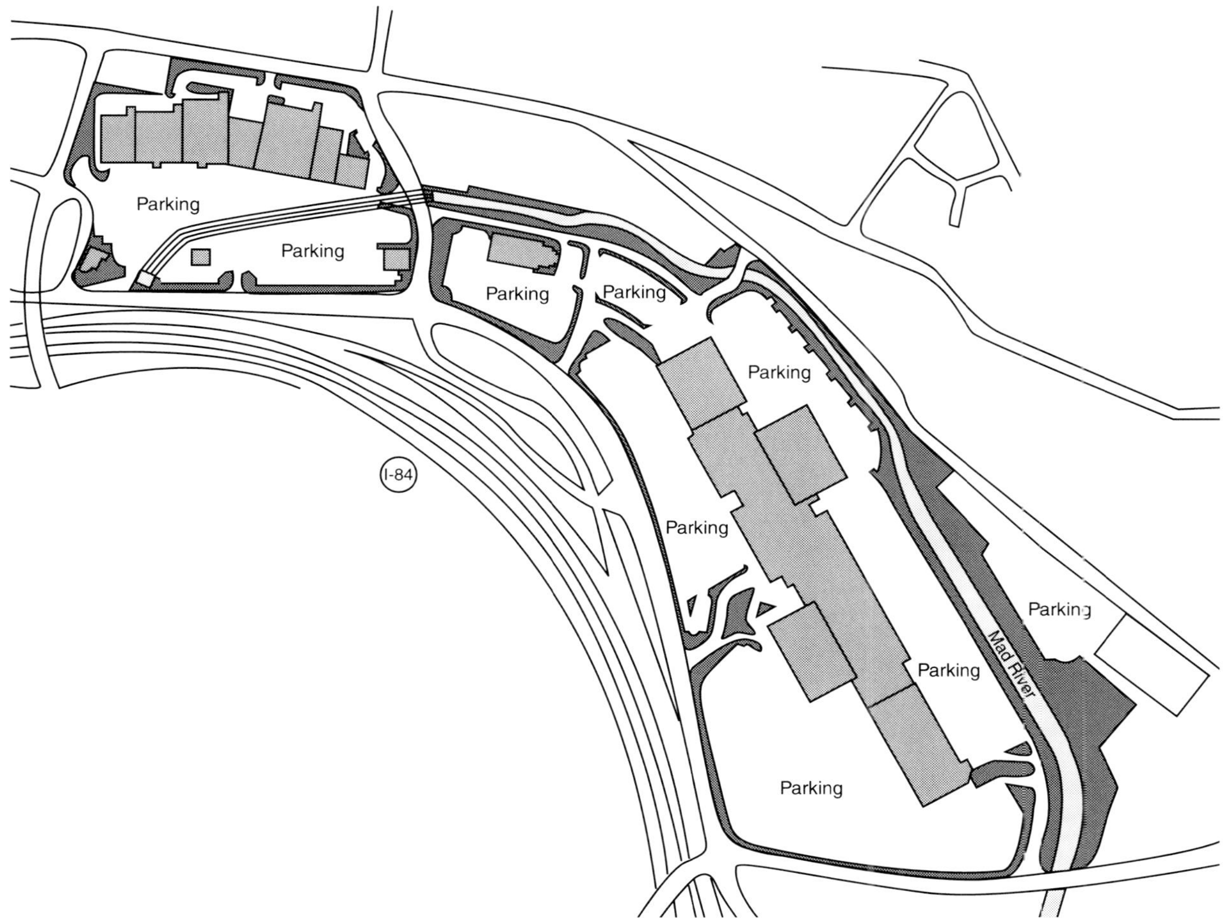

brances or because cleanup expenses are perceived to exceed market value.

Local Economic Conditions

According to *City-County Data Book*,[1] the city of Waterbury had a population of 106,900 in 1992, up 3.5 percent from 1980. About 81 percent of the population is white. The median age is 33.1 years, very close to the state figure. The crime rate (serious crimes known to police) was 9,300 per 100,000, almost double the state rate. Median family income was $37,900, or 77 percent of the state average. Nearly 10 percent of families (9.9 percent) lived below the poverty line, double the state average.

The city has lost a substantial number of jobs. In 1987, the city was home to 242 manufacturing companies with 11,400 employees. That figure was down 17 percent from 1982 and down by almost half from 1963, when 20,300 employees worked in 261 manufacturing firms. Retail growth has also been negative; 820 retail companies with a payroll in the city in 1963 dropped 13 percent to 713 establishments with a payroll in 1987.

To plan for development of the downtown area in general and the Brass Mill site in particular, the Naugatuck Valley Development Corporation (NVDC) was formed and became active in developing the site in 1992. NVDC was a key player in guiding site development. Its director spearheaded the site's entry into USRAP (then a pilot program) and established NVDC as a conduit for state remediation funding. The director kept the parties talking and at the table, and was a steadying influence when new faces came and went. He also helped solidify the city's role of substantial support through tax increment financing and indemnification for the developer.

Project Description

Homart Development Corporation selected the Brass Works site for a shopping mall and optioned it in 1993.

It had about $10 million in the project when General Growth Partners, Inc. (GGP), acquired the firm and its portfolio in 1995. GGP's strategy is to build the project and hold it for the long term for its own portfolio or for that of its associated REIT. The project's intended use is 1.2 million square feet of retail and commercial space—a 1 million-square-foot regional mall and a 200,000-square-foot big-box community center. The project opened in 1997.

According to the project director, the regional mall will have four anchors: Filene's, JCPenney, Sears, and Leachmere (with all leases signed and funds in escrow) plus a 12-screen theater complex and about 150 other shops in 330,000 square feet. As of November 1996, all mall anchors and a substantial amount of the mall's in-line retail space had been preleased. The community shopping center is expected to feature a Barnes & Noble bookstore, Circuit City electronics, and some restaurants. Smaller stores in the regional mall pay rents of $34.00 to $35.00 per square foot, triple net. Rents in the community shopping center will be $14.00 to $16.00 per square foot, triple net. The layout of the shopping center is shown in Figure 10.2.

As a result of its excellent location, the project's retail trade area extends well beyond Waterbury, with the nearest competitors of a similar scale 15 to 25 miles away. About 340,000 persons in 130,000 households live in the primary market area; average household income in 1996 was $58,000.

A significant feature of the Brass Mill site is the Mad River, which flows through the northern portion of the property. About $2.2 million was allocated to deal with contaminated river sediment.

The Skovill Brass Works mill that occupied the site before redevelopment was contaminated with lead paint and asbestos.

Site Remediation

The site was used as a factory as far back as the early 1800s but last used in 1986. Its primary use was as a manufacturer of brass products and brass buttons for military uniforms. The site included several structures, many unsound and few suitable for reuse, with 2.2 million square feet of space. Over half the space was in one enormous rolling mill. The buildings were filled with lead paint residue and asbestos. Century Brass partially remediated the site and contained sludge contaminated with metal hydroxide off site in an RCRA landfill referred to as a "PIRNO" (property in receivership nobody owns, or property I'd rather not own, depending on the source). Other types of contamination included oily soils, volatile organic compounds, and PCBs. No underground storage tanks were found on site. Fifteen to 20 percent of the site contained soils contaminated with hazardous materials

The guiding principle of GGP–Brass Mill, Inc., from the beginning was to avoid being the entity who could be held liable for prior contamination. GGP's project director insisted on full cleanup to residential standards because of the parent company's concerns about liability and the condition specified by the mall's anchor tenants, which did not want deed restrictions on the property. (At least one of the anchors will own its own store.) The requirement for residential cleanliness increased the cost of cleanup substantially, prompting the state to take an aggressive role in financing the project. At the time DEP approved the plan for remediation in April 1994, the expected cost of remediation was about $20 million; Homart had already spent over $10 million, which could not be recouped if the deal fell through. Additional funds were needed to improve surface infrastructure and clean up the Mad River, which contained some contaminated sediments and was to be partially opened as an amenity.

Contaminants on the Brass Mill site included oily soils, volatile organic compounds, and PCBs.

GGP's concerns about liability required the creation of another nonprofit corporation, Brass Center Ltd. (BCL), to conduct the actual remediation on site. Cleaning the site was made more complex by the presence of the Mad River, which runs through most of the site along its northern boundary. Because the river had been draining offsite properties upstream over many years, its sediment had accumulated contaminated materials. The bulk of the remediation remaining took about two years. DEP

A portion of the Mad River that had been piped through the Skovill Brass Works (upper right) was reopened to the surface as a water amenity for the Brass Mill Center.

signed off on completion of remediation in June 1996, a CNTS was issued that same week, and EPA issued a "comfort letter" at about the same time. Because ongoing monitoring is necessary, the property received a Form 4 transfer under the CTA. An NFA letter is expected when environmental monitoring is finished in three to five years, and the Form 4 is expected to be changed to Form 2 (no further environmental action required).

Remediation expenses from the point Homart/GGP got involved (excluding the partial remediation conducted by Century Brass) totaled $22 million, excluding soft costs but including $10 million for ridding the buildings of substantial amounts of asbestos and lead paint before demolition and another $7 million to demolish the buildings, and haul away and bury the debris.

The material was deposited in a city landfill, which is to be closed, saving money by reducing transportation costs for the debris. GGP put $350,000 in escrow to help cover the expense of closing the landfill. Use of the landfill represents an in-kind contribution from the city to the project.

Another $3 million was needed to remediate subsurface soil and about $800,000 to handle PCBs. The balance was allotted to dealing with the river sediment. The total cost of remediation for the project, $22 million excluding infrastructure improvements, works out to $5.81 per square foot of land, or about 10.5 percent of total project costs.

The Developer's Financing of the Project

Up to the point when the project was acquired, remediated, and about 50 percent constructed, the developer had financed the retail center with internal financing. GGP had substantial money at risk: It had spent $10 million by the time the remediation plan was approved in 1994, including consultants' fees and testing. The developers also used their own funds to pay for a substantial portion of construction and development of the site. At the point when the construction loan was put in place, the developers had over $50 million of GGP funds in the project, which included part of the construction costs and site improvements. Remediation and infrastructure,

The total remediation cost of $22 million is $5.81 per square foot over the site's 87 acres, or about 10.5 percent of the total cost.

FIGURE 10.3

PROJECT DATA—BRASS MILL REGIONAL SHOPPING CENTER

Land Use Information
Site Area: 87 acres (3,789,720 square feet)
Floor/Area Ratio (FAR): 0.32
Net Leasable Building Area: 1,200,000 square feet
Number of Tenants: 160
Site Preparation Time: 24 months

Development Cost Information		
Land Acquisition Cost	$15,379,000	($4.06 per square foot)
Site Preparation Costs		
Remediation	$22,000,000	($5.81 per square foot)
Other site preparation (river)	30,501,000	($8.05 per square foot)
Construction Costs		
Building hard costs	$96,000,000	($80 per building square foot), aboveground
Construction losses (2%)	1,920,000	
Soft Costs		
Back taxes to city	$5,000,000	
Architect, legal, planning (6% of hard and site costs)	8,000,000	
Environmental consultants	6,000,000	
Construction loan/carrying costs (0.7 LTV)	7,000,000	
Developer's fee (10%)	17,200,000	
Total Development Cost	**$209,000,000**	($174.17 per square foot)
Minus Public Subsidy (remediation grants, state and federal aid)	– 45,000,000	
Net Cost to Developer	**$164,000,000**	($136.67 per building square foot)
Operating Cash Flow		
Market Rent (average)	$18,400,000	($15.33 per square foot, triple net)
Market Vacancy Rate (5% of tenant space)	(600,000)	
Security Costs	300,000	($0.25 per square foot)
Environmental Monitoring	50,000	
Net Operating Income (stable in year 3)	**$17,450,000**	
Financing and Investment		
Value (NOI/cap rate of 0.09)	$164,170,000	
Before-Tax Cash Flow	$17,450,000	
Equity Requirement	$164,000,000	
Return on Equity	10.6%	

however, were paid for largely with public money (see Figure 10.3).

Public Funds

This project received funds from the federal government, four state departments, and the city of Waterbury. Subsidies totaled at least $45 million, or 22 percent of total project costs.

The federal role was limited to the $4.8 million in federal funds provided for abatement of asbestos. The state DEP helped the developers acquire the funds, which were funneled through NVDC. Unfortunately, this federal program is no longer available.

The state financed a total of $31 million for environmental remediation and related site improvements with Connecticut Development Authority bonds. GGP must reimburse the state for $31 million if it fails to deliver a shopping center by the agreed-upon date. Thus, a total of $35.8 million was channeled through NVDC. The state Department of Transportation also provided GGP with up to $2 million in an allowance for off-site infrastructure improvements.

The city of Waterbury provided $7.2 million for the project, financed through tax increment financing from future property tax revenues from the project.

Construction Loan

In late 1996, the project obtained a construction loan from a consortium of banks led by Wells Fargo. Terms included a loan-to-value ratio of 0.7, a principal amount of $117 million, and an interest rate of 10 percent. The total amount of interest expense was expected to be $7 million.

Robert E. Mikrut

Robert E. Mikrut

Brass Mill Center is a 1.2 million-square-foot regional mall with 200,000 square feet of community shopping. General Growth Partners, Inc., the builder of the project, secured four anchors for the mall: Filene's, JCPenney, Sears, and Leachmere. It also has a 12-screen theater complex and about 150 other shops in 330,000 square feet.

Permanent Financing

Net operating income was expected to be about $17.5 million, providing an 11 percent rate of return on the developer's $164 million in equity. Permanent financing could increase the return through leverage. Return could also be increased when the project is fully leased because it will be of institutional investment quality, it has no deed restrictions, and a CNTS from the state accompanies the property. The project's long-term rate of return (excluding the developer's fee) is expected to be about 11 percent, above the required break-even point.

Strategies to Reduce Liability

The deal was structured to minimize liability to the new owner, GGP. Closing occurred in June 1996, just after site remediation was completed. At the beginning of the project, when the remediation plan was approved, GGP had assigned its option on the property to the remediation entity BCL. Two years later, BCL exercised the option and bought the property from the current owners, New Waterbury, Inc. After BCL stepped into the chain of title, it resold the property to GGP on the same day, helping to maintain GGP's prime directive of avoiding liability.

The main protection for GGP was the city of Waterbury's indemnification of GGP (or other present or future owners) from environmental liability for 30 years through BCL, which is to be kept alive solely for this purpose. The city's contingent liability is capped at 50 percent of its TIF revenues. Environmental insurance was never seriously considered as an option to reduce liability. And although the CNTS from the state was a nice bonus, it was not an important factor in deciding to proceed with the deal because it was not known to be available at the beginning of the development process.

Return on Public Funds

State and local shares of project funding were a very substantial $40.2 million, or 19 percent of the project's overall costs. According to estimates from DECD and NVDC, the direct fiscal return is substantial: The fully developed property is expected to pay over $3 million per year in personal and real property taxes by 2000. Economic benefits are also substantial, with approxi-

Robert E. Mikrut

Robert E. Mikrut

The designers of Brass Mill Center, Arrowstreet, Inc., of Somerville, Massachusetts, used the brass works theme as a design element throughout the project.

mately 1,700 construction jobs created over two to three years and $46 million in salaries pumped into the local economy. In addition, 2,600 full- and part-time permanent retail sales and management positions will be created. Moreover, the potential exists for additional development on adjacent parcels, with overall positive effects on downtown Waterbury. Development of the project has also had intangible benefits, such as elimination of blight and reuse of a major urban property adjacent to Waterbury's central business district.

Market Acceptance

Leasing stayed on track. Ten months before the expected grand opening, all four anchor tenants had signed on with funds in escrow, 40 percent of the tenant space in the regional mall had been committed, and 60 percent of the space in the community center had been committed. Today, the mall is fully leased. Rents at the mall are at or above industry standards. In short, the project's past as a brownfield has not impaired its ability to market space to tenants.

Lessons Learned

Having proceeded at a time when Connecticut's brownfield program was still evolving, the project's key to its successful outcome is flexibility. This site has several important aspects, including excellent access and visibility from I-84 and the large size of the assembled parcel, which made the deal attractive to the developer. Its next most important feature, from the developer's perspective, was indemnification from the city of Waterbury and the creation of BCL to conduct the remediation and absorb potential future environmental liability. The fact that no deed restrictions were in place was key to this project, although this condition required cleanup to residential standards, which increased site remediation costs to the point where the state had to provide a substantial subsidy. Still important (but of lesser concern) to the developer were the DEP's role in negotiating the remediation plan early in the process and the "comfort letter" from EPA Region 1. The state's CNTS (which came late in the game) and the transfer Form 4 status were good to have but did not affect the decision to proceed with the deal because they were unavailable at that time. The return to the developer is above the break-even point, and the deal is expected to be a financial and operational home run. The state's investment of about $33 million in the project is justified by its potential fiscal, economic, and political benefits.

At its peak in the 1940s, Olin employed about 20,000 people in this sprawling industrial complex. It included over 25 large buildings and numerous other smaller structures, many of which are functionally obsolete by contemporary standards.

Science Park Winchester Factory

Background

Science Park is an 80-acre industrial complex in the Newhallville neighborhood of New Haven, Connecticut. Suitable for an industrial area (see Figure 10.4), the site is located just off I-91, five to ten minutes northeast of downtown in a particularly depressed part of town. Although its location is not spectacular, the site has adequate highway access and fair visibility. Because of its relatively mediocre location, however, land prices in the area are fairly low, about $1.00 to $2.00 per square foot.

The case involves a large, sequentially abandoned industrial site, a responsible former owner (Olin Corp.), and a not-for-profit land developer. Olin had partly remediated and indemnified the site of the Winchester factory, a 15-acre piece of Science Park. The state had a prominent role in environmental approvals, the financing of remediation, and tax incentives. The project involved a land lease to reduce liability for the new user; it retained over 500 jobs in a very economically depressed area.

As a Connecticut-based corporation, Olin wanted to retain as many jobs as possible in the state. It also receives some financial benefits to offset expenses, namely, a tax write-off for the land and remediation expenses. Olin is a scientifically sophisticated firm, allowing more confidence in the assessment of potential problems associated with site development. Moreover, it can veto potential new users, thereby avoiding new contamination on the site and reducing the potential future liability.

The Market

New Haven's population in 1992 was 124,000 people, down 1.7 percent from 1980. About 57 percent of the population is white. The median age is 29.2 years, much younger than the state figure of 35.7 years, and many small children live there. The crime rate (serious crimes known to police) was 14,900 per 100,000, almost triple the state average. The city is economically depressed, with median family income $31,200, or only 63 percent of the state average. In 1992, 14.6 percent of families lived below the poverty line, almost triple the state average. The unemployment rate was 7.6 percent in 1991, slightly higher than the state average.

The city has lost a substantial number of jobs. In 1987, the city contained 186 manufacturing companies with 8,600 employees, down 27 percent from 1982 and more than two-thirds from 1963, when 29,700 employees worked in 389 manufacturing firms. Retail growth has also been negative. The city was home to 852 establishments with payroll in 1987, down one-quarter from 1,152 retail companies with payroll in 1963. Thus, retaining jobs was a very high priority for both the city and the state.

Science Park Development Corporation Site

The Winchester Company (the U.S. Repeating Arms Company or USRAC) had operated on what is now the site of the SPDC, making guns and ammunition since before the turn of the century and through both World War I and World War II. In 1931, Winchester became a division of Olin Corp. Later, it also made roller skates, batteries, and flashlights. At its peak in the 1940s, Olin operated with about 20,000 employees on about 80 acres in this sprawling industrial complex, which included over 25 large buildings plus numerous other smaller structures, many of which are functionally obsolete by contemporary standards. Over 15 of the structures had five or more stories. The site also had its own power plant, with a signature smokestack. By the 1970s, Olin had been closing buildings because they were no longer needed and the property's decline was substantial. The unused structures were contaminated with asbestos, lead, and other materials, and contaminated soils were present in various locations throughout the complex. In 1981, USRAC was spun off from Olin. USRAC continued to operate in a large, multistory building on part of the site. Olin, which continues as a major diversified corporation based in Norwalk, Connecticut, still operates a metallurgical research laboratory on part of the site. Despite Olin's continued presence, however, the neighborhood fell into

Reggie Jackson

Science Park is an 80-acre industrial complex in the Newhallville neighborhood of New Haven, Connecticut. The site is located just off I-91, five to ten minutes northeast of downtown.

decline with its attendant high unemployment rate and urban blight.

Science Park Development Corporation (SPDC) was formed in early 1983 as a not-for-profit corporation to develop the area and serve as a vehicle for Olin's responsible divestiture of the property. SPDC is a joint venture of the city of New Haven, Yale University, and Olin, the property owner. According to SPDC officials, "Olin would remediate portions of the site and donate them to SPDC to develop and manage, Yale could use the site as an incubator, and the city would provide infrastructure and tax breaks." SPDC would have multiple tasks: to assemble property, to run an industrial incubator, to act as general contractor for site remediation and channel state and other funds, and eventually to develop and own the 15-acre USRAC site, which is an entirely new project (see Figure 10.5).[2]

SPDC is very sensitive about serving the needs of the Newhallville neighborhood. Local residents are on SPDC's governing board and have a voice in important decisions such as local road access through the complex and guidelines for hiring minorities. In general, neighbors have been very supportive of the project, which provides rel-

FIGURE 10.4

NEW HAVEN, CONNECTICUT

FIGURE 10.5

Science Park and USRAC

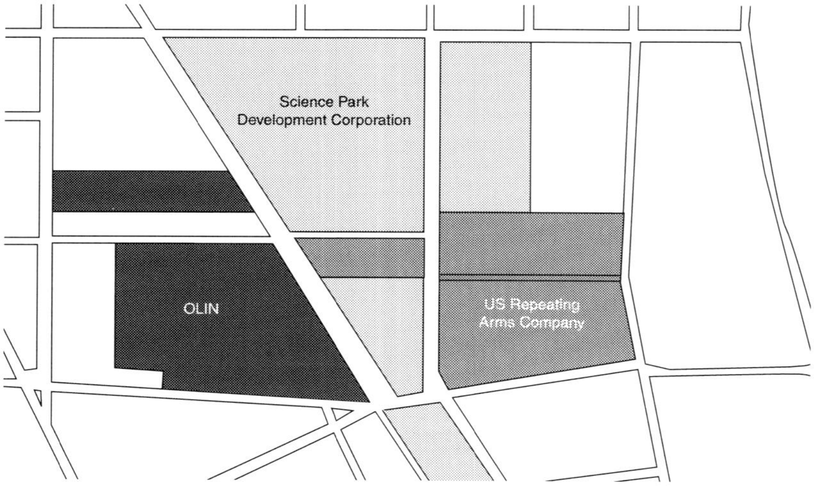

incubator has 300 employees, about 20 percent of whom are minorities.

Ironically, the success of the project's tenants is a problem for SPDC's bottom line as landlords, as successful firms must leave the project to grow. Overall, however, despite years of positive cash flow, SPDC still needs regular capital subsidies and periodic infusions of operating funds to maintain a favorable financial position. Part of this dilemma is by design. To maintain its role as recipient of unused Olin structures, SPDC needs to maintain economic viability. On the other hand, its role as an environmental remediator is risky, and having limited assets is a good strategy for this purpose.

In addition to reusing vacant buildings for the incubator, SPDC also acquired vacant pieces of the old Winchester property. It has renovated and leased another 304,000 square feet of space in two low-rise industrial buildings donated by Olin, and it has leased a ten- to 15-acre parcel containing several old research buildings that it plans to sublet as appropriate light manufacturing tenants become available. In 1992, SPDC took on a new role as facilitator, when Olin engaged SPDC as a remediation contractor and a conduit for DECD funds for the new 15-acre USRAC factory site.

atively high-paying jobs and the current type of industry that is perceived to be cleaner than the old, smoke-belching industry.

SPDC started developing the complex in 1983, with the incubator project first. By 1986, Olin had donated three multistory buildings, and SPDC had cleaned them up and was managing them. The incubator building contained a total of 300,000 square feet on ten acres. Eighty firms occupying 175,000 square feet were located there. By 1992, the incubator project had attained an occupancy rate of 85 to 90 percent and was charging nearly market rents—about $10.00 per square foot per year, gross, for office space, $15.00 to $18.00 per square foot for labs, and $5.00 per square foot for manufacturing space. According to the facilities manager at SPDC, the

The New USRAC Factory

In 1992, USRAC, which had been acquired by GIAT Industries, a large European concern, was operating very inefficiently in antiquated five-story buildings. USRAC threatened to move to South Carolina to find more efficient quarters. To retain the jobs in Connecticut, DECD offered to help reclaim the adjacent contaminated site and move USRAC to a new factory there. The city of New Haven offered tax inducements, and Olin acknowl-

A joint venture of the city of New Haven, Yale University, and Olin, Science Park Development Corporation was founded in 1983 as a not-for-profit corporation to develop the area and serve as a vehicle for Olin's responsible divestiture of the property.

edged it would share in responsibility for the project. That year a partnership was formed, with SPDC playing a key role.

Site Remediation

The site's history included manufacture of guns, ammunition, roller skates, batteries, and flashlights. Based on environmental studies from as far back as 1986, the 15-acre site was revealed to have about two acres of hot spots, mostly of lead-tainted soil, and nonvolatile polyaromatic hydrocarbons. According to HRP Associates, the environmental firm that performed the studies, the groundwater situation was favorable. Its average depth was 18 feet below the surface, and it fell into Connecticut's urban groundwater status (nonpotable groundwater, public water supply readily available). The site also had several standing buildings totaling 650,000 square feet and containing asbestos wrapped around utility pipes, and underground storage tanks, which explains the presence of light petroleum and fuel oil in the soil. Tunnels had been dug under the buildings on the site, but because it was a war plant, no records had been kept of where they were.

From the start, the players agreed on a basic division of responsibility. Olin agreed to remediate the soil, and the state, acting through SPDC, would handle asbestos abatement and demolition of the buildings. Further, SPDC would own the land once remediation was complete. The strategy for soil remediation was to excavate selected hot spots down to four to six feet and then apply a structural slab (a form of cap) over the remaining contaminated soil. A contractor set up an active pumping system to extract fuel oil from the soil. Groundwater monitoring was initiated using a subset of the original 54 monitoring wells and is to be conducted for at least five years. According to HRP, monitoring reveals that the level of contaminants has decreased. The frequency of groundwater monitoring is likely to be cut back soon.

Olin had already been working toward remediating the site for several years when the site became part of the state's Urban Sites Remedial Action Program in 1992 to retain the factory's jobs in Connecticut. Because the project was on a fast track, DEP approved the remedial action plan, including the structural cap over the contaminated soil, and provided an early version of an NFA letter in August 1992. A pre-CTA version of the deed restriction was filed on the property in June 1993. As part of the closure agreement, Olin provided an indemnification letter to future buyers concerning known contamination.

The U.S. Repeating Arms Company, manufacturers of Winchester firearms, is a subsidiary of Olin and has occupied this site since before the turn of the century and through both world wars.

Financing Remediation

Olin, acting voluntarily, paid for the environmental studies, estimated at $230,000. According to an official of the company, excavating the contaminated hot spots, demolishing the power plant, and installing the structural cap (which was minimal because it was part of the building's floor and parking lot) cost a total of $1 million. The petroleum extraction system cost $100,000. Thus, Olin's share of remediation totaled $1.1 million plus environmental consulting. The state financed the demolition of the buildings and removal of asbestos, through SPDC, at a cost of $2.3 million. Overall remediation costs, therefore, were $5.20 per square foot of land. Olin continues to pay for groundwater monitoring, an average of $50,000 per year.

Building and Financing the Factory

After SPDC took title to the land in 1992, it agreed to lease the land to USRAC for $130,000 per year, a strategy that reduces risk to future lien holders and owners. USRAC acted as its own developer and hired a general contractor, the FIP Corporation of Cheshire, Connecticut, which built the project over two years. Under construction by 1993, the factory opened in October 1994.

USRAC's manufacturing and assembly plant cost a total of $22.3 million, with $4 million of the amount for factory machinery and equipment, and business lost during the move; the cost to develop the site and of real estate improvements was thus $18.3 million. Of this amount, $13 million, before government subsidies, went for construction of the new 225,000-square-foot factory.

The public role was substantial. According to SPDC and DECD, the state provided $2.3 million to remove asbestos and demolish the structures on the site, and DECD provided an extra $2 million grant in aid for plant equipment and $150,000 more for road improvements and landscaping. The city of New Haven put up $850,000 to improve infrastructure, such as curbs and drainage. To sweeten the bottom line, the state also gave USRAC a personal property tax abatement, and the city provided real property tax abatement. Thus, the project received a total of $5.3 million in state and local funds. Including Olin's $1.1 million for remediation and $230,000 for environmental consulting fees, USRAC's total cost was $15.7 million. Deducting the $2 million public subsidy for equipment leaves a net cost to USRAC for the real estate and site improvements of $13.7 million.

According to USRAC's comptroller, the firm was committed to a site in New Haven, where the market rent was $6.00 per square foot, triple net. Subtracting the $130,000 in land lease payments to SPDC, the property tax abatement, and the subsidy for Olin's environmental monitoring yields a net operating income of $1.2 million per year.

Permanent financing for the USRAC plant was provided by an $11 million industrial development bond issued by the city of New Haven. The loan-to-value ratio is 0.77. With the subsidy, the interest rate is 5.3 percent, with a 30-year amortization period. The bond was guaranteed by a letter of credit from BNP, a French bank.

As general remediation contractor for building cleanup at the site, Science Park Development Corporation retains some of the liability for cleanup. By leasing the land, the tenants are insulated from future liability. USRAC is further protected by Olin's indemnification.

The parent company, GIAT Industries, also stands behind the callable bonds. Annual debt service is $573,000. After debt service, before-tax cash flow to USRAC is $647,000 per year. It needs $2.7 million capital for the project, generating an annual rate of return of 24 percent.

The public share of the project was $5.3 million, or 23.4 percent of overall costs (real estate plus equipment). (Tax abatements or subsidies resulting from the industrial development bonds are not included in this amount.) Of the $5.3 million, $4.3 million was state money. For this investment, 500 permanent, full-time jobs were retained, about 25 percent of which are held by minorities who live nearby. Because personal and property taxes are abated for ten years and state corporate taxes are lowered for up to 20 years (the property is in an enterprise zone), the near-term impact of property tax is negligible. The intangible aspects, however—retaining jobs and votes in an economically depressed area—are substantial. The project has also had substantial public relations impact: it is the largest new factory built in Connecticut in the past 20 years, and the critical mass this project generated for SPDC's overall development is also an important benefit.

Market Acceptance

The project is functioning at full capacity, subject to the market. The modern, efficient plant allows USRAC to compete effectively in the international marketplace.

Lessons Learned

This case shows the importance of a not-for-profit developer, SPDC, in recycling contaminated property. SPDC acted as a catalyst for the project in receiving land and buildings from a willing and responsible former owner, Olin Corp., maintaining its ability to take advantage of tax benefits and insulate past and future users from liability. From a business perspective, maintaining flexibility is very important. While USRAC was not originally envisioned as a likely candidate for the business park because it did not serve as moveup space for a biomedical or pharmaceutical incubator, USRAC is a highly visible corporation, funds were available, and political pressure was apparent. And for SPDC, empty buildings are an opportunity: the factory abandoned by USRAC in 1994 is now SPDC's next project.

As general remediation contractor for cleaning up the building, SPDC retains some of the liability for cleanup. Owning the land and leasing it to USRAC insulates USRAC from some future liability. USRAC is further insulated by Olin's indemnification, which minimizes the importance

FIGURE 10.6

PROJECT DATA—U.S. REPEATING ARMS COMPANY

Land Use Information		
Site Area: 15 acres (653,400 square feet)		
Floor/Area Ratio: 0.39		
Building Area: 225,000 square feet		
Development Cost Information		
Land Acquisition Cost	0	(leased from SPDC)
Site Preparation Costs		
Remediation	$3,400,000	($5.20 per square foot)
Other site preparation	1,070,000	($1.64 per square foot)
Construction Costs		
Building hard costs	$13,000,000	($57.78 per building square foot)
Machinery and equipment	3,000,000	
Soft Costs		
Business lost	$1,000,000	
Legal, architect, planning (3% of hard costs)	390,000	
Environmental consultants	230,000	
Construction loan/carrying costs (internally financed)	0	
Developer's fee	100,000	
Total Development Cost	**$22,300,000**	($99.11 per square foot)
Minus Public Subsidy (remediation grants, state and city aid)	– 5,300,000	
Minus Olin's Share	– 1,330,000	
Net Cost to USRAC	**$15,670,000**	($69.64 per square foot for real estate and equipment)
Net Cost to USRAC	**$13,670,000**	($60.76 per square foot for real estate only)
Operating Cash Flow		
Rent to USRAC ($6 per square foot, triple net)	$1,350,000	
Land Lease from SPDC	130,000	
Environmental Monitoring	0	(paid for by Olin Corp.)
Net Operating Income	**$1,220,000**	
Financing and Investment		
Value (NOI/cap rate of 0.085)	$14,352,000	
Loan Amount (loan-to-value ratio of 0.77)	$11,000,000	
Debt Service (industrial development bond at 5.3%)	$573,000	
Debt Service Coverage Ratio	2.13	
Before-Tax Cash Flow	$647,000	
Equity Requirement	$2,670,000	
Return on Equity	24.2%	

of state closure documents that are less thorough than those issued today.

DECD played a large role in financing the project, despite limited financial return, counting instead on the political returns of retaining jobs in a depressed economy. DEP was flexible, allowing a structural cap well before permanent guidelines for risk-based, site-specific corrective actions were enacted in early 1996. But the greatest factor is the difference a responsible former owner (Olin) can make by allowing for an orderly and funded transition between abandonment and development, maintaining a relatively secure site, and indemnifying future users.

Notes

1. U.S. Bureau of the Census, *City-County Data Book 1963* (Washington, D.C.: U.S. Dept. of Commerce, 1963); and U.S. Bureau of the Census, *City-County Data Book 1994* (Washington, D.C.: U.S. Dept. of Commerce, 1994).

2. See Charles Bartsch and Elizabeth Collaton, "Industrial Site Reuse and Urban Development: An Overview," *Cityscape* 2(3), September 1996, pp. 17–61, for a summary of SPDC's evolution and development.

11 Two Brownfield Development Projects in Michigan

Michigan's program governing contaminated sites now has all the essential pieces in place, and it is expected to become a national leader in brownfield development. Detroit, located on the Detroit River across from Windsor, Ontario, is Michigan's largest market area. The city has been economically depressed, although the situation is improving. Michigan's top-down approach to brownfield development encourages a substantial role for local government and excellent coordination among the federal, state, and local sectors. The state actively funds site assessment and remediation.

Both cases in this chapter were marginally impacted by contamination. One site contained construction and demolition debris from prior residential development. The other had LUSTs. The Michigan Department of Environmental Quality (MDEQ) was the lead agency in these cases, and the Michigan State Housing Development Authority (MSHDA) continues to play a major role in financing housing development. Despite the fact that Michigan's voluntary cleanup program is fairly new, it has seen substantial activity: as of year-end 1996, 385 volunteers were in the pipeline.

The two modestly sized projects featured in this chapter were both developed by not-for-profit corporations. The Helen Odean Butler Apartments is a subsidized low-income housing project constructed on an old urban renewal site. MSHDA played a major role in financing the development. The Detroit Community Health Center is an inner-city medical clinic, a portion of which is built on an old gas station site. It received private sector financing, guaranteed by a major medical provider.

Michigan's Regulatory Environment

Michigan has one of the most comprehensive VCPs in the country. The state government primes the pump for site assessment and remediation, and coordinates management of a project using an intragovernmental action team called the REUS–A Team. The Michigan Department of Environmental Quality supervises both the VCP and the UST program, which were finalized in 1995 and early 1996, respectively. Michigan's terminal document allows a limited number of situations requiring reopeners, provides a CNTS, and gives lenders and new owners who successfully complete remediation solid liability exemptions. The state government also has enacted flexible new site-specific cleanup standards. EPA Region 5 grants formal memorandums of understanding for brownfield projects. Because of the existing program's comprehensive nature, no major new environmental legislation is pending.

The Voluntary Cleanup Program

Michigan's voluntary cleanup program dates from 1995. A site must first go through a baseline environmental assessment (BEA). According to MDEQ, the agency had processed 734 BEA applicants by year-end 1996. Of this number, 447 were petitions for MDEQ to determine the cleanliness of a (presumably) noncontaminated property. The remaining 287 BEAs were submitted by volunteers entering the VCP. After the BEA, Michigan's brownfield program takes one of two tracks. The volunteer may seek to contain the contamination and ask MDEQ to review and approve a "due care plan," or actively seek to remediate the site, having MDEQ review the remediation plan and issue its findings. As noted, the program entails strong closure documents.

Michigan's formal MOU with EPA Region 5 states that EPA does not anticipate action against recipients of the state-issued CNTS, except for exceptional circumstances. The MOU should provide lenders and future owners with more security than a "comfort letter."

Michigan's LUST Program

Michigan's LUST program is part of MDEQ, which regulates the monitoring and cleanup of underground storage tanks. Sites with both LUSTs and other contamination can go through the Environmental Response Division's VCP, while sites with only LUSTs come under a different program, which can issue an NFA letter upon completion of the cleanup. New owners of LUSTs may also get an exemption from liability if they did not cause the contamination. Michigan also administers an insurance fund for remediation of USTs, but the fund has encountered financial problems.

Financial Incentives

Michigan grants substantial financial inducements to fund up-front costs. A state bond fund (with a one-time issuance of bonds) subsidizes environmental site assessment and remediation. The money goes to local governments, which nominate properties for funding. In 1996, for example, $20 million was available statewide for site assessment and remediation of brownfields. Since the funding became available, MDEQ has supported 86 site assessments for a total state expenditure of $9.5 million, plus another $17.4 million to remediate 35 brownfield sites.[1] Brownfield TIF districts have also been authorized, subject to creation of local brownfield redevelopment authorities by municipalities or counties.

Cleanup Standards

The state's new risk-based corrective action, site-specific approach to remediation has specified acceptable levels for a long list of contaminants since late 1995. Different standards apply to residential, commercial, and industrial uses. Successfully remediated sites may receive unlimited residential or other land use status if they have been cleared of high levels of lead. Alternatively, they may receive "limited-use status" for a particular use with exposure barriers *and* institutional controls required. Deed restrictions become part of the property's permanent record.

Liability Exemptions

Liability exemptions for lenders have been explicitly available by statute since early 1996. Like new owners, lenders who foreclose on a property must conduct a BEA within 45 days to be exempt from liability. This requirement is consistent with new federal legislation stating that if new owners or lenders conduct a BEA, they are exempt from liability for preexisting contamination.

Intragovernmental Coordination

MDEQ and brownfield officials in Detroit (and other communities) meet monthly to coordinate solutions to problems, hasten the approval process, and provide site assessment funds for many projects. This working group, the REUS–Action Team, usually includes 15 to 20 upper managers in an all-day meeting. The REUS–A Team moves quickly to shepherd both simple and complex projects through the funding and regulatory quagmire. For a typical session, the agenda might include eight to 12 active projects, with a few new ones added or completed and removed from further consideration. Funds are allocated, intra- and intergovernmental problems identified, and solutions devised. According to a city attorney assigned to Detroit's Planning and Development Department, "The REUS–A Team has played a role in at least 40 projects since its creation in 1995. The group's particular value is to identify and focus on barriers to development at specific sites by bringing the technical expertise and background of various personnel together to solve site-specific problems."

State Housing Finance

Like many other states, Michigan supports housing projects through the Michigan State Housing Development Authority. MSHDA's many programs include construction and permanent financing for housing projects that serve low- to moderate-income residents and administration of the federal low-income housing tax credit (LIHTC) program for the state, which makes tax credits available to projects on a competitive basis. MSHDA has an open pipeline for mortgage loans for multifamily housing.

According to MSHDA's deputy director and chief underwriter, MSHDA's primary mission is to provide low- to moderate-income housing. The agency does not seek out brownfield properties, but it has usually been able to finance housing production on them when the properties meet the other required criteria. Proximity to anchor institutions, such as major employers, and location in an area with well-maintained residential structures are characteristics that increase a site's appeal to MSHDA. Like any lender, MSHDA looks at what is in the ground and how unacceptable environmental conditions can be mitigated or remediated. MSHDA generally requires sites to be cleaned to residential standards.[2] It requires developers to submit a Phase 1 environmental study, and its in-house staff evaluate environmental risks and advise when additional testing or remediation is needed. The agency carefully evaluates relevant exposure pathways and identifies areas that need to be remediated to residential standards.

Michigan's new brownfield regulations make it somewhat easier for MSHDA to finance formerly contaminated lands (especially to grant lenders exemption from liability), although MSHDA was comfortable financing projects before the recent changes to state environmental law (featuring the CNTS) were introduced in late 1995.[3] MSHDA has not needed to foreclose on any formerly contaminated sites. For active loan workouts, MSHDA would conduct additional environmental analysis before taking title.

MSHDA has been active in the Detroit area and throughout the state since the 1970s. In Detroit, MSHDA is financing 76 low- to moderate-income housing projects comprising more than 9,000 units. In addition to the project featured in this case study, MSHDA recently financed a 30/70 housing project (30 percent low- to moderate-income/70 percent market rate) in the city, and it is actively underwriting several other projects, all on sites with some previous level of contamination. MSHDA has extensive experience with financing housing developments on sites formerly occupied by gas stations.

Local Economic Conditions

The city of Detroit has lost a substantial number of jobs in the past three and one-half decades. In 1987, the city was home to 1,255 manufacturing companies with 102,200 employees, down 3 percent from 1982 and down almost by half from 1963, when 200,600 employees worked in 3,370 manufacturing firms. Retail growth has also been negative. The city contained 3,847 establishments with payroll in 1987, down 63 percent from 10,300 retail companies with payroll in 1963.

This contraction in jobs has led to a parallel decrease in population. Detroit's population in 1992 was 1 million, down 15.9 percent from 1980. Nearly 80 percent of the population are minorities. The median age is 30.8 years, about two years younger than the comparable state figure. The crime rate (serious crimes known to police) in 1990 was 12,300 per 100,000, double the state average. Median family income was $22,600, or 62 percent of the state average. Twenty-nine percent of families lived below the poverty line in 1992, about triple the state average. The housing stock has decreased rapidly: In 1990, there were 410,000 units, down 13 percent from 1980. Fifty-three percent of units were owner-occupied, well below the state figure of 71 percent, with the median dollar value of an owned unit $25,600, or 42 percent of the state median, in 1990.

The Helen Odean Butler Apartments is a 133-unit low- to moderate-income housing complex in the Elmwood Park neighborhood of Detroit. Located about five minutes from downtown and one-half mile from the river, it is adjacent to the Detroit empowerment zone.

The Helen Odean Butler Apartments

Background

The Helen Odean Butler Apartments is a 133-unit low- to moderate-income housing complex in the Elmwood Park neighborhood in the city of Detroit. Located about five minutes from downtown, it is one-half mile from the river, just adjacent to the Detroit empowerment zone. The developer and management entity is V.I.S.I.O.N.S., Inc., a not-for-profit, church-based entity. The complex contains all low- to moderate-income apartments (for residents earning 30 to 60 percent of the area's gross income) and thus is heavily subsidized by the Michigan State Housing Development Authority. Figure 11.1 shows the location of the project.

According to its project director, V.I.S.I.O.N.S. (Vital Investments Serving In Our NeighborhoodS) was founded in 1985 by the "visionary" pastor of New Calvary Baptist Church in Detroit as a vehicle to reverse the blight, decline, and outward migration in the church's service area, whose residents were fleeing the city's eroding tax base and services. V.I.S.I.O.N.S. started small, buying and rehabilitating ten single- and multi-family structures in the vicinity of the church property over seven years. The Helen Odean Butler project, named after the pastor's wife, represented a big jump in difficulty over previous efforts, but V.I.S.I.O.N.S. did not stop there. It recently acquired 218,000 square feet of industrial/manufacturing space on 20 acres in its service area at a bankruptcy sale. Part of the property has already been leased to two auto-related warehouse users. Because New Calvary has a tithing congregation, V.I.S.I.O.N.S. has more capital than many other not-for-profit development corporations.

Development Plan

The entire development site contains 11.4 acres. It is adjacent to the venerable Elmwood Cemetery and abuts more expensive market-rate housing projects, Circle Drive I and II. Across the street, in Detroit's empowerment zone, is a tract of vacant land for a planned Phase 3 residential project. The first phase, which includes 96 rental units (plus a manager's unit and community center/party room) on eight acres is complete and completely occupied.

FIGURE 11.1

LOCATION OF HELEN ODEAN BUTLER APARTMENTS IN DETROIT

FIGURE 11.2

HELEN ODEAN BUTLER APARTMENTS—SITE PLAN, PHASE 1

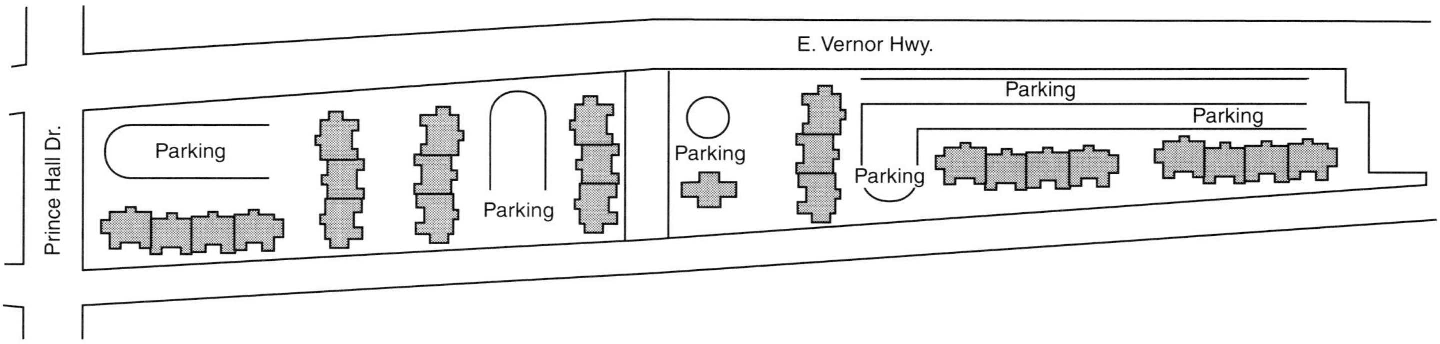

Phase 2 will contain 36 units on almost three acres. The focus of this case study is Phase 1.

The project comprises seven garden apartment buildings (not including the community center) built on slabs, with modern conveniences such as washers and dryers in each unit, security alarms, and dishwashers. The 12- and 16-unit, two-story buildings have no basements but do have a small entryway. Open parking is available on site. Figure 11.2 shows the site plan.

According to V.I.S.I.O.N.S., the smaller two-bedroom, one-bathroom units contain 850 square feet of living space and rent from a low of $250 per month to a more current $463 per month. The 1,180-square-foot three-bedroom, two-bathroom units rent for $539 per month. All rents are well below the $650 to $875 per month market rents charged in nearby developments. Almost all of the project's 96 heads of household are employed, and 90 of the units have at least one child present. MSHDA requires annual household incomes of $18,500 to $34,850, depending on the number of occupants. The project received 700 applications before construction was half finished, and maintains a waiting list of over 500 names.

Site History

Nearly all the site was formerly an urban renewal site from the 1960s. It was owned by the city of Detroit, with a local church owning an outparcel. For a long time, the site had been bypassed for development because of perceived contamination. Recently, two other developers attempted to put together deals but failed because of concerns about liability and the lack of good information about the site's owners.

The site was formerly residential, with about 50 houses on it. Part of the site contained a dry cleaning establishment. It is located along a main auto thoroughfare, which led to a thin layer of lead from leaded gasoline emissions over the years. The city of Detroit managed remediation, then sold the cleaned land to V.I.S.I.O.N.S. for $137,000.

Remediation

This site was one of the last to go through the old regulatory system. Contamination consisted mostly of lead, presumably from lead paint and vehicle emissions, and a trace of arsenic here and there. As is typical for most of the city of Detroit, clay soil was found several feet under the surface. About two acres of the surface soils of the 11.4-acre site had hot spots where lead was above acceptable limits. These contaminated soils were removed to a landfill. The rest of the site contained acceptably low levels of contamination.

The developer had to pay for the initial site assessment, but the city conducted and paid for actual reme-

The developer and management entity is V.I.S.I.O.N.S., Inc., a not-for-profit, church-based entity that was founded in 1985 by the New Calvary Baptist Church as a vehicle to reverse the blight, decline, and outward migration in the community.

diation of the site with a $100,000 grant from the state Department of Commerce. The site received a Type B closure letter under the old system after remediation was completed (similar to an NFA letter), stating that the site was cleaned and suitable for residential use. The site's design ensures the safety of residents, as it allows limited pathways for residual contamination to affect occupants. For example, buildings are located away from residual contamination, the site plan uses buffers, and the slab construction and lack of basements limit possible contact with contamination.

Although the REUS–A Team did not directly manage cleanup, cleanup was relatively fast: eight months to negotiate the remediation plan and another six months for remediation and testing. The overall expense of cleanup (excluding the demolition of 50 houses, which took place in the 1960s) was $100,000, or $50,000 per acre. Although no deed restrictions are involved, the operator has agreed not to move any soils off the site without proper testing.

The REUS–A Team took an interest in this case because of the policy issue concerning lead pathways. The consultant used statistical measures to determine realistic average exposure levels. Because there were no problems with groundwater and the project used municipal drinking water, the team proposed (and the state DEQ agreed) that remediation until the lead did not pose a direct contact hazard was satisfactory. Hence, lead levels are safe for the use of the site.

The developer paid initial site assessment consulting costs, but the city conducted the actual remediation of the site at a cost of $100,000, paid for with a grant from the state Department of Commerce.

Financing Site Development

Overall, remediation was fairly inexpensive. The city paid $100,000, and during construction the developer paid another $66,000 for removal of debris, for a total of $166,000 (again excluding demolition during the 1960s). If the $50,000 in environmental consulting fees is added, the expense works out to $0.58 per square foot of land. Cost of the land for Phase 1 to the city was $118,000. The developer had to pay only 10 percent down, with the balance due upon closing of the construction loan.

Site preparation involved run-of-the-mill construction of parking lots and landscaping, except that some soil had to be taken to a controlled landfill. Most of the soil was used for on-site berming. Site preparation expenses totaled $645,000, or $1.74 per square foot of land (see Figure 11.3).

Construction Costs

MSHDA provided both construction and permanent loans for the project. Construction took a little over one year, with the units built, rented, and occupied as they came on line to improve cash flow for the developer. MSHDA required the builder, Liberty Construction, to provide a maximum price contract for the units. Of the $5.5 million devoted to improvements, direct building hard costs totaled nearly $4.3 million, mostly for the structures ($3.9 million) but also including the community center and fixtures, and compliance with the city code.

Legal soft costs were fairly low ($30,000), mostly because the project director is an attorney. Other soft costs for planning, architecture, city fees, insurance, and marketing totaled $339,000. MSHDA took a total of $147,000, $33,000 of which was 1 percent interest on the construction loan.

MSHDA's pro forma includes an allowance for the builder's overhead and profit, which together totaled $300,000 for this project. V.I.S.I.O.N.S. was allowed 5 percent (in this case $285,000) for putting the deal together. These funds were a major source of the developer's equity for permanent financing. Overall, the project cost $6.4 million. Net cost to the developer after the $100,000 city subsidy was $6.3 million, or $65,300 per unit.

Operating Cash Flow and Investment

Projected cash flow, in a future stable year, will be driven by revenues totaling $597,000 per year, nearly $520 per month per unit. In the near term, projected revenues are $490,000 per year, or $425 per month per unit. Although the project is 100 percent occupied and has a long waiting list, an allowance is made for uncollectible rents and vacancies of a month here and there as units are reno-

FIGURE 11.3

Project Data—Helen Odean Butler Apartments

Land Use Information		
Site Area: 8½ acres (370,260 square feet)		
Floor/Area Ratio (FAR): 0.27		
Building Area: 96,000 square feet (96 1,000-square-foot units)		
Number of Tenants: 96		
Development Cost Information		
Land Acquisition Cost	$118,500	($0.32 per square foot)
Site Preparation Costs		
Remediation	$166,000	($0.45 per square foot)
Other site preparation	645,000	($1.74 per square foot)
Construction Costs		
Building hard costs	$4,289,000	($44.68 per square foot)
Demolition	0	
Soft Costs		
Legal	$30,000	
Architect, planning, miscellaneous (5% of project costs)	339,000	
Environmental consultants	50,000	
Construction loan/fees/carrying costs (1% MSHDA loan, fees)	147,000	
Developer's fee (5% to V.I.S.I.O.N.S.)	285,000	
Builder's overhead and profit (7% of hard cost)	300,000	
Total Development Cost	**$6,369,500**	($66.35 per square foot)
Minus Public Subsidy	–100,000	
Net Cost to Developer	**$6,269,000**	($65.31 per building square foot)
Operating Cash Flow (stable year)		
Subsidized Rents	$597,000	($250–540/unit/month plus utilities)
Vacancies	(25,000)	
Minus Operating Costs	–287,000	($3 per square foot)
Net Operating Income	**$285,000**	
Financing and Investment		
Value (cost approach)	$6,369,000	
Loan Amount (0.90 LTV ratio)	$5,711,000	
Debt Service (1% for 30 years)	$220,000	
Debt Service Coverage Ratio	1.01 to 1.30	
Before-Tax Cash Flow	$65,000	
V.I.S.I.O.N.S. Equity Requirement	$654,300	
Return on V.I.S.I.O.N.S.'s Equity	9.9%	

vated when tenants move out. Future expenses of $250 per unit per month, including replacement reserves, come to an estimated $287,000 per year. Net operating income before debt service in the future stable year is projected to be $285,000, compared with just over $220,000 per year in the near term.

MSHDA's permanent loan was for 30 years at 1 percent interest. The developer's return is capped at 12 percent, with a 1 percent annual increase allowed until a final cap of 25 percent is reached. Prepayment of the mortgage loan is prohibited, and MSHDA requires the property to be used for low- to moderate-income renters for 30 years. MSHDA also has the right of first refusal if V.I.S.I.O.N.S. decides to sell the project.

MSHDA's estimate of the project's value is based on the cost approach (considering the tightly regulated building conditions described earlier), plus a developer's fee. Thus, for determining the loan-to-value ratio, the project's value is $6.4 million. V.I.S.I.O.N.S. borrowed $5.7 million, for an LTV ratio of 0.90. The project's debt service, with its highly subsidized interest rate and long amortization period, is just $220,000 per year. The remaining $65,000 is the project's before-tax cash flow, providing the lender with a debt service coverage ratio of 1.3 in a future stable year. MSHDA, however, allowed the developers to have a debt service coverage ratio of just over 1.0 in the early years of the project.

Low-Income Housing Tax Credits

A large part of the project's equity was derived from low-income housing tax credits. This complex national program is administered in Michigan by MSHDA. In general, long-term requirements for low income restrict the project's cash flow, permitting owners and outside investors to receive a federal income tax credit related to the costs of construction. The tax credits generated by this project provide $264,000 per year in income tax credits for ten years. The developers found corporate investors and tax credit trust players willing to pay about $1.3 million for this stream of benefits, or 56 percent of the credits' face value. The funds are to be paid directly to V.I.S.I.O.N.S. in four to five payments within three years of the first structure's completion. The MSHDA agency that administers the tax-credit program advises MSHDA underwriters with respect to available equity and monitors compliance with program restrictions, such as limitations on the developer's fees, income levels, and rental rates.

Taking out the $100,000 in remediation cost paid for by the city, V.I.S.I.O.N.S. is left with $654,300 equity in the project. Its projected rate of return in a future stable year is just under 10 percent, although for the first several years, the rate of return is likely to be under 5 percent.

Return on Public Investment

Not counting funds paid to condemn and clear the property, this project used a negligible amount of local funds (even the $100,000 for remediation was contributed by the state) and a large, state-subsidized mortgage. It also uses federal low-income housing tax credits. While the property pays local property taxes, its fiscal returns alone cannot justify the large public investment. The benefits from the project are social, providing dignified and stable housing for the working poor in the city of Detroit and stabilizing the neighborhood.

Market Acceptance

With full occupancy and a waiting list of 500, this project has been accepted in the market. Contamination left from the site's previous use has not negatively affected marketing.

Lessons Learned

Although the site had been overlooked for a long time, the cost of remediation was quite low and the issue of brownfields perceived rather than actual. Designing the units without basements was a smart way to reduce transmission pathways for contamination and save construction costs. Leaving some soil on site, away from structures and under common areas, also saved costs.

The state absorbs risk, if any, on the back end of the deal. Syndicated tax-credit equity was a major source of equity for the not-for-profit developer, who also makes an adequate rate of return, which it can plow back into achieving its social goals. The builder also made an adequate profit and was able to cover overhead. The group achieving the most benefit, however, is the project's low- to moderate-income residents, who got new housing at affordable rental rates.

The Detroit Community Health Connection

Background

Detroit Community Health Connection, Inc. (DCHC), a private, not-for-profit corporation, has been providing primary, preventive public health care services to Detroit's indigent population since 1988. When it became obvious a few years ago that a new site was needed, DCHC leaders began looking for a second site upon which to build a new 13,700-square-foot facility in the city of Detroit that would be accessible to its client base. They settled on a site of slightly less than one acre on Jefferson, a major thoroughfare at the southeastern edge of the city near Grosse Point Park. The site has good traffic flows, is on many bus routes, and is highly visible (see Figure 11.4).

Part of the site was formerly used as a gas station. Most of the site was owned by the city, and the rest was controlled by a church. Land prices in the area were $0.50 to $1.50 per square foot. DCHC was the developer, although it retained attorneys to handle the environmental and site assembly parts of the deal. The clinic has opened its doors, and medical care is being provided to patients. The professional staff includes four medical doctors, a certified physician assistant and midwife, nurses, and other medical technical and office staff.

FIGURE 11.4

DCHC VICINITY MAP

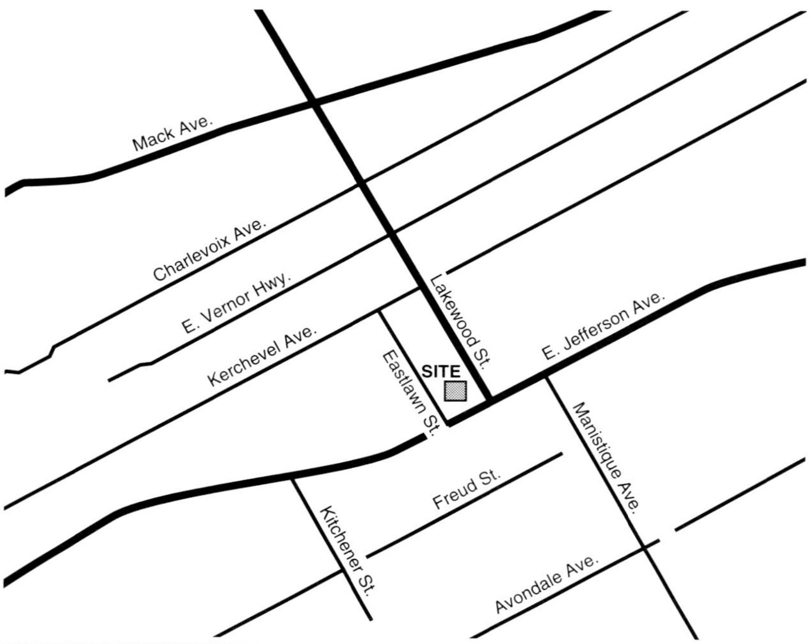

Development Plan

The 39,800-square-foot (0.9-acre) site has 235 feet of frontage on Jefferson; it is in six parcels with two owners. The new building has 13,700 square feet of space and ample off-street parking. The project's floor/area ratio is 0.35.

Site History

The site has been in use since before the Civil War. The eastern part of the site on the corner was used as a gas and auto service station on and off since 1916. The site was also used for various retail stores, a bowling alley, and a parking lot for a nearby church. In the 1970s, the property was abandoned, and the city demolished the structures and obtained control of two-thirds of the site through the urban renewal program and foreclosure of the properties because of delinquent property taxes. By the early 1990s, the site was vacant, and the church was using the middle portion of the site for a parking lot.

In June 1994, DCHC retained an attorney to begin assembling the site on its behalf. Within a month, an agreement had been struck to acquire the church parcel. The request to acquire the balance of the site from the city was submitted in September 1994, but it took until November 1995 to close the land deal because it was necessary to have both the development agreement and environmental problems clarified. All the parcels had some form of clouded title. DCHC's total cost for land was $42,000, or $1.06 per square foot, for a site that was both legally clear and environmentally clean.

Site Remediation

Two main types of contamination were present. Investigations in early 1995 by DCHC's environmental consultant found BTEX (benzene, toluene, ethylbenzene, xylene), PNAs (polynuclear aromatics), and various metals on one part of the site. A magnetometer detected metal from USTs from the gas station on the corner, which involved contacting the Michigan UST agency and the fire marshal. The church parcel contained little of environmental concern. The city-directed remediation included removal of six underground tanks and 470 cubic yards of BTEX-saturated soil in the immediate vicinity of the tank pit. Clay soil precluded any concern about groundwater contamination, with municipal drinking water brought to the site. The PNAs were left on site and capped under the parking lot. The city funded a portion of the remediation, mainly removal of the USTs, using money from the state's revolving fund for removal of LUSTs. Overall, the city paid about $90,000 to remediate the site. Later, during construction, two more

USTs were found, adding another $18,000 to the cost of remediation.

Overall, environmental remediation and consulting fees (excluding environmental attorneys who worked on the CNTS) totaled $128,000, or $3.23 per square foot of land. When remediation was complete, the site received a CNTS from MDEQ in 1996 in the form of an administrative order by consent, signed by the state attorney general, which formalized the agreement among MDEQ, the city of Detroit, and DCHC.

The REUS–A Team handled the project, which designated the site for action and helped guide remediation. The team was primarily educator and facilitator. Later, REUS–A Team members met with Comerica Bank about providing permanent financing for the project. The team's input was key in addressing the bank's concerns about liability and the costs of remediating the USTs on site. The loan was granted after the REUS–A Team helped set up loan guarantees.

The city removed eight underground storage tanks and 470 cubic yards of BTEX-saturated soil in the immediate vicinity of the tank pit. PNAs were left on site and capped under the parking lot.

Construction

Construction began soon after the real estate closing and lasted one year. Pouring concrete during the winter months slowed progress. During excavation for building footings, it was necessary to excavate old concrete slabs and debris from prior structures. Backfill was added to stabilize the new concrete foundation. The two extra USTs were discovered during excavation for the sewer line. Later, when the plumbing contractor applied for a plumbing permit from the city of Detroit, seven liens, totaling $850 and dating from 1895, for unpaid disconnect charges were revealed. The liens were not of record, and the city eventually forgave them.

Overall, other site work (excluding remediation) cost $120,000, primarily to prepare the site, pave the parking lot, and put up a fence. Hard costs for the structure totaled $1.4 million, or $105 per building square foot. Architectural fees approximated 7 percent of hard costs. Soft costs for real estate and environmental legal services totaled $80,000. DCHC took no development fee, and interest on the construction loan and fees totaled an estimated $70,000. Overall, the project cost slightly less than $2 million. After the public subsidy for remediation, the cost to DCHC was $1.9 million, or about $138 per building square foot (see Figure 11.5).

Financing

DCHC acted as its own not-for-profit developer for the project. The bulk of the construction and permanent financing came from one future advance mortgage loan of $950,000 from Comerica Bank. The term of the loan was ten years at a loan-to-value ratio of 0.5. A major regional health care provider supplied a loan guarantee for the first mortgage and is helping DCHC obtain grants from philanthropic foundations and other sources for its share of the equity. At the conclusion of fundraising, DCHC's equity stake is expected to be $539,000 (of its own funds), with the balance ($400,000) coming from grants.

Assuming market rent for comparable clinic space would be $9.00 per square foot, triple net, the net operating income for the center as real estate would be $170,000 per year. After paying debt service (estimated to be $145,000 in a typical year), the center would have before-tax cash flow of $25,000 per year, a 4.6 percent return on DCHC's equity.

The debt service coverage ratio of about 1.17 for this project is misleading, because DCHC also obtained a federal grant from the Department of Health and Human Services to cover the majority of the debt service payments for the ten-year life of the Comerica loan.

Return on Public Investment

The amount of state and local public funds in this project was fairly modest: only the cost of remediation and demolition, which was partially offset by sale of the property. Because the project is a not-for-profit venture, no property taxes are paid. Although it created only a few new permanent jobs (because DCHC closed its other

FIGURE 11.5

PROJECT DATA—DETROIT COMMUNITY HEALTH CONNECTION

Land Use Information
Site Area: 0.9 acre (39,800 square feet)
Floor/Area Ratio: 0.35
Building Area: 13,700 square feet
Number of Tenants: 1 user, no vacancies

Development Cost Information		
Land Acquisition Cost	$42,000	($1.06 per square foot)
Site Preparation Costs		
Remediation	$108,000	($2.71 per square foot)
Other site preparation	120,000	($3.02 per square foot)
Construction Costs		
Building hard costs	$1,438,000	($105 per square foot)
Demolition	0	
Soft Costs		
Legal, real estate, environmental	$80,000	
Environmental consultants	20,000	
Architect, planning (7% of hard costs)	101,000	
Construction loan/carrying costs	70,000	
Developer's fee	0	
Total Development Cost	**$1,979,000**	($144.45 per building square foot)
Minus Public Subsidy	–90,000	
Net Cost to Developer	**$1,889,000**	($137.88 per building square foot)
Operating Cash Flow		
Market Rent	$180,000	($9 per square foot, triple net)
Security	(10,000)	($ 0.50 per square foot)
Net Operating Income	**$170,000**	
Financing and Investment		
Value (NOI/cap rate of 0.09)	$1,888,900	
Loan Amount (0.50 loan-to-value ratio)	$950,000	
Annual Debt Service (10%)	$145,000	
Debt Service Coverage Ratio	1.17	
Before-Tax Cash Flow	$25,000	
Equity Requirement (excluding grants of $400,000)	$539,000	
Return on Equity	4.6%	

inefficient clinic), the project serves an important community need.

Market Acceptance

The project opened its doors in December 1996. The clinic has been well received by patients and staff and is an important link in the chain of health care providers in Detroit.

Lessons Learned

With the appropriate loan guarantees and backing and a state-issued covenant not to sue, private capital can be attracted to this type of inner-city project. Capping PNAs under the parking lot helped keep remediation costs down. After the city took care of remediation, the project has been well accepted in the market.

Despite its relatively small dollar amount, this project, with its clouded title, environmental remediation, loan guarantees, and CNTS, was highly complex. The amount of investigation and soft costs required was close to that for a much larger project. Counsel, REUS–A Team members, and the DCHC director and staff spent an extensive amount of time obtaining the loan, loan guarantees, and equity grants.

Notes

1. Claudia Kerbawy, Michigan Dept. of Environmental Quality, telephone interview, January 1997.
2. Rich Pennings, deputy director and chief underwriter, Michigan State Housing Development Authority, telephone interview, February 1997.
3. Ibid.
4. Ibid.

12 Brownfield Development in Suburban Cleveland: Expansion Of a Shopping Center

Ohio's VCP is relatively new, the last pieces of the program having been put in place in late 1996. Like most progressive brownfield programs, Ohio's Voluntary Action Program (VAP) employs risk-based cleanup standards and provides good terminal documents. Unlike in many states, however, Ohio's approach is very much driven by the private sector, which potentially could allow a large number of sites through the system with minimal state supervision. Because of Ohio's long history of industrialization, much of it support of auto manufacturing, the state has a large supply of brownfields in cities such as Cleveland, Toledo, Dayton, Cincinnati, Akron, and Youngstown. Much of the northern part of the state has a high water table because of its location on Lake Erie. The privately oriented VCP, which has little in the way of public grants, features tax credits and loans. Ohio has aggressively used local property tax abatement for a number of years.

The Ohio Environmental Protection Agency (OEPA) employs a bottom-up approach to brownfield development. While it does not maintain a formal registry of brownfield sites, OEPA does maintain a list of hazardous waste sites in the state. The state environmental unit employs flexible, site-sensitive remediation rules, including encapsulation of contamination where appropriate. Certified environmental consultants prepare the necessary documents, clean up the site without direct supervision by OEPA, and issue the NFA letter. OEPA then issues a CNTS. Successful brownfield developers may take a tax credit and apply to various loan funds for money to finance remediation. This approach is new, and fewer than ten projects had received a CNTS as of year-end 1996.

This case study describes the expansion of a shopping center in an inner suburb of Cleveland (no actual names are used because the deal is still in progress). This privately funded project has received its CNTS and, as of December 1997, was in the early stages of construction. Remediation began under interim guidelines from the state. The market has not yet accepted the project.

Ohio's Regulatory Environment

Ohio began preparing a voluntary cleanup program to remediate and develop industrial sites in 1994. The program was finalized in late 1996, although some challenges to rules for RBCA are still pending. OEPA is the lead agency, and cleanups are supervised by the Site Remediation Program. The state also has a number of other laws pertaining to the cleanup of contaminated sites, such as laws governing underground storage tanks. Moreover, under state statute ORC 3734 addressing hazardous wastes, OEPA can use administrative consent orders to force responsible parties to clean up known contaminated sites. Potentially responsible parties may take part in the VAP if they have no mandatory state or federal cleanup actions in progress. The Bureau of Underground Storage Tank Regulations (BUSTR), housed in the Ohio Department of Commerce, administers USTs; it also keeps the state's list of LUSTs. Ohio's VAP does not accept USTs, but sites with ongoing cleanup can seek an NFA letter from BUSTR, then enter the VAP.

Consistent with the government's initiative on the development of urban land, OEPA encourages economic development of contaminated lands using site remediation techniques that minimize costs, and letting the private sector direct remediation. To ensure quality outcomes, OEPA certifies environmental consultants based on academic credentials, work experience, and ethical criteria. OEPA has set up the program so that consultants have their own long-range interests in mind. The system provides safeguards that require consultants to balance their clients' needs while maintaining their own reputations. About 60 individuals are currently certified, including some based outside Ohio. In addition, the VAP maintains quality control by requiring 25 percent of the projects issued CNTS letters to be audited, including scientific laboratory records. Certified consultants must keep their files available to OEPA for ten years.

Approximately 60 sites have participated or are participating in the VAP. Through early 1997, 18 had received an NFA letter, and seven had obtained a CNTS.

The VAP and Closure Documents

The first step in remediating a site for a brownfield developer is to hire a certified environmental consultant to evaluate the site. With no formal initial contact with OEPA required, the consultant prepares the studies for Phases I and II, then moves on to Phase III remediation, with minimal input from OEPA. The site is then remediated, potentially using the RBCAs discussed in the next subsection. When the site has been remediated to the specified levels, the consultant issues an NFA letter, after which the consultant and developer submit the NFA letter to OEPA, which can then issue the CNTS. The CNTS currently takes the form of findings and orders signed by the director of OEPA. The CNTS binds other state agencies from using specific statutes to pursue further action against the parties involved in cleanup. It does not, however, provide any protection against third-party lawsuits. Large complex sites may receive an NFA letter and CNTS for each phase, as construction is completed. Reopeners are possible in the event of fraud or the failure to meet applicable standards in place at the time the CNTS was issued (ORC 3746.12).

Ohio has not yet obtained a formal MOU from EPA Region 5, although "comfort letters" are available. Quality control is reportedly one reason that Ohio is the only Region 5 state without an MOU from EPA. Discussions are in progress, however, and OEPA believes its program ensures sufficient environmental protection for EPA to be comfortable with it.

Cleanup Standards

The state recently promulgated a set of regulations, in place since December 1996, allowing cleanup to background or risk-based levels, whichever are higher, based on certain site-specific criteria (OAC 3745.300 et seq.). Water quality is a big issue because of the high water table in many parts of the state, and different sets of criteria apply to use of potable and nonpotable groundwater. Designation as an "urban setting," with less restrictive, risk-based cleanup requirements, is also available.

Different standards for specific substances pertain to residential, commercial, and industrial uses. Encapsulation is permitted on sites with historically contaminated fill, but capped sites may involve additional monitoring, a restriction filed with the county as part of the deed to the property, and being the subject of state disclosure regulations.

Protection from Liability

The CNTS from Ohio's VAP includes protection from liability for new owners. This protection runs with the land and thus is transferable to future owners. Protection from liability for lenders is fairly strong. Lenders who foreclose are not liable for environmental damage that occurred before they took control of the property. Lenders generally can incur liability only if they negligently contribute to pollution on the site.

FIGURE 12.1

SITE REMEDIATION, SHOWING AREAS WITH CONTAMINATED GROUNDWATER

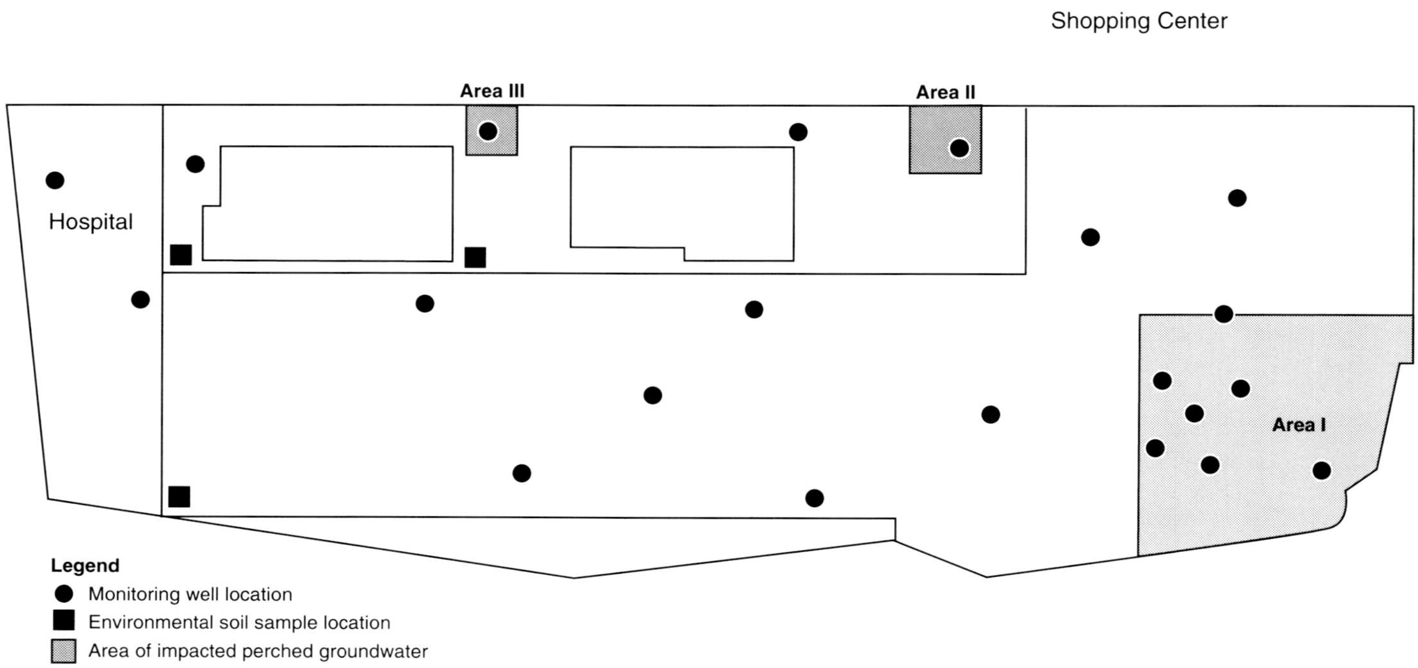

Financial Inducements

Because Ohio brownfield developers enter the VAP late in the game, no up-front program is available to fund site assessment or remediation. Low-interest loans for investigation and remediation have been available since 1994, however, through the Ohio Department of Development, OEPA's Ohio Water Pollution Control Loan Fund, and the Ohio Water Development Authority, among others. The latter two agencies have loaned at least $300 million of these revolving funds, with about $30 million earmarked for brownfields. In late 1996, the Ohio Department of Development initiated a grant program to reimburse community development corporations and local government agencies for the investigation and remediation of brownfields.

Local property taxes can be abated for ten years on built improvements on brownfield projects that achieve a CNTS. Use of property tax abatements is a common economic and community development tool in Ohio.

Ohio is one of the first states to offer tax credits for the remediation of brownfields. A 10 percent corporate income tax credit is allowed for qualifying remediation activities, up to $500,000. That amount is increased to 15 percent and $750,000 for sites in designated "disadvantaged" areas. The credit, which is not transferable to other parties, can be spread out over five years.

Pending Actions

Because Ohio's VAP has just been completed, OEPA intends to observe how it operates before it takes on any new initiatives. Financial incentive programs, however, are high on the list for both the governor and lieutenant governor.

Ohio's VCP will be closely watched because it could be useful in the rest of the country. Its approach to site remediation is driven by the private sector, and the state has a much smaller role than in most other states with VCPs. If issues related to the certification of environmental consultants and the auditing of consultants' findings can be satisfactorily resolved, Ohio's approach can potentially generate a large quantity of remediated sites with limited oversight from the state and relatively little up-front subsidy.

EastRock Shopping Center

Background

This site of the former Acme manufacturing plant is located on 19 acres in an inner suburb of Cleveland about five miles from downtown on an interstate highway. Adjacent to an existing 240,000-square-foot shopping mall, the project at completion would contain 287,000 square feet of retail space, at a total investment of about

$30 million (hard costs). Because it is an expansion of an existing center, its eventual market success is virtually assured. The experienced developer has an established relationship with a bank. The project is under development, and state approvals have been granted and financing lined up, but the final plan has not yet been approved.

The site, in its checkered past, was used by a number of manufacturing companies and commercial tenants for over 80 years. Although a few tenants still occupied small buildings on the site until this project was initiated, most of the site had been abandoned when the developer expressed interest in it in 1986. The developer had developed the nearby shopping center, which was doing quite well.

The site extends along the north side of an interstate highway and is accessible from a major interchange nearby. Many big-box retailers and a suburban medical facility are located nearby. The project's location is suitable for a community shopping center. Land prices in the area for a comparable site over ten acres assembled from parcels with negligible contamination (if any are available) range from $6.00 to $10.00 per square foot.

Local Economic Conditions

According to the U.S. Census, the suburb's population in 1990 was just over 11,000 people, down 5 percent from 1980.[1] Virtually all of the population is white. The median age is 41 years, much higher than the state figure of 33.3 years. Median family income is about $27,000, or 93 percent of the state average. About 5 percent of households lived below the poverty line in 1990, less than half the state average. Typical of a bedroom community, the city's employment base is small. The city had fewer than 100 retail establishments, with total sales of about $200 million, in 1992.[2] Several big-box retailers have moved in since then, however.

Because of its excellent location and the drawing power of the existing center, the project's retail trade area extends well beyond the local suburb into Cleveland and other suburbs.

Project Description

The project's intended use is 287,000 square feet of retail and commercial space. The center would contain two or three big-box retailers and other stores suitable for a community shopping center. The strategy is to build the project and hold it for the long term for the owner's portfolio. As of December 1997, no leases had been signed. Market acceptance is an issue, as big-box tenants have been reluctant to make commitments based on their perception that on-site contamination could be an issue.

According to the project director, the site was assembled and acquired using real estate options over the past several years. Three separate parcels were involved. One property was acquired using a "1031 land swap," which required the developer to find a suitable piece of land to swap with the seller. The developer paid $2.8 million for the 19 acres, as is, or about $3.40 per square foot.

FIGURE 12.2

REMEDIATION OF THE EASTROCK SITE, SHOWING EXTENT OF FOUNDRY SAND

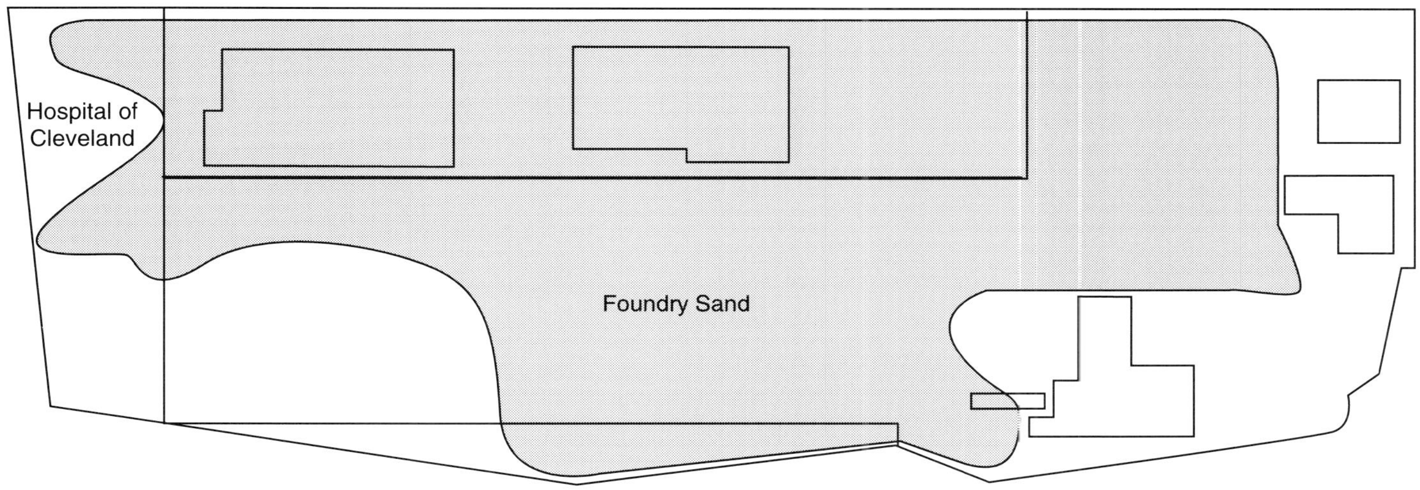

In addition to the contamination caused by on-site polluters, the site was used as a dump for foundry sand, construction debris, and other fill materials, including lead and other heavy metals and asbestos.

Plans are proceeding more slowly than expected, however, because the local planning board has not yet approved the project, despite the fact that retailing is an allowable use under the existing industrial zoning. The community is concerned about replacing lost industrial jobs and wants a denser project. Typical of many Ohio suburban communities, the community would obtain a large fiscal benefit from local income taxes and only a moderate benefit from property taxes. On the other hand, very little revenue would accrue to the community from retail sales taxes because of the way the state allocates this income. This tax structure encourages the construction of office and industrial space, to the detriment of retail uses. Thus, state law plays a role in the community's fiscal motivation to approve the project.

Like other Ohio communities, this suburb faces substantial costs to close its municipal landfill to comply with the state's solid waste laws. Therefore, projects in planning, especially those that may use scarce landfills like brownfields, may be vulnerable to extended discussions and potential delay. This suburb is also seeking resources from the state for an unrelated matter, and the shopping center is caught in the cross fire.

Site Remediation

The site was used as a factory as far back as 1914. Since then, occupants have included a plastics factory, an asphalt-manufacturing plant, a metal-refurbishing plant, warehouses, and machine shops. The site shows evidence of at least ten structures and several hundred thousand square feet of building space, although not all this space necessarily was occupied at the same time.

In addition to the contamination caused by on-site polluters, the site was used as a dump for foundry sand, construction debris, and other fill materials. One of the primary environmental problems was that lead and other heavy metals had permeated the fill material that had been deposited throughout the site. Debris from the buildings contained asbestos. And perched groundwater in several well-defined areas of the site contained solvents and dissolved metals. Piles of tires and barrels of hazardous materials of unknown origin were scattered throughout the site. In all, over 50 piles of material on the site had to be dealt with.

Five other environmental consultants had looked at the site before the current group did. They had already conducted Phase I and II studies. The Phase II analyses included samples on 100-, 15-, and ten-foot grids. The consultants came up with completely different results, with estimates for remediating the site ranging from virtually nothing to $13 million. The higher figure reflects the cost to dig out all contaminated material and haul it to a hazardous waste landfill about 100 miles away. All told, the developer has spent about $600,000 on environmental consulting fees for this project.

To sort out the environmental problems and determine whether developing the site is feasible, the developer in late 1994 retained Hemisphere Corporation, a Cleveland-based brownfield development and investment company, to manage site remediation. According to its president, Hemisphere's strategy for remediation from the beginning was to use a risk-based approach, employing both engineering and institutional controls. A vice president of the company says that problems in remediating the project were resolved by performing an extensive Phase II investigation and a risk assessment. Once the level of risk was identified, Hemisphere determined that contaminated material could largely be left in place, so long as a suitable barrier was constructed, and still meet applicable state standards.

Initial contact with OEPA was minimal, and the consultants went right to work in 1995 by extensively investigating the site. The next step was the NFA letter, which the consultant issued in August 1996. OEPA reviewed the NFA letter and issued a CNTS in December 1996 for the parts of the project that did not contain contaminated groundwater. The CNTS prescribes procedures to be taken if additional contamination is discovered under buildings on the site during later stages of construction. Because some contamination remains on site, a deed restricting land use to commercial or industrial will be filed with the county before occupancy.

The main feature of remediation was the use of a cap to contain contamination on site. In most parts of the site, this cap will take the form of a parking lot. The developer has entered into an operation and maintenance agreement with OEPA to preserve the integrity of the cap in perpetuity, which includes criteria for financial performance. These arrangements are required to preserve the CNTS. The operation and maintenance agreement requires an annual inspection to verify that the cap is intact.

Part of the problem involved in managing site remediation was that OEPA's rules were changing during remediation, specifically those with respect to groundwater in urban areas. At the beginning of site remediation, interim rules from the VAP were in place, which generated uncertainty about how to deal with groundwater at the site.

This uncertainty was overcome by splitting off the three small areas of the site where groundwater was an issue and applying the VAP to the remainder of the site. Thus, the vast majority of the site obtained the consultant's NFA letter and was issued a CNTS by OEPA, enabling marketing to proceed. When new rules concerning groundwater took effect in December 1996, the balance of the site underwent the VAP. An NFA letter has been issued for this part of the site, and OEPA is reviewing the request for the CNTS. The total cost of remediation for the project using a cap, including the consultant's fees, is $4.1 million, or just under $5.00 per square foot. See Figure 12.1 for a more in-depth illustration of remediation strategies showing general location, building footprints, soil test pits, and groundwater monitoring wells. The figure delineates the three areas (indicated by roman numerals) that were broken off from the main parcel for the CNTS.

Because of potential tenants' reluctance to lease the property, the developer is exploring a fallback strategy for remediation, which is to segregate contaminated soil onto about two to three acres, leaving 16 acres clean enough to build on. Although the CNTS is flexible enough to permit the developer to take this approach, this strategy would likely increase remediation costs by about $1.5 million, to $5 million. Thus, total remediation costs, including environmental consulting fees, are likely to be $5.6 million, or $6.77 per square foot, or approximately 18 to 20 percent of the total projected cost of about $30 million. Future site development costs may be substantially reduced, however, because much of the cost of remediation will go toward a parking lot. And the net remediation cost to the developers should be reduced by up to $500,000 because of the tax credit from the state.

FIGURE 12.3

PROJECT DATA—EXPANSION OF AN EXISTING SHOPPING CENTER

Land Use Information		
Site Area: 19 acres (827,640 square feet)		
Floor/Area Ratio: 0.35		
Net Leasable Building Area: 287,000 square feet		
Development Cost Information		
Land Acquisition Cost	$2,800,000	($3.38 per square foot)
Site Preparation Costs		
Remediation	$5,000,000	($6.04 per square foot)
Other site preparation	NA	
Construction Costs		
Building hard costs	NA	
Other (construction losses)	NA	
Soft Costs		
Architect, legal, planning	NA	
Environmental consultants	$600,000	
Construction loan/carrying costs	NA	
Brownfields consulting fee	NA	
Developer's fee	NA	
Total Development Cost	**$30,000,000**	($104.53 per building square foot)
Minus Public Subsidy	–500,000	State brownfield tax credits
Net Cost to Developer	**$29,500,000**	($102.79 per building square foot)
Operating Cash Flow		
Market Rent	NA	
Market Vacancy	NA	
Security Costs	NA	
Environmental Monitoring	NA	
Tax Abatement (75%, over 10 years)	$450,000	
Financing and Investment		
Value (NOI/cap rate)	NA	
Private Loan Amount (0.6 loan-to-value ratio)	NA	
Private Debt Service	NA	
Debt Service on Public Loan from Ohio Water Pollution Control Loan Fund	$574,000	
Debt Service Coverage ratio	NA	
Before-Tax Cash Flow	NA	
Equity Requirement	NA	
Return on Equity		

The strategy of segregating the soil has a positive side. The cost increase may be partially offset by the fact that using a cap and leaving the foundry soil in place (see Figure 12.2) would have increased construction costs because the foundry sand is unsuitable to support a building. A structural foundation, using footers sunk down through the foundry sand to the soil or bedrock below, would be required for adequate support.

Deal Structure

In the long run, the project will be financed 60 percent through private financing, 20 percent through a loan from the state, and 20 percent with private equity. The project has lined up a major national bank to provide construction and permanent financing for the project contingent upon obtaining signed leases. When the project is complete, the real estate will secure the loan. In the meantime, the partners are funding the remediation with a personal loan, at an interest rate of 10 percent.

Public financing to cover costs of remediation will be provided by the Ohio Water Development Authority and OEPA's Ohio Water Pollution Control Loan Fund. These agencies have committed a total of $5.3 million in subordinated loans to finance remediation. The loans will be amortized over 20 years at a subsidized interest rate of approximately 4 percent (see Figure 12.3).

Strategies to Reduce Liability

The state's CNTS is the main vehicle to reduce liability. It is too soon to determine, however, whether or not the market will accept the concept and importance of this instrument. The lack of an MOU is also a factor, but EPA Region 5 has provided a "comfort letter" for the project.

Splitting the parcel into parts and keeping land under buildings essentially clean from contaminated soil may prove to be necessary. The developer is also exploring the possibility of obtaining environmental insurance on the property.

Return on Public Funds

Ohio generally rewards private sector investment with cost reductions after the fact. Three separate sources of public subsidy are available.

First is the brownfield remediation tax credit from the state, which would save the developer approximately $500,000 of site development costs. It would be taken off the developer's corporate income tax within the first several years of the project. Second are subsidized state loans to reduce operating cash flow. The loans would be used to fund site remediation of up to $5.3 million, amortized over a 20-year period at approximately 4 percent. This approach would reduce debt service of about $230,000 per year over a market-rate loan. The present value of the public subsidy required to bring this loan down from market rates to the rate paid is approximately $2 million. Third is property tax abatement of $450,000 per year from local government, reflecting a reduction of 75 percent of the value of the improvements over ten years. The present value of this subsidy would be about $3 million. The overall public subsidy for this project would be $5.5 million, or about 18 percent of the project's total cost.

The public return on the project would be substantial, especially after the ten-year property tax abatement is over. The fully developed property is expected to pay over $600,000 per year in personal and real property taxes by 2010. Economic benefits are also large: Approximately 350 construction jobs would be created over two to three years, pumping $10 million or more in salaries into the local economy. In addition, the new retail stores would create 400 full- and part-time permanent retail sales and management jobs. Development of the project also has intangible benefits, such as elimination of blight and reuse of an important suburban property.

Market Acceptance

Potential tenants' not accepting the project is its major hurdle at this time. The center hopes to attract big-box retail tenants by segregating contaminated soil onto other parts of the site.

Lessons Learned

This site has several attractive features, including excellent access and visibility from the interstate and a large assembled parcel. Because the center is essentially an extension of an established shopping center, it should be accepted in the long run.

The fact that the site received one of Ohio's first CNTS documents is both a strength and a weakness at this point. The CNTS allowed the project to proceed at a time when Ohio's VAP was just getting established, and splitting out the groundwater and soil components of the project enabled the developer to begin marketing the project under the interim regulations. But as long as contamination is not removed from the site, the market may take some time to recognize the value of the CNTS or other closure documents.

The local planning body is reluctant to approve the project, despite the fact that retail use is allowable under existing zoning and retailing is most likely the property's highest and best use. State tax laws that allow local governments to rely heavily on income taxes and little on sales tax may be a factor. The state may also be seeking to extract funds from the developer for the future costs of closing landfills.

Notes

1. U.S. Bureau of the Census, *Census of Population and Housing* (Washington D.C.: U.S. Dept. of Commerce, 1990).

2. U.S. Bureau of the Census, *Census of Retail Trade* (Washington, D.C.: U.S. Dept. of Commerce, 1992).

13 Brownfield Development in New Jersey: Port Imperial Housing Project

Since it first initiated a voluntary remediation program (VRP) a few years ago, New Jersey has been aggressively encouraging development of contaminated property. A component of the VRP addresses only brownfields. New Jersey's location in the northeast corridor near both New York City and Philadelphia means that many parts of the state are within commuting distance of these cities as well as Newark, one of the largest ports on the East Coast. New Jersey was for decades an industrial powerhouse, which led to large tracts of contaminated property. Much of the low-lying northern part of the state has a very high water table. Faced with the national recession of the early 1990s, New Jersey took an active role in encouraging development of industrial sites. The new programs are more flexible than the state's earlier efforts at environmental cleanup, enacted in the early 1980s.

The state's top-down approach to brownfield development involves keeping a list of contaminated sites. The state environmental unit's flexible rules allow encapsulation of contaminated material and provide up-front money for VCPs. Thus, New Jersey has a relatively large volume of sites. More than 2,300 sites have entered the broadly defined program since 1994, including sites with underground storage tanks. At least 20 brownfield sites have received terminal documents and are under construction.

Port Imperial at West New York is a large housing complex located on the Hudson River overlooking midtown Manhattan. This privately funded project has received approvals from the state and began construction at the end of 1996.

New Jersey's Regulatory Environment

New Jersey created a voluntary cleanup program to remediate and develop industrial sites in 1993, and laws were updated as recently as early 1996. The New Jersey

Department of Environmental Protection (NJDEP) is the lead agency, with cleanups supervised by the Site Remediation Program. Other laws, such as the New Jersey Spill Act, govern petroleum leaks. Moreover, NJDEP can use administrative consent orders to force responsible parties to clean up known contaminated sites under the Industrial Site Recovery Act, which triggers a procedure for the sale of industrial property. The broad VCP accepts USTs and potentially responsible parties who step forward to remediate contaminated lands, as well as more traditional brownfield sites. NJDEP's flexible risk-based corrective actions allow and encourage saving costs through the use of impermeable caps where they are a cost-effective measure.

For the voluntary program for brownfield sites, the state's roles involve oversight and sign-off of site investigation, issuance of an NFA letter, and funding investigation and remediation of brownfield sites through the Hazardous Discharge Site Remediation Fund. The brownfield component of the program is not intended for potentially responsible parties. In New Jersey, brownfield deals have proceeded without a formal memorandum of understanding from EPA Region 2, although an informal arrangement has existed for some time.

Consistent with the governor's initiative on the development of urban land, NJDEP maintains an aggressive, proactive approach that encourages economic development of contaminated lands with cost-minimizing site remediation techniques (especially encapsulation), financial inducements, and expedited approval. NJDEP keeps a publicly available list of about 7,000 known contaminated sites. Of the 2,300 projects in the broader system through mid-1996, over 650 had received NFA letters. And of the 20 projects that had received terminal documents and construction had been completed, at least eight involve housing as the new use, and several employ encapsulation techniques.

The first step after a brownfield project enters the VRP is the memorandum of agreement between the volunteer and NJDEP, agreeing on the general framework for NJDEP's oversight. Planning includes preliminary and site assessments (roughly equivalent to Phase I and II environmental studies), followed by the remedial assessment to quantify costs. With this information in hand, the environmental consultant and NJDEP negotiate the remediation action workplan, which guides the strategy for and implementation of site cleanup. Once cleanup is over, officials from the VRP review the remedial action report that has been prepared and offer the brownfield developer an NFA letter from NJDEP for parcels successfully remediated by other than PRPs. Large, complex sites may receive NFA letters for each phase as construction is completed. Reopeners are possible in two cases: if the NFA letter does not cover prior undiscovered contamination and if the safety standard decreases by a factor of ten. In these cases, the state may compel a PRP to clean up the site.

The state's new risk-based approach to remediation includes a comprehensive and user-friendly technical guide, *Guidance Document for the Remediation of Contaminated Soils,* which allows cleanup to background levels based on site-specific criteria. The guide, which has been available since 1995, is periodically updated. Encapsulation is permitted on sites where the source of contamination is known, which NJDEP approves when it approves the plan for remediation. Specific cost criteria apply to the approval of encapsulation. For example, NJDEP has regularly approved remediation plans in which the cost of the cap is less than one-half of the cost to remove all contaminated materials, and levels of risk are comparable. Capped sites, however, involve additional monitoring and a declaration of environmental restriction from NJDEP, which is filed with the county as part of the deed to the property and is subject to state regulations covering disclosures about real estate. Different standards pertain to residential and nonresidential uses. Water quality is a big issue because of the high water table in many parts of the state.

Exemption from Liability

Exemption from liability for new owners is generally considered adequate, but a version now pending before the state assembly would strengthen it even more. Some brownfield developers in New Jersey have used a limited liability corporation, a vehicle that blends partnership and corporate forms of ownership, to limit their liability. Exemptions from liability for lenders are fairly strong. Lenders who foreclose are not liable for environmental damage that occurred before they took control of the property, only if they are proved to have been negligent.

Financial Inducements

Another reason for the large volume of deals through the VRP in New Jersey is the availability of up-front funding through the Hazardous Discharge Site Remediation Fund. Low-interest loans and grants for remediation have been available since 1993; in addition, municipalities are eligible for site investigation grants, and private parties who are not PRPs are eligible for up to $1 million. The New Jersey Economic Development Authority has awarded at least $15 million of these funds, and another

FIGURE 13.1

THE WEST NEW YORK, NEW JERSEY, AREA

FIGURE 13.2

SITE LAYOUT

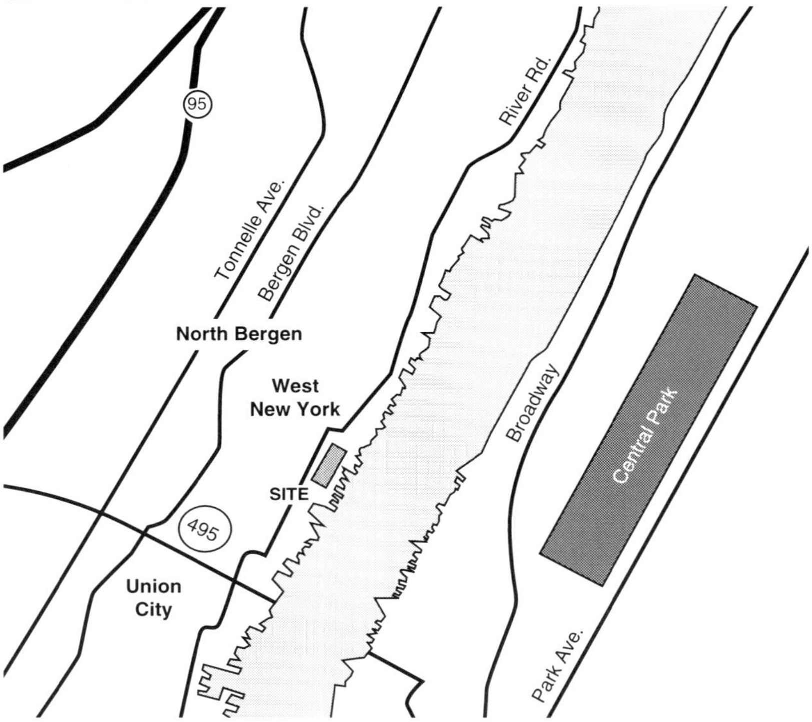

$40 million is available. Property tax abatement for nonresidential development in designated environmental opportunity zones has been available since 1996.

Pending Actions

New Jersey environmental regulators are making it easier for lenders and new owners to take part in brownfield deals by helping quantify the risks of liability. As of mid-1996, NJDEP had no formal CNTS, but legislation is pending to create one that would also deal with existing reopeners. One option is to finance possible future cleanups resulting from undiscovered prior contamination through an insurance premium or other fee to be paid by the successful remediator upon receipt of the NFA letter.

The state is also considering separating soil remediation from groundwater cleanup in areas where contamination is high and water is not used for human consumption. A future legislative initiative may include effective exemption for remediators from third-party liability resulting from off-site groundwater contamination.

Port Imperial at West New York

Background

Port Imperial at West New York is a 158-acre site in West New York, New Jersey, less than half an hour from New York City by ferry or train. The developer is Roseland Property Company of Roseland, New Jersey. The site has 4,900 feet of frontage on the Hudson River, and 94 acres of the total 158 are buildable uplands, out of the Hudson River floodplain. The site, less than one mile from Route 495, has good highway access and superb visibility, and offers views of the midtown Manhattan skyline. Its location is ideal for housing. A ferry to Manhattan docks on the property (see Figures 13.1 and 13.2). Comparable land in the area, where available, has a market value of about $6.00 to $8.00 per square foot, depending on views and access. The property is in a controlled waterfront development zone, and housing is a permitted use.

Local Economic Conditions

The population of West New York, New Jersey, in 1992 was 37,500 people, down 4.4 percent from 1980. West New York is largely a bedroom community for Manhattan, which over the same period gained almost 61,000 persons, an increase of 4.3 percent over 1980. According to *City-County Data Book,*[1] over 70 percent of the population of West New York is Hispanic, compared with one-quarter in both Manhattan and New York City.

The median age is 34.7, very close to the state figure and slightly below Manhattan's 35.9. Slightly over 30 percent (31.3 percent) of West New York's population is 25 to 44 years old, compared with 39.2 percent of Manhattan's total population. The crime rate (serious crimes known to police) in West New York was 6,400 per 100,000 in 1992, a bit higher than the rest of New Jersey's average but only two-thirds of that for New York City as a whole. Median family income was $26,400, or 18 percent lower than in Manhattan.

Over 75 percent (77.2 percent) of West New York workers over age 16 worked outside the town in 1990. In contrast, only 6.4 percent of Manhattan residents left the borough for work that same year. The town's housing market also has been stagnant: only a handful of new housing units were built in West New York between 1990 and 1992. The median rent paid, counting all apartments in 1990 in West New York, was $439, 15 percent lower than in Manhattan (including rent-controlled units), and values of owner-occupied housing were 35 percent lower than in Manhattan.

Development Plan

Port Imperial at West New York is expected to be built in three phases over ten years. At completion, the project will have 4,100 housing units. Roseland Property Company is acting primarily as master developer, although it will also be builder/developer of portions of the site. Phase I consists of three parts: one section of townhouses and two of rental units. The first section, Bull's Ferry, has been approved for 258 for-sale townhouses and is to be developed by K. Hovnanian Enterprises. The two- and three-bedroom townhouses are expected to be 1,600 to 2,500 square feet and sell for $260,000 to $450,000 (about $170 per square foot). Roseland will provide prepared building sites and infrastructure for the community. The second neighborhood will consist of 570 market-rate rental units, to be developed by Related Companies of New York. Roseland will also provide a prepared building site for this project. The third neighborhood, The Landings at Port Imperial, is a joint venture between Roseland and Prudential. It has been approved for 276 market-rate rental units in generally low- and mid-rise buildings. The one-, two-, and three-bedroom apartments will average 1,100 square feet and rent for $1.75 per square foot per month, about 30 to 40 percent below market-rate rents in Manhattan.

Site History

Since just before the turn of the century, the site had been used as a freight and marine terminal for the transfer of coal; railway cars were emptied, washed, and loaded there. A Phase I environmental study revealed that an ice house for a granite company was also located there in the early 1900s. Grain elevators and a pier for loading coal were also present, although by 1936 they had become inactive. Railroad tracks crisscrossed the site, and fill dirt was imported long ago to support the

A stunning view of Manhattan gives Port Imperial real value as residential real estate.

tracks; rail operations ceased on the site in about 1982. The site also contained aboveground storage tanks and building materials. The site's location on the Hudson River and within its floodplain (at an elevation of ten feet) makes the project subject to New Jersey's regulations on coastal zone management and waterfront development, also under the direction of NJDEP.

After the site fell into disuse, another entity acquired its 158 acres and an adjacent large tract of land. It attempted to develop the site but ran into difficulty and eventually defaulted on the mortgage. In 1995, Roseland acquired the mortgages from the former lender and then obtained ownership of the property through a deed in lieu of foreclosure at a cost of approximately $21 million.

Site Remediation

The site had already undergone extensive environmental testing before Roseland obtained it. Four previous consultants had worked the site before 1995, when the developer's environmental consultant, Ecol Sciences, took over the project. These prior studies included about 100 test pits at a combined cost of $150,000, but no remediation plan at the time proved economically feasible in terms of real estate development. Phase II environmental studies revealed that discharges from the rail cars, contaminated fill brought in from off site to support the tracks, and coal and grain residues had generated relatively even levels of nonvolatile, base-neutral compounds, primarily polyaromatic hydrocarbons, throughout the site.

Ecol Sciences, during summer 1995, picked up where the other consultants left off. Roseland had preliminarily decided to acquire the property and needed, within one month, a determination of potential remediation costs on which to base its decision to proceed or not. With a review of prior work and a little more testing, Ecol Sciences helped the developer enter New Jersey's VRP. Fortunately, the environmental consulting team, which included Ecol Sciences and the law firm of Bennett and Yoskin, had experience with a similar remediation plan that had been approved for a nearby property. The memorandum of agreement, which covered mainly which documents NJDEP would review, was obtained shortly thereafter, in fall 1995.

NJDEP approved the remedial action workplan in March 1996. Based on samples from preliminary and site investigations, Ecol concluded that the impact on groundwater did not exceed acceptable levels and that the contamination was not mobile or volatile. Thus, the consultant demonstrated to NJDEP that encapsulation was appropriate, and the state agreed. Indeed, the cost to completely remediate the site by hauling and burying the contaminated soil would have been about $74 million, enough to kill the deal. In contrast, the total cost of the agreed-upon cap is about $3 million (less than 5 percent of the cost of hauling away and burying the soil), with over $2 million of this expense used for a cap that is part of normal foundation work and impermeable sublayers of parking lots and roads, which make up 70 percent of the site's surface area. The only net additional expense to prepare a cap is for landscaping for the 30 percent of the site where it will be needed. These areas will have a thin felt membrane, covered with 18 inches of clean fill dirt. Thus, net remediation costs are an estimated $900,000, or $0.13 per square foot. Moreover, remediation will take place as part of normal construction, removing any delay that would occur waiting for remediation to be completed. Once the caps have been successfully put in place, the project will receive an NFA letter from the state for each phase as the project is built out. Ecol will maintain a health and safety official on site during construction, and later NJDEP will periodically monitor the cap to ensure its integrity. The site will receive a Declaration of Environmental Restriction from the state, which serves as notification that contamination on site exceeds cleanup criteria for residential use. According to the attorney who assisted Ecol Sciences and the developer in getting the necessary approvals from NJDEP for site cleanup and waterfront development, and related approvals from the U.S. Army Corps of Engineers, NJDEP's approval of the remediation action workplan was the milestone for the project, because it formalized the state's acceptance of encapsulation and made the project feasible.

The low additional expense for remediation means that the developers are using no public funds for site assessment or remediation.

Financing

The project was on track as of December 1996, when preconstruction soil compacting was taking place. As of this writing, the developer had obtained all necessary state approvals except that for waterfront development. The developer's plan is to get a construction loan for development of infrastructure—major sewer and water lines and roads—and for some of the built improvements in Phase I.

The developer is considering several sources for construction loans, including PNC Bank. According to PNC, providing a construction loan for the project would make sense because the extensive knowledge about the site limits unknowns for the bank. The project's excellent market fundamentals and competitive position in the

Port Imperial fronts on 4,900 feet of the Hudson River. Ninety-four acres of the total are buildable uplands, out of the Hudson River floodplain.

marketplace enhance its position. Moreover, the borrower could offer the land, valued at about $50 million, as collateral. The developer expects that construction loans would be taken out by permanent financing later.

The costs of remediation and financing are summarized in Figure 13.3. The developer acquired the property for $21 million and estimates that installing roads, and sewer and water lines for all three phases will cost $8 million. Installing infrastructure will allow the developer to sell buildable tracts to outside builders or to develop lots in joint ventures with others. Adding fees for remediation and the environmental consultant of $1.4 million, plus other soft costs for legal counsel and other consultants, means that the developer's stake in the project is estimated to be just over $31 million, before construction financing and any developer's fee are considered.

The developer has already lined up buyers for the land for the first three neighborhoods. While information about land sales is proprietary, the developer will be able to recover all its equity plus make a substantial profit from just the land sales of the project's first phase.

For The Landings at Port Imperial, the rental housing project that is a joint venture between Roseland and Prudential, total costs to the joint venture are a projected $33 million, or about $109 per building square foot. This figure includes all hard and soft costs, including land, and infrastructure improvements.

Market Acceptance

The project is currently in the early stages of construction. The fact that the developer has lined up major buyers for the neighborhood sites in Phase I and has found another major entity to enter a joint venture with is a strong, positive market signal. Further, the developer believes that the target rental market (young professionals) will not care that the site comes with a Declaration of Environmental Restriction and will focus instead on the site's views and easy access to Manhattan.

Lessons Learned

Market amenities are important in a housing project with an ideal location that can emphasize views and access. Projects with a superior location such as this one can rely on pent-up demand to drive strong sale prices and brisk absorption.

The developer retained environmental and legal consultants who had experience with the state regulatory system and with similar sites. Their guidance helped prepare proposals that responded to objections before they were raised and was instrumental in acquiring state approvals. Remediation was made very inexpensive through the use of caps and other cost-minimizing techniques. These savings, coupled with the developer's strategy of buying low, made the project feasible.

New Jersey banks have concluded deals without a CNTS or MOU (often required by lenders in other states) in place because of the state's signing off on a project and adequate collateral. They are sophisticated enough to be interested in providing construction loans to this project despite the fact that an NFA letter (which would come after completion of each construction phase) would not be issued at the time the bank would provide the

FIGURE 13.3

PROJECT DATA—PORT IMPERIAL AT WEST NEW YORK: LAND DEVELOPMENT, PHASE I

Land Use Information
Site Area: 158 acres (6,882,500 square feet)
Floor/Area Ratio: 0.67 (3 phases)
Building Area:
  Total Project: 4.6 million square feet
  Phase I: 1.5 million square feet
Site Preparation Time: 24 to 36 months

Development Cost Information	
Land Acquisition Cost	
Deed in lieu of foreclosure	$21,000,000 ($3.05 per square foot)
Site Preparation Costs	
Net additional remediation costs	$900,000 ($0.13 per square foot)
Other site preparation (infrastructure)	8,000,000 ($1.15 per square foot)
Soft Costs	
Architect, legal, planning	$1,000,000
Environmental consultants	400,000
Total Development Cost	**$31,300,000** ($4.50 per land square foot)
Net Cost to Developer	**$31,300,000**
Financing and Investment	
Equity Requirement	$31,300,000

Note: Because of the project's complexity, the developer's dual roles as master developer and joint venture builder of part of the project, the deal's still-evolving status, and the developer's not using any public funds, the financial analysis of this project is less complete than those for other case studies in this book.

Port Imperial is less than half an hour from New York City by ferry or train.

loan. Therefore, what is "bankable" from the lender's standpoint depends on which state the project and bank are in. Care should be taken not to generalize the importance of an NFA letter; in one state, it may mean a lot, in others much less.

Note

1. U.S. Bureau of the Census, *City-County Data Book 1963* (Washington, D.C.: U.S. Dept. of Commerce, 1963); and U.S. Bureau of the Census, *City-County Data Book 1994* (Washington, D.C.: U.S. Dept. of Commerce, 1994).

14 Brownfield Development in California: A Research Park in Emeryville

California has one of the most developed VCPs of any state. The first of its major programs was put in place in 1993. California's more general VCP is based on risk-based corrective actions and provides good terminal documents. Its urban-oriented, selective Expedited Remedial Action Program (ERAP) provides substantial financial support and excellent terminal documents. Recent initiatives include certifying private consultants to conduct simple remediations outside the voluntary cleanup process and improving the quality of terminal documents for the VCP. Regional water quality control boards also offer brownfield programs.

California's diverse and large economy, with a history of industrialization, military bases, and agriculture, indicates that the state probably has the largest supply of brownfields in the country. The state's location on the Pacific Rim, excellent weather, and natural beauty indicate that demand for these brownfields, especially in larger metropolitan areas such as Los Angeles and San Francisco/Oakland, is relatively high. Because of their proximity to the Pacific Ocean, substantial portions of these urban areas have a high water table. Hence, the State Water Resources Control Board (SWRCB), through its nine regional offices, is also a major player in brownfield development in California. Some regional water boards, in fact, run a parallel brownfield program, and developers can choose one or both main state agencies to work with on their brownfield project.

California's approach to brownfield development is generally top down. The state maintains a formal registry of brownfield sites (CALSITES), consistent with a list of hazardous waste sites. Efforts have been made recently to remove erroneously classified sites. State environmental units' rules for remediation are flexible and site sensitive, and permit encapsulation of contamination. The California Environmental Protection Agency's Department of Toxic Substances Control (DTSC) and regional water quality agencies coordinate their work closely with local governments and the public during remediation. The California system has achieved an impressive number of cleaned sites, with about 100 projects having received a terminal document as of year-end 1996.

The focus of this case study is northern California, in particular the San Francisco Bay Area and the city of Emeryville, a small community with an innovative EPA pilot program for brownfields. The subject, the Chiron Corporation Research and Development Park, is a 25-acre campus-style office and R&D complex on a former oil company facility in the San Francisco Bay Area near Oakland. The first phase of the park, to be occupied by Chiron, has received its terminal documents and is under construction, with occupancy expected in 1998. Foreign banks financed the project.

California's Regulatory Environment

California passed its first legislation covering VCPs to remediate and develop traditional brownfield sites in 1993. ERAP was initiated as a heavily subsidized urban pilot program in 1994. The lead agency for both programs is the Department of Toxic Substances Control, which supervises cleanups. The state also has a number of other laws that pertain to the cleanup of contaminated sites, including the state's Superfund program, also administered by the California EPA. Under this law, DTSC can use administrative consent orders to force responsible parties to clean up known contaminated sites.

In general, DTSC is responsible for soil-related environmental issues, while the State Water Resources Control Board is involved in brownfield development projects in areas where groundwater is concerned. Although both DTSC and SWRCB are part of the California EPA, they maintain separate identities and approaches to environmental management with respect to formal public participation, universal compliance with nationally recognized third-party cost-recovery procedures, and other issues. Thus, many brownfield projects in areas where demand is high, like the San Francisco Bay Area, are on a dual regulatory track for brownfield development.

DTSC's supportive, proactive approach to encouraging economic development of contaminated lands uses flexible, cost-minimizing techniques for site remediation. Of the 200 or more projects in VCPs as of early 1997, about 100 had received completion letters. For the 30 sites that were farthest along the pipeline, including those cleaned up under the state's Superfund program, DTSC has guided the development of over 1,400 acres, which will accommodate over 13 million square feet of commercial, recreational, and industrial space and 5,200 units of housing. Much of it is under construction or already occupied.[1]

DTSC's San Francisco office is in charge of the 60 or so projects currently in the VCP pipeline there (about half of which are involved in rebuilding the I-880 freeway damaged during the earthquake in 1989). Of those not associated with the roadway, about 15 have received a remedial action certification or NFA letter; the typical processing time is six months to two years. About 70 percent of the brownfield projects in the San Francisco region are also involved with the San Francisco Regional Water Quality Control Board (RWQCB).

California's Voluntary Cleanup Program

California's streamlined VCP allows DTSC to review, maintain oversight of, and sign off on specific remediation activities for voluntary participants. Successful projects receive a remedial action certification at the end of the process. DTSC may coordinate activities closely with one of the nine regional water quality control boards on projects containing contaminated groundwater, including those on most urban sites.

The VCP does not accept UST sites with petroleum-only waste problems. Remediation of such sites rests with the SWRCB, which keeps the state's list of LUSTs. Likewise, the VCP is not intended for responsible parties in the federal or state Superfund programs.

The brownfield developer must first contact DTSC and seek to be admitted to the program. After its eligibility has been established, the volunteer prepares a preliminary endangerment assessment, which describes the extent of contamination. If no remediation is needed and the site is essentially clean, DTSC may issue an NFA letter. If remediation is required, however, then the volunteer must prepare a remedial action workplan (for projects whose remediation will cost under $1 million) or a remediation action plan (for larger cleanups). Typically, these plans would include Phase I and II environmental studies. Both the workplan and the plan require a formal one-month period for public comments. Once DTSC has approved the workplan or the plan and the parties agree to DTSC's reimbursement for oversight, remediation can begin. A DTSC officer oversees the environmental consultant's efforts during remediation. Normally, DTSC uses risk-based corrective actions to keep costs of remediation down. Once remediation is complete, the volunteer may receive a remedial action certification, a closure document similar to an NFA letter in other states.

A CNTS is not available for participants in the VCP, but California is currently in the early stages of implementing a prospective purchaser agreement which functions much like a CNTS. A site in the VCP may receive closure documents for phases of a project, as construction is completed. The remedial action certification or NFA letter may specify any land use restrictions, environmental monitoring or mitigation activities required, or deed restrictions. The remedial action certification can be reopened for fraud and contamination discovered later.

The Expedited Remedial Action Program

ERAP was established as a pilot program under Senate Bill 923 in 1994. It is restricted to 30 sites, which must meet requirements for eligibility set by DTSC. It allows for risk-based remediation strategies and flexible cleanup standards, and considers the site's end use. Applicants, which may include parties partly responsible for the contamination, also prepare a preliminary endangerment assessment and remediation action plan. As lead agency for a project, DTSC provides consolidated permitting for sites in the program. DTSC may also apportion liability for cleanup, and the state may provide funding for up to ten sites with "orphan" shares, where responsible parties are insolvent or cannot be identified. Successful applicants receive a CNTS from the state, which is stronger than the remedial action certification generally available under the VCP. A component of ERAP can be used to expedite cleanup through resolution of disputes and arbitration. As of year-end 1996, ten sites had been selected, three of them with orphan shares.[2]

Memorandum of Understanding with EPA

California has been negotiating a formal agreement with the U.S. EPA covering sites in the VCP and ERAP. This agreement, a state memorandum of agreement, states that EPA will adopt a hands-off approach once DTSC signs off on a site. The state memorandum of agreement is an endorsement of an overall program rather than a site-by-site approval. DTSC and EPA expect to finalize the state MOA soon.[3]

Cleanup Standards

The state's approach to remediation is risk based, and the standards pertain to all California programs. DTSC, SWRCB, and regional water quality agencies play a major role in setting cleanup standards. All the entities generally employ the U.S. EPA's guidelines for site cleanup. Division 20 of the California Health and Safety Code, updated every year, contains specific thresholds for contamination. These standards allow cleanup to background levels based on site-specific criteria, while different standards for specific substances pertain to residential and nonresidential uses. Although encapsulation is permitted on sites that were filled with contaminated soil sometime in the past, capped sites typically involve additional monitoring and require a deed restriction filed with the local authority.

SWRCB's Role

California law also enumerates flexible standards for cleanups, applicable to both petroleum-based and other contamination, in areas with substantial groundwater contamination, such as the San Francisco area. SWRCB is charged with regulating underground storage tanks, with management of the regulation and remediation of USTs generally delegated to the regional water quality control board. In over 100 locations throughout the state, however, a city or county, rather than the regional board, is the local implementing agency for compliance with regulations for USTs. Because of the large number of UST regulators, regional boards may also play the role of educator. In the San Francisco Bay Area, for example, the water board's toxicologist has trained over 800 regulators, responsible parties, and consultants in risk management and environmental decision making.

Flexible groundwater management in California can most readily be accomplished in designated groundwater management zones. In these areas, the regional water quality control boards may apply economic and technical criteria for risk management where cleaned groundwater is less than perfectly clean but below limits requiring action, or cleanup cannot reasonably be achieved, or the site is low risk and contamination is not moving. The key issue usually is whether or not the groundwater can be used as drinking water in the foreseeable future. This flexibility has allowed development of many brownfield properties, based on the principle of establishing groundwater nonattainment zones, where rules for the cleanup are risk based rather than based on standards and closure documents are generally not available.

The autonomy granted to regional water quality control boards allows them to oversee a regulatory process that in many ways parallels DTSC's approach but for some users is more flexible and may allow a shorter time to attain closure documents. In the San Francisco Bay Area, the chief of the regional water quality control board's Toxics Division directs the flexible, risk-management approach to cleanup of groundwater that has enticed many brownfield developers to designate the regional water quality control board as the lead governmental contact for environmental cleanup. The board's objectives are to maintain a healthy level of water quality in the short and long terms, based on the reasonably likely future use of the property and the groundwater beneath it. In determining the appropriate strategy for a potential brownfield project where the groundwater is not expected to be potable, the chief and the toxicologist first conduct a risk-based assessment to determine whether any pathways or receptors exist that could endanger humans. Available technology is then efficiently allocated based on risk management rather than on using the best available (and often most expensive) technology. Remediation can thus focus on reducing risk on the site to acceptable levels and directing funds more efficiently to remediation rather than to investigation. This approach can shorten the time needed to achieve an acceptable solution.

This approach to the question of what to do with brownfields requires educating participants in risk management. Stakeholders—developers, neighboring property owners, lenders, planners, and even elected officials—in nearby communities need to be educated about the details, science, issues, political factors, and tradeoffs involved in risk management. This challenge limits implementation of groundwater management for the San Francisco Bay Area's regional water quality control board.

The local water quality control board and DTSC are engaged in a cordially cooperative but competitive stance with respect to brownfield sites. Brownfield developers can choose one agency or the other as lead, depending on their time and concerns about third-party liability. A provision in California law for "supercertification" allows a property owner to officially designate one agency or the other as lead, based on the condition of soil and groundwater and prior remediation on site.

Exemptions from Liability

The VCP terminates in a remedial action certification, which provides some protection for new owners but not a release from liability. Implementation of a prospective purchaser agreement would improve this situation considerably. Participants in ERAP receive very good exemption from liability for new owners through the CNTS. In cases where local governments actively remediated sites that satisfied requirements of DTSC and the regional water quality control board, any exemption from liability or immunity the local jurisdiction received is extended to successive property owners or lenders.[4]

The picture for lenders is somewhat comforting. SB 1285, Hazardous Material Liability of Lenders and Fiduciaries, provides limited liability for lenders and fiduciaries that have a legal interest but did not "directly" contribute to the release or potential release of a hazardous substance.[5]

Financial Inducements

Except for projects in ERAP, California has no major state-led initiatives for funding the up-front costs of site assessment or remediation. Amendments to the Community Facilities Act (AB 2610), however, permit the creation of community facilities districts, which can levy taxes for the cleanup of brownfields. This tax increment financing program provides long-term financing.[6]

Another important local financing tool is the Mello-Roos Community Facilities Act, which allows local governments to set up special taxing districts to issue bonds and then use the proceeds to remediate contaminated property.

Recent Initiatives

California is also creating a new program that would issue credentials to private site managers who oversee cleanup of sites with lower levels of contamination.[7] DTSC would have very little oversight of sites in the program.

California's new policy for prospective purchasers enhances the quality of its closure documents for participants in the VCP. A few have already been issued. The prospective purchaser agreement issued is equivalent to a CNTS, but the agreement binds only DTSC. SWRCB recently issued similar guidance on prospective purchaser agreements.[8]

The Bay Area contains many examples of innovative brownfield remediation. The city of Richmond, for example, has guided the development of large amounts of brownfield property on a former shipyard, which was also a state Superfund site. The city of Richmond acquired the 200-acre Marina Bay development project in the early 1980s, remediated it, and transformed it into a large housing and recreation complex.

In Oakland, where a brownfield site is under development, the city enacted the Urban Land Redevelopment Program to address the risks inherent in brownfield development. The program includes the tracking of development permits and creation of a table of remediation activities for inner-city sites, based on local hydrology and soil conditions. Standards were set up through collaboration of the San Francisco Regional Water Quality Control Board, DTSC, and the U.S. EPA. If a site has been remediated for a specific use, say commercial development, then a nearby commercial site (perhaps two blocks away) need only show that its environmental conditions are nearly equivalent to be approved for the same cleanup procedure. The municipality grants this approval, provided the developer agrees to remediate the property to predetermined levels. Properties taking this route can also obtain an NFA letter, rather than a deed restriction on the property, from the city.

The city of Emeryville, a small commercial community on the eastern shore of the San Francisco Bay, has become a leader in brownfield remediation, following a path compatible with SB 1248. SB 1248 formally recognizes cleanups by local agencies and the power that local health authorities can exercise in supervising and certifying cleanups of brownfields. The Chiron project is just one of several active projects in Emeryville.

Emeryville's Leadership In the Remediation of Urban Brownfields

Much of Emeryville's one and one-half square miles contains property with a past history of environmental contamination and development. In 1996, Emeryville won a pilot grant from the U.S. EPA to develop an inventory of brownfield sites and initiatives for brownfield development. Emeryville's economic development director envisions that the Emeryville Redevelopment Authority (ERA) will soon be the main permitting entity for brownfield development within its borders, coordinating actions with DTSC and the regional water quality control board. Thus, Emeryville will be charged with actively guiding development by making itself both lead planner and remediation permitter. The inventory is currently under development, and ERA plans to implement a risk-based approach to brownfield development by defining groundwater management zones. Such zones would allow development without totally cleaning up the underlying groundwater in the East Bay, provided future site users and the environment are protected. The Emeryville Redevelopment Authority also wants to create a set of financial tools to aid in brownfield development, including a contingency and mitigation fund. To set up such a fund is a challenge, given the community's annual budget of only about $18 million.

According to U.S. Census data, the city of Emeryville's population in 1990 was 5,700, up 55 percent from 1980. About 42 percent of the population is white. The median age is 34.4 years, roughly comparable with the state figure. Median family income was $35,700. Fifteen percent of families lived below the poverty line in 1990, slightly higher than the state figure of about 13 percent. Job growth was also substantial; the city had nearly 14,000 jobs in 1990, up about 12 percent from 1980.

Emeryville is generally progrowth. The community's position is nearly ideal geographically (close to both Oakland and San Francisco) and politically (small and easy to do business in, with flexible planning approvals for many projects). Emeryville is creating hybrid legislation that falls between California's SB 1248 and a California community redevelopment law known as the Polanco Act, passed in 1990. This act gives development authorities the power to investigate sites, order cleanup, or clean the site themselves and charge responsible parties for the cost. Redevelopment authorities may also implement cleanup of brownfields if they have a cleanup plan. The agency can obtain immunity from past contamination and pass the immunity along to future owners, giving development authorities both a carrot (immunity) and a stick (the threat of action or a payment) to entice responsible parties to participate in an area's overall groundwater management strategy.

Emeryville plans to spur brownfield development by taking over operational responsibility for both soil remediation and groundwater management. For soil contamination problems, ERA plans primarily to use DTSC regulations and standards so that if a developer agrees to remediate a site to those standards, ERA would have the authority to issue environmental permits. ERA intends to pursue the acquisition of memorandums of understanding with DTSC and the regional water board, and a "letter of no interest" from the U.S. EPA.

For the more complicated issue of groundwater, part of the pilot project would set up a groundwater monitoring and mitigation plan. Parties who participate in a funding mechanism to collectively pay for improving groundwater quality would receive immunity from future action. Funding options currently being reviewed include establishing development fees, soliciting responsible parties' participation, creating a special assessment district, making insurance available, and budgeting funds from project reserves. The intent is to do away with site-by-site investigation and cleanup of groundwater, saving time and money for developers. The money saved would go to pay for improving quality of the groundwater. Officials expected to present the plan to the San Francisco Regional Water Quality Control Board for approval late in 1997. Developers unwilling to pursue ERA's approach would have the option of going to DTSC for environmental approval for soil issues or to the San Francisco Regional Water Quality Control Board for groundwater issues. For most projects, doing so would be more expensive and time-consuming.

Emeryville's approach has already borne fruit. Since the late 1980s, Emeryville has assisted in the development of over 70 acres of brownfields containing almost 900,000 square feet of nonresidential space and about 750 housing units, not including the Chiron project. Implementing the new program should increase the rate of brownfield development substantially.

The Chiron Life Sciences Center in Emeryville

Background

This 25-acre site was home to a former oil research facility in Emeryville, about five miles from downtown Oakland and eight miles from downtown San Francisco. It is adjacent to an industrial/warehouse district and located near a railroad track spur.

At completion, the project will contain 2.2 million square feet of research and development and office space in an office park–type environment for an expected investment of $700 million (1997 dollars). Chiron Corporation will occupy the facility for its own use.

Formed in the early 1980s by three researchers from nearby University of California–Berkeley, Chiron Corporation is a biotechnology company that manufactures cancer-fighting drugs and other products. The firm's products include genetically engineered vaccines used to treat Hepatitis B, whooping cough, and multiple sclerosis. The company's operations are based in Emeryville, where research, development, and manufacturing are conducted. Since 1993, Chiron has employed approximately 930 people in several buildings scattered around the city. Most of them were located on a 15-acre site that is part of the proposed 25-acre complex. In 1995, European drug giant Ciba-Geigy provided Chiron with diagnostics business and bought half of Chiron's shares. Chiron is now controlled by Novartes, formed from Ciba-Geigy and another large European drug firm, Sandoz.

The first phase of the project, consisting of about 300,000 square feet on four and one-half acres, is cur-

FIGURE 14.1

CHIRON PROJECT AND VICINITY

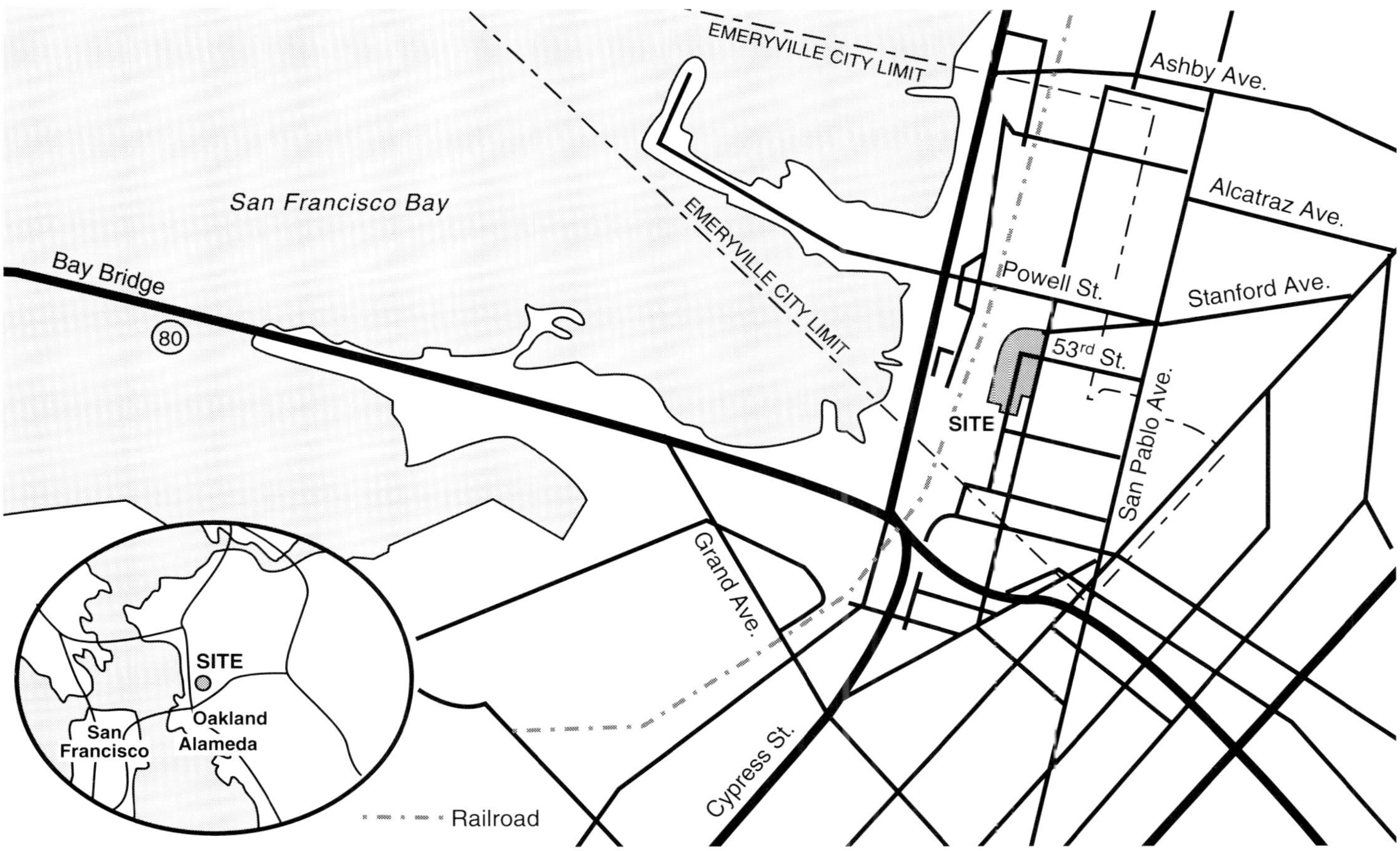

Architect's model of the Chiron project.

rently under construction. The city of Emeryville played a major role in site development, helping to retain Chiron as a corporate resident of the community by offering to offset environmental mitigation expenses through substantial property tax incentives.

The site had been used by oil and power companies for R&D and by a power company for storage since the 1920s. Chiron first became involved with the project a few years after the site was abandoned in the early 1980s, occupying part of the site in the mid-1980s. It currently occupies or owns about 20 acres (80 percent of the overall site). Fifteen acres underlie the existing facility. Chiron acquired an additional five acres from the city of Emeryville, which had obtained the parcel from a local power company and remediated it. In all, six separate owners are involved, including a company called BGR that owns some of the ground under the 15 acres containing the existing Chiron buildings. The total cost to acquire the 25-acre site is expected to be $24 million, or $22.00 per square foot.

The site is about one-half mile from I-80 and is accessible from a major interchange at Powell Street, giving it good highway access and fair visibility. Its location takes advantage of nearby residential communities and daytime support services. Land in Emeryville for assembled parcels of ten or more acres zoned for commercial or mixed use, with negligible contamination, costs $25.00 to $30.00 per square foot, if such parcels are available. Figure 14.1 shows the location of the project in the city of Emeryville on the eastern part of San Francisco Bay.

Project Description

Chiron's 2.2 million-square-foot R&D facility will contain mostly four- to six-story buildings, although a few office towers may be as high as 20 stories. The overall floor/area ratio will be 2.0. Amenities will include views of the bay, an auditorium, upgraded landscaping, and public open space. At completion, approximately 4,200 people will be employed in the complex. Chiron's financial strategy is to build the project and occupy it for the long term for its own use. It does not intend to rent space to others. The first phase of the project, 300,000 square feet on four and one-half acres adjacent to Chiron's existing grounds, is under construction, with opening planned for 1998. Figures 14.2 and 14.3 show the project's existing and projected development.

In searching for a permanent home, Chiron had three main concerns: to build a new facility at an urban site, to build it quickly and cost effectively, and to resolve environmental issues associated with past industrial use. The company faced a serious decision in the late 1980s: whether to stay in Emeryville or move elsewhere. The firm made it known that the cost of staying where it was and remaining competitive implied increased expenses of about $200 million. The city of Emeryville rose to the challenge with property tax incentives meant to offset certain costs, subsidizing the costs of utilities, infrastructure, site cleanup, relocation, and land acquisition. Emeryville also managed the public development review and provided density incentives for the development plan, which was approved in 1995.

The company's background in biotechnology is germane to the project's site remediation and development plan. To carry out environmental objectives, Chiron adopted a risk-management plan that divided risk exposure into short term and long term. Short-term issues dealt with construction workers and the timing of remediation. Workers were educated about tolerance levels, and the site was tightly controlled, with workers' clothing confined to the site and vehicles washed often. The remediation plan, supervised by the San Francisco Regional Water Quality Control Board, was sufficiently flexible so that when the inevitable surprises occurred, they would not substantially delay remediation and construction of the new buildings.

The long-term strategy involved keeping employees' exposure at extremely low levels and minimizing disruption to the soil if the need arose to reach utilities. Thus, all utilities were placed above ground, in a pedestal, and the site was designed around contamination remaining on site (contaminated soil was not put under buildings, for example). This approach to risk management was sufficient to attract a consortium of European banks to finance the first phase of the project.

Site History and Remediation

Shell Oil used the site for research and development as far back as the 1920s. Pacific Gas & Electric (PG&E) also owned part of the larger site (where Phase I of the project is located) and stored transformers there; it cleaned the site in the late 1980s. A former paint factory is located next to Chiron's site. The site includes a total of about

FIGURE 14.2

EXISTING SITE

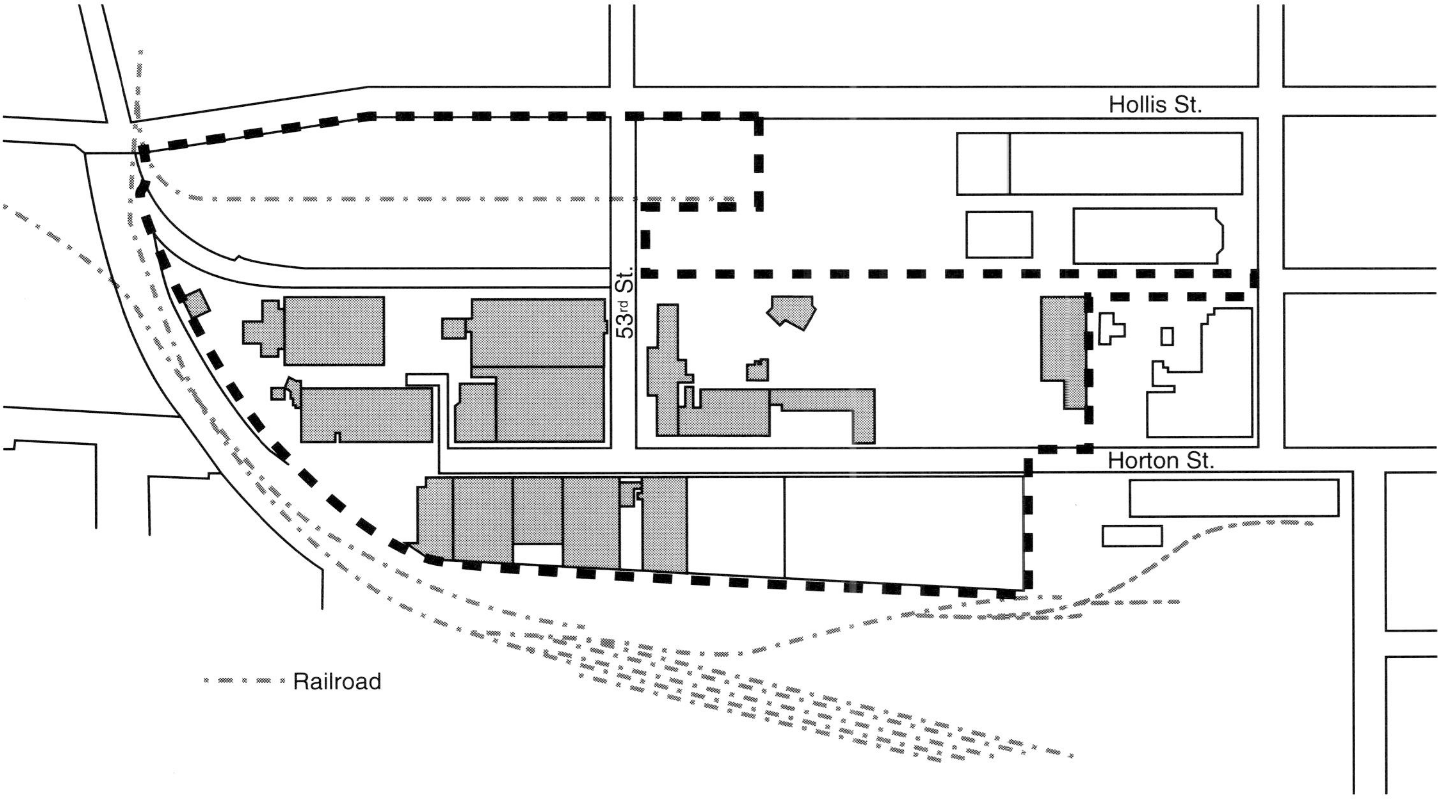

ten structures, with about 400,000 square feet of building space. Demolition has been minimal.

In addition to the contamination caused by on-site polluters, the site's groundwater was contaminated by the adjacent paint factory (litigation continues). One of the primary environmental problems is USTs: at one time over 50 were located on the 25-acre site. Petroleum hydrocarbons permeated the site. Lead and other heavy metals, such as arsenic, also permeated the fill material that had been deposited throughout the site. Debris from the buildings contained asbestos.

Remediation for the project took two tracks, one with the San Francisco Regional Water Quality Control Board for the USTs and groundwater, and another with DTSC for the soil. To sort out the problems and determine whether development was feasible, Chiron retained Erler and Kalinowski, Inc., a California environmental consulting firm familiar with brownfield remediation in the Bay Area, to manage site remediation. The strategy from the beginning was to employ risk-based remediation, using both engineering and institutional controls.

PG&E had closed its transformer storage facility in the mid-1980s. At that time, PG&E investigated the site, found hot spots of PCBs, and removed them in 1987 and 1988. Its subsequent confirmation sampling found tolerable levels (below 25 parts per million), and PG&E received a remedial action certification from DTSC in 1989, before inception of the VCP. The city of Emeryville bought the parcel from PG&E, which tested "clean," and then conveyed it to Chiron by 1991. While building a parking lot, Chiron took some soil samples as part of its investigation with the San Francisco Regional Water Quality Control Board and found contamination at 5,400 parts per million. Thus, Chiron had to reopen its remedial action certification with DTSC, and it performed more extensive testing over the next several years.

Chiron then became part of California's VCP. Because the case involved reopening a certification, Chiron did not have to go through a preliminary endangerment assessment. In April 1996, Chiron and DTSC arrived at a voluntary cleanup agreement pertaining to document review and payment for services. By July, Chiron was receiving public comments, and soon afterward DTSC approved its remedial action workplan (cleanup costs for this part of the project were about $700,000). Chiron removed a total of 10,000 cubic yards of PCB-laden soil

FIGURE 14.3

MASTER PLAN

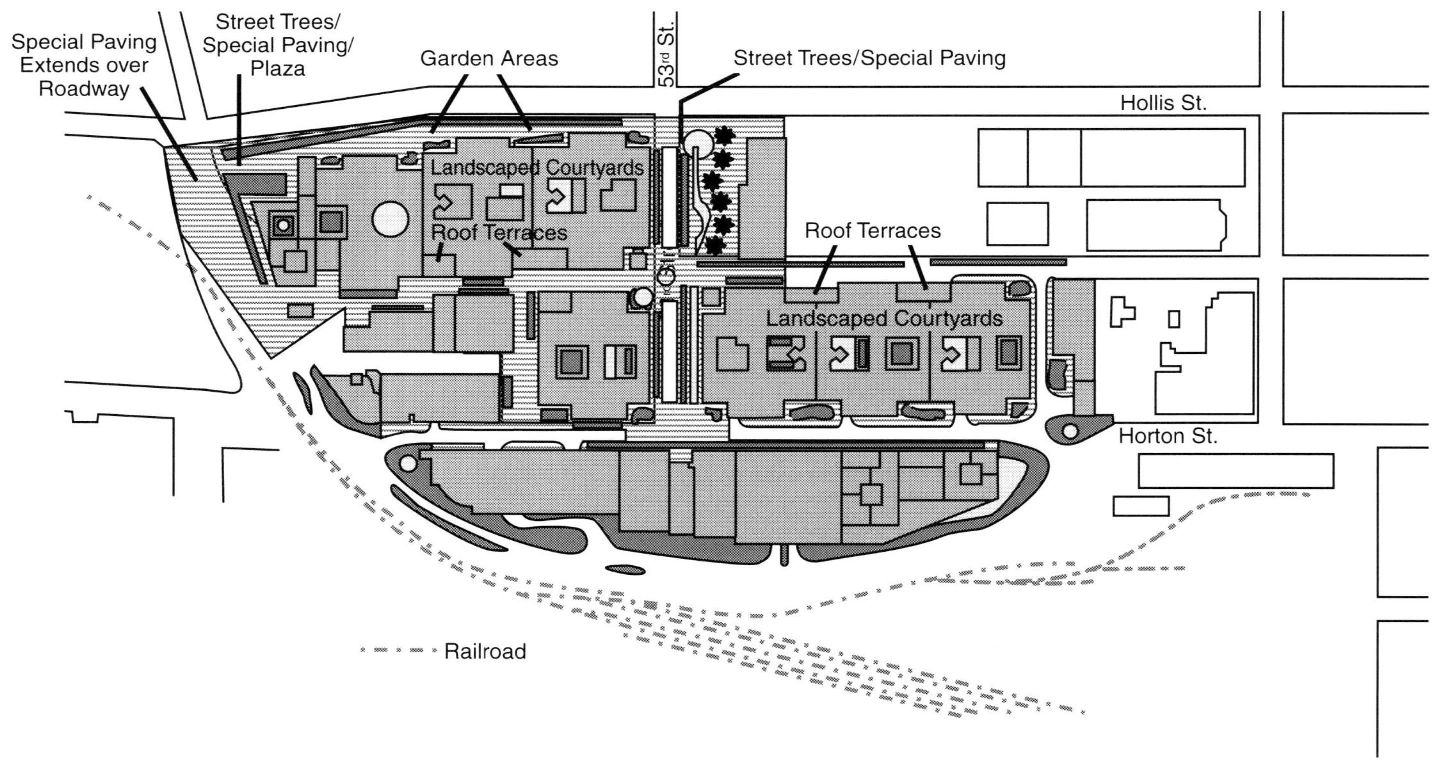

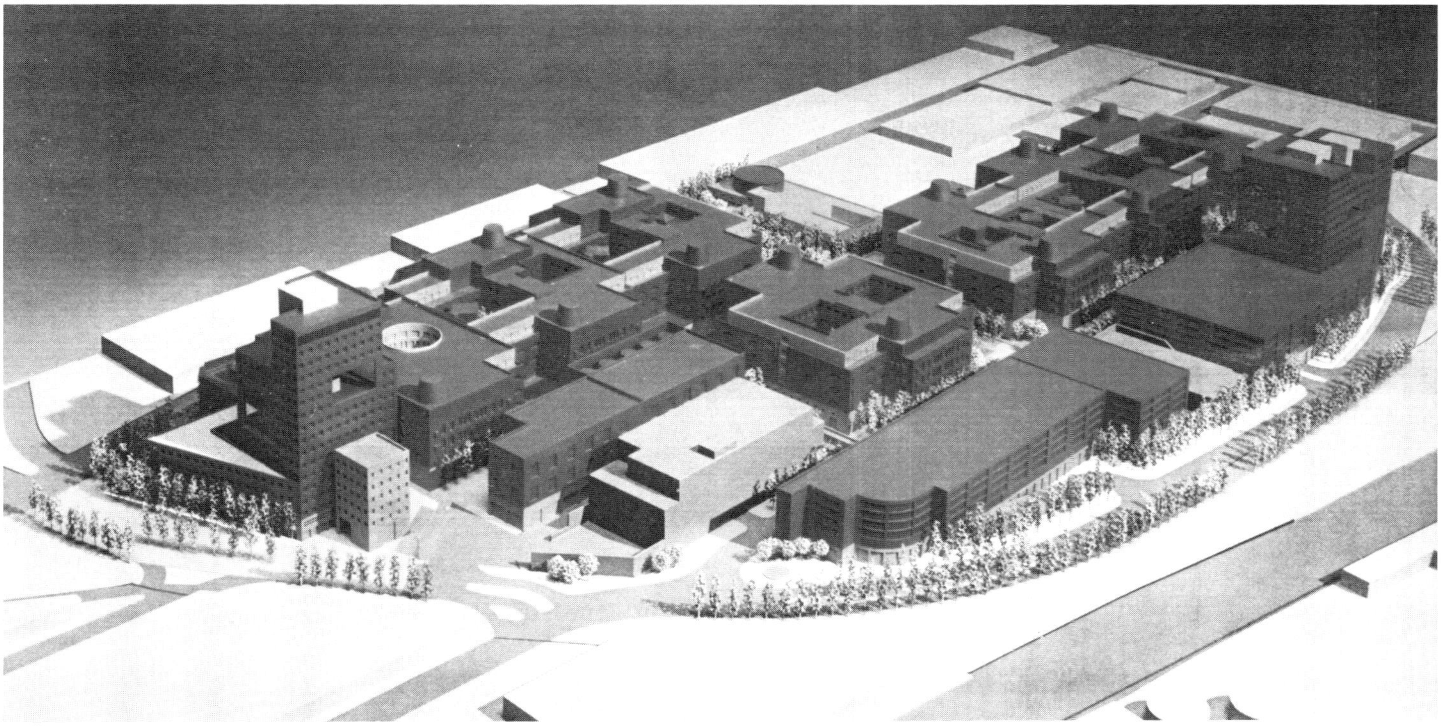

The Chiron Life Sciences Center is a 25-acre campus-style complex on a former oil company facility in the San Francisco Bay Area, near Oakland. At completion, the project will contain over 2 million square feet of R&D and office space and employ approximately 4,200 people.

(ten feet deep in spots), which was taken to off-site landfills. Soil remediation of the four and one-half acres is believed to be complete, and DTSC expected to issue a remedial action certification as soon as June 1997, subject to the deed restriction's being filed.

Groundwater in several well-defined areas of the site had been impacted by isolated floating hydrocarbons associated with former USTs, isolated plumes of volatile organic compounds, and random occurrences of metals. The San Francisco Regional Water Quality Control Board was designated the lead agency in 1994. Its overall strategy for groundwater is risk management; groundwater in the Emeryville area is not expected to be potable, so rather than making it as clean as drinking water, the goal was to manage the contamination. Thus, the plan was to render any groundwater contamination stable or to shrink its plume at a concentration at or below the level suitable for Chiron's intended use of the property as an R&D and office complex.

The Alameda County Department of Environmental Health and the San Francisco Regional Water Quality Control Board completed their respective reviews of Chiron's environmental risk assessment in March 1995 and found the report to be consistent with the San Francisco Regional Water Quality Control Board's guidelines for a groundwater nonattainment zone. Under those guidelines, the agencies continue to guide Chiron's remediation activities. While not an NFA letter or a CNTS, the document spells out the remediation strategy for Chiron's project, relieving a great deal of uncertainty about groundwater remediation.

The site was designed to accommodate contamination remaining on site. The utilities will be placed above ground in a pedestal under buildings, the buildings will have no basements, and parking lots will cap groundwater contamination. Built improvements are limited to areas that will not be disrupted if utilities must be reached at some future date. The intent is to minimize the possibility that any building will ever need to be closed and operations disrupted if environmental standards require future investigation of the site.

Chiron was able to save money during Phase I of the project by sampling soil quality of those contaminated soils destined for the landfills itself. DTSC reviewed the data and issued a letter confirming the validity of the sampling procedure. Thus, Chiron was able to get a better price from the landfill and was also assured that removal would proceed without delay. Overall direct environmental remediation of the larger project is expected to be about $10 million. Total cost of remediation for the project, including consultants' fees but excluding infrastructure improvements, is estimated to be

FIGURE 14.4

PROJECT DATA—CHIRON LIFE SCIENCES CENTER

Land Use Information		
Site Area: 25 acres (1,089,000 square feet)		
Floor/Area Ratio: 2.0		
Gross Building Area: 2.2 million square feet		
Development Cost Information		
Land Acquisition Cost	$24,000,000	($22.04 per square foot)
Site Preparation Costs		
Remediation	$10,000,000	($9.20 per square foot)
Roads, parking, utilities	15,000,000	($13.75 per square foot)
Construction Costs		
Hard costs	$569,000,000	($259 per building square foot)
Soft Costs		
Architect, legal, planning	$36,000,000	(6% of hard and site costs)
Environmental consultants	1,000,000	
Exactions and impact fees to city	3,000,000	
Construction loan/carrying costs	12,000,000	(5% interest, 2% of costs)
Builder's/developer's fee	30,000,000	
Total Development Cost	**$700,000,000**	($318 per building square foot)
Minus Public Subsidy (parking structure)	–5,000,000	
Net Cost to Developer	**$695,000,000**	($316 per building square foot)
Operating Cash Flow (in 1997 dollars)		
Market Rent	$57,200,000	($26 per square foot, triple net, average)
Market Vacancy	570,000	(1% of total)
Environmental Monitoring	300,000	
TIF Property Tax Rebate	2,800,000	
Net Operating Income	**$59,130,000**	
Financing and Investment		
Value (NOI/0.09 cap rate)	$657,000,000	
Loan Amount (0.8 loan-to-value ratio)	$525,560,000	
Private Debt/Sale Leaseback	$47,304,000	
Debt Service Coverage Ratio	1.25	
Before-Tax Cash Flow	$11,800,000	
Equity Requirement	$169,440,000	
Return on Equity	7.0%	

$11 million, about $10.10 per square foot, or about 2 percent of total project costs.

Public Participation

Public participation covered the remediation of PCBs, approval of the plan, financial inducements, and groundwater issues. DTSC handled the process, which focused on controlling dust during removal of PCBs and cleaning to a higher level on parts of the site near residential areas. In return for supplying buffers, more landscaping, and other forms of environmental mitigation, Chiron was awarded substantial increases in density for the project, about double the original proposal. Detailed agreements covering development and financial responsibility between the city of Emeryville and Chiron were finalized in December 1995.

Financial Structure for Phase I

Phase I of the Chiron Life Sciences Center includes development of approximately 300,000 square feet of building space on four and one-half acres. It also includes some property acquisition, remediation, and design and planning for the larger 25-acre project. The total cost is budgeted at just over $138 million. Chiron and its parent companies sought financing for the project, with a working agreement from state regulators (primarily the San Francisco Regional Water Quality Control Board) in hand, but U.S. banks were reluctant to finance the project. Chiron's European connections brought a consortium of Swiss and French banks to the negotiating table.

The main player in bridging the gap between financiers and Chiron was Elizabeth Ward, president of Washington Advisors, Inc., based in San Francisco. Ward has a strong background in environmental science (having worked for the U.S. EPA) and finance (with an MBA and experience in banking). Her main task was to reallocate the project's risks so that all parties could feel comfortable:

> We identified what the real risks were. The groundwater issue was quantifiable. The real risks to the banks were the regulators' not allowing occupancy of the building or a situation that would make Chiron take the building down at some future point. Once we obtained regulators' concurrence regarding groundwater management and remediation in writing, the banks were comfortable.

Ward explained the project's risks to the lenders in quantifiable terms, convincing them that the utility pedestal and caps virtually assured that the building could be productively occupied. Thus, negotiations paved the way for other risk-reducing strategies.

After this major hurdle had been cleared, the key factor in financing the first phase of the property was an indemnification (for lease payments) provided by Chiron's parent company. This indemnification enabled Chiron to borrow $198 million, more than the value of the underlying improvements, turning Phase I of the project into a "credit deal" rather than strictly a real estate–secured deal. Terms included a sale-leaseback so the tax benefits of depreciation would be available to the lenders. The initial lease runs five years, with the banks expecting a 5 percent rate of return on loaned funds.

Still other risk-reducing strategies were used in Phase I. First, the land lease stipulated that the land and any remaining environmental liability rested with Chiron or other local landowners and would not directly affect the quality of the building as collateral. Second, Emeryville's taking title to the former PG&E parcel meant that the city would absorb future liability for issues involving groundwater.

Projected Construction, Deal, and Financing for the 25-Acre Site

In addition to the site acquisition and remediation costs noted earlier, other expenses for site preparation—roads, landscaping, utilities, and so on—are likely to cost $15 million. Thus, development and site preparation of the 25-acre project is expected to be $50 million (see Figure 14.4).

Hard costs for the 2.2 million square feet of building space, including utility pedestals, high-quality security and temperature control, and laboratory equipment, is expected to amount to $259 per building square foot, or a total of $569 million. Because of the large amount of sophisticated equipment involved and the stringent controls required for scientific experimentation, this cost is much higher than for a typical real estate project. Soft costs, including impact fees and exactions to the city of Emeryville and soft costs for development services, approximate $39 million. Overall construction financing would likely be about 2 percent of the total project cost. Finally, Chiron is taking a development fee of about 5 percent for its role in implementing development. The total project cost of $700 million would be reduced by $5 million in the form of a development subsidy from the city for a parking structure. Therefore, the total project cost to Chiron will be $695 million, or $316 per building square foot.

The deal will be structured with 80 percent private financing and 20 percent Chiron's equity. The market rent for comparable R&D/office space is about $26.00 per square foot per year, triple net. Thus, Chiron would derive approximately $57.2 million per year from occupying the project. After accounting for environmental monitoring costs and adding back in the annual TIF property tax rebate from the city of $2.8 million, net operating income for this project, for a stable year well into the 21st century, would be about $59 million (in 1997 dollars).

The market value of a project with this NOI, assuming a cap rate of 0.09, would be $657 million. Assuming the lease conditions emulate the standard industry loan-to-value ratio of 0.8 and debt service coverage ratio of 1.25, the lease payment for the equivalent debt service coverage for this project would be $47.3 million per year. While the specific terms of the deal have not yet been set, this payment stream should allow the lending consortium to achieve its required 5 percent return while simultaneously meeting the requirements for loan-to-value ratio and debt service coverage. Before-tax cash flow would then be $11.8 million per year, providing a 7 percent rate of return on Chiron's $169.4 million in equity.

Return on Public Funds

No state funds were used for this project. Emeryville's innovative strategy to offset Chiron's additional expenses will be funded through reimbursements. Chiron will pay the expenses for eligible line items, such as utilities, cleanup, and infrastructure, and then report them to Emeryville quarterly. The city will credit Chiron with interest on these expenses and then, through tax increment financing, rebate a proportionate share of taxes to Chiron, amounting to a property tax abatement. Emery-

The Chiron campus, in the left center foreground, has good access and visibility, and is directly adjacent to its existing facility. Relatively high land values in Emeryville mean that the project can absorb substantial remediation costs and remain financially viable.

ville has also offered to assist Chiron with a parking structure worth about $5 million. The future tax break for Chiron will be approximately $2.8 million per year out of a total possible local share of $7 million in property taxes. Tax increment financing will be capped at $95 million. Overall, public investment will be about $100 million, or about 14 percent of the total cost of the project at completion.

Public return on the project is substantial, especially after property tax payments are completed. The fully developed property is expected to pay over $12 million per year in personal and real property taxes by 2020. Economic benefits are also substantial, including several thousand hours of construction employment over the project's extended construction period. In the long run, the additional 3,300 jobs are expected to pump well over $100 million per year in salaries into the local economy. In addition, over 900 permanent jobs will be retained. Development of the project has also had intangible benefits, such as elimination of blight and reuse of a large portion of Emeryville's tax base.

Market Acceptance

Based on the project's receiving financing and the beginning of construction, the site's past as a brownfield has not impaired its ability to market space to tenants.

Lessons Learned

This site's good access and visibility, and its location near Chiron's existing facility were advantages. Relatively high land values in Emeryville mean the project can absorb substantial remediation costs and still be financially viable.

The approach to risk management set forth by the San Francisco Regional Water Quality Control Board allowed remediation to go forward relatively quickly, and Chiron could develop the facility in a timely manner and maintain a competitive edge. Emeryville's proposed special assessment district for groundwater remediation, in which groundwater would be treated as a common good and liability absorbed by the city, supported the notion that a collective solution was likely and diminished any concerns about future reopeners.

The key factor in financing the first phase of the property was the indemnity provided by Chiron's parent company, making this portion of the project a "credit deal" rather than strictly a real estate–secured deal. The land lease, sale-leaseback, and building's design (which virtually ensures that the building can be productively occupied) reduced risks sufficiently to calm the lending consortium's fears. The consultant played an important role in translating scientific data to quantifiable risks for lenders.

Notes

1. "Environmental Renewal and Economic Revitalization Successes," California EPA, Dept. of Toxic Substances Control, March 1996, p. 1.

2. "Fact Sheet: Senate Bill 923," California EPA, Dept. of Toxic Substances Control, January 1997.

3. "Update: Redevelopment and Revitalization of Brownfields. DTSC Initiatives," California EPA, Dept. of Toxic Substances Control, August 1996.

4. "Fact Sheet: Brownfield Initiatives," California EPA, Dept. of Toxic Substances Control, February 1997.

5. Ibid.

6. Ibid.

7. "Update: Redevelopment and Revitalization of Brownfields."

8. "Fact Sheet: Prospective Purchaser Policy," California EPA, Dept. of Toxic Substances Control, October 1996.

15 Development of Contaminated Urban Land in New Zealand

Located in the southern hemisphere about 1,000 miles (1,600 km) east of Australia, New Zealand's two main islands (North Island and South Island) cover a total land area of 102,700 square miles (266,100 km^2), about the size of the state of Colorado. New Zealand's constitutional history can be traced back to its colonization by the British in the early 1800s with the Treaty of Waitangi, signed in 1840 with the aboriginal Maori chiefs. The treaty transferred sovereignty to the Crown for the guarantees given by the treaty, and New Zealand became a British colony. It is now an independent democracy with a parliamentary system of government, but New Zealand is still part of the British commonwealth. Queen Elizabeth II is represented by the Governor General as the head of state who summons and dissolves parliament and gives royal assent to legislation passed by the House of Parliament.

New Zealand, with a population of 3.6 million, is a capitalist economy. Its relies on forestry, dairy, wool, and meat products as its main exports. Horticulture, fishing, manufacturing, and tourism are also significant industries, and New Zealand markets itself abroad as "clean and green." The temperate weather helps promote tourism year round.

The city of Auckland, the focus of this chapter, is located toward the northern end of North Island and is the most urbanized city in New Zealand. Population of the metropolitan area is just over 1 million residents, 350,000 of whom live in the centrally located Auckland City, one of four contiguous cities and two district councils in the metropolitan area. The mean daily temperature is 75ºF (24ºC) in January (mid-summer) and 59ºF (15ºC) in July (mid-winter), with 43 inches (1,100 mm) of rainfall annually. The temperate climate allows property development year round without any breaks for cold weather.

Auckland is located on an isthmus between the Waitemata Harbor off the Pacific Ocean to the east and Manukau Harbor off the Tasman Sea to the west. On the Pacific "Rim of Fire," Auckland is built amid over 70 extinct volcanoes, whose distinctive dead cones dot the landscape. Rich in minerals such as nickel, the volcanic soils are largely basalt and scoria and may be porous with fissures and fractures. Artesian water is used for the domestic water supply in some parts of town. Much of the downtown central business district and port area were reclaimed from Waitemata Harbor about 100 years ago.

New Zealanders are easygoing. Life is pleasurable and a national health service takes care of most medical costs. The easygoing attitude extends to litigation; in nearly all cases, it is not permitted to sue for personal injury damages (say, from a car accident), because a compulsory accident compensation scheme to which all income earners contribute meets the expenses and pays compensation. New Zealand's being a less litigious society appears to affect how lenders view the risk and stigma of developing contaminated lands.

Property Markets

New Zealand has a close relationship with Australia, across the Tasman Sea, as well as with other parts of the Pacific Rim. Many banks and professional organizations in the two countries are closely linked, and environmental regulations in New Zealand closely parallel those in some Australian states, especially in New South Wales. Investors, tourists, and immigrants from Malaysia, Hong Kong, Korea, Singapore, Taiwan, Japan, and China are commonly seen in New Zealand. In early 1998, the exchange rate was $1.00 to NZ$1.75.

Interest and lending rates are similar to those in the United States. In 1997, ten-year government bonds yielded 7.5 percent, domestic first mortgage rates were 9 to 10 percent, and inflation was between 2 and 3 percent. Incomes are lower than in the United States. In Auckland, the average weekly wage is $375 (NZ$659), or $19,580 (NZ$34,270) per year. Growth in gross domestic product in New Zealand recently was 2.5 percent, compared with 2.2 percent in the United States. Income tax rates are also similar to those in the United States, with a progressive marginal tax rate topping out at 33 percent. A 12.5 percent value-added tax for goods and services is also levied on virtually all transactions, including property.[1]

The homeownership rate in New Zealand is over 70 percent, slightly higher than in the United States. Housing sale prices are generally higher than in the United States. According to a recent report on Auckland's economy prepared by the Strategic Development Group of the Auckland City Council, the average house price in the region in 1996 was $143,400 (NZ$251,000). Rental units are also more expensive than in most U.S. markets. Apartments in Auckland's CBD typically rent for $230 to $400 (NZ$400 to NZ$700) per week for a two- to three-bedroom unit.

Sale prices for residential lots in the suburbs are somewhat higher than in most U.S. urban markets, ranging from $68,600 to $142,900 (NZ$120,000 to NZ$250,000) for a 4,300- to 5,400-square-foot (400- to 500-m^2) lot. Premiums for water or harbor views are high. Land for condominium (apartment) buildings in the CBD ranges from $28,600 to $68,600 (NZ$50,000 to NZ$120,000) per unit. Commercial land is more expensive than in the United States. Land for retail buildings in the suburbs, for example, ranges from $16.00 to $26.55 per square foot (NZ$300 to NZ$500/m^2), depending on size, visibility, and location.

A freehold system of land title applies. Multistory condominium units are usually held under strata titles called "unit titles." Townhouses are more frequently held under a strata title or "crossed lease," in which each owner has an undivided interest in the freehold land and leases back his or her defined building and surroundings on a footprint defined in a deposited plan, with a "composite title" issued for the freehold/leasehold combined interests.

Ground leases under long-term (usually 21-year) perpetually renewable leases are an old but common form of tenure in New Zealand. The lessee pays ground rent to the landowner and "owns" the building held under a leasehold title. Much of Auckland's CBD and reclaimed land are held under ground leases, as are substantial portions of the residential suburbs.

The Structure of Environmental Regulation in New Zealand

New Zealand has three tiers of government: national, regional, and local. The national Ministry for the Environment guides overall direction by issuing policy statements, setting environmental standards, and issuing documents defining site cleanliness. The Crown also holds title to large amounts of land, some of which is contaminated, primarily through state-owned enterprises. The regional level is similar to regional planning authorities in the United States; it is responsible for oversight of environmental issues, such as discharge of contaminants to land, water, and air. Local government authorities are responsible for local control of health and safety issues and the effects of land use. They also grant planning, zoning, building, and environmental approvals. Both regional and local authorities own property. New Zealand has no layer comparable to states in the United States.

National Government

The primary environmental legislation addressing regulation and development of contaminated property is the Resource Management Act of 1991 (RMA), which sets policy and guidelines for managing discharges, remediation, financial responsibility, and development of contaminated property. The RMA features joint and several liability, focusing on finding polluters and making them clean up and pay for remediation. It does not prescribe specific standards of cleanliness for hazardous substances but sets forth a public process by which they could be achieved.

The RMA contains several important components, including land use control exercised by local authorities through district plans, which provide a regime of permitted, controlled, discretionary, noncompliant, and prohibited uses. A resource and/or planning consent is required if a plan does not specifically refer to a potential use as a permitted use.

Abatement notices under Sections 322 to 328 or enforcement notices under Sections 314 to 321 can be served by an enforcement officer for noncomplying uses and environmental contamination, with appeal possible to the Environmental Court. Notices can be served on an owner, occupant, or operator, requiring cessation of the activity, and remedy or mitigation of adverse effects. Failure to comply incurs civil liability not only for costs of compliance, but also for fines of up to $114,300 (NZ$200,000) plus $5,700 (NZ$10,000) per day for continuing offenses, or imprisonment of responsible individuals for up to two years. The major defenses under Section 341 are limited to emergencies or uncontrollable events. Liability extends to principals, managers, directors, agents, employees, and anyone involved in management of a concern, and it can extend to lenders if they are active in the management of a property through foreclosure.

The RMA has guided several recent national initiatives, including assessment of liability, and standards of cleanliness for gasworks, property owned by the timber industry, and remediation of service stations. Standards are set to be consistent with Australian and New Zealand environmental standards, but according to the Auckland Regional Council, no licensing is currently available for soil investigation firms. Some Australian states are moving to establish licensing arrangements,[2] however, and it is likely that New Zealand will also follow this path.

The portion of the RMA most relevant to land development is Section 15 on discharge of contaminants into the environment. This section allows regional planning entities to enter the regulatory loop if they are concerned about on- or off-site contamination of ground- or surface water. Such discharges require a permit. Aside from this requirement, the RMA delegates the bulk of authority over matters involving contaminated land to individual local authorities.

The national government has commissioned an inventory of property by type for each of New Zealand's 14 regional areas. As of late 1995, almost 8,000 sites had been identified, of which 1,500 may present a serious problem regarding cleanup and health risk.[3] Consistent with past urban development in New Zealand, many of these sites were contaminated by coal gasification works, service stations, and industrial waste. Moreover, this figure probably underestimates the actual number of sites.[4]

The Crown, acting through the national government, also owns many contaminated dump sites. Many of them are rural, typically chemical and insecticide dumps, and timber processing waste dumps. Consultants are currently submitting proposals for the contract to assist the main asset-holding state-owned enterprises in determining what to do with this portfolio of properties.[5] The related issue of what to do with orphan sites (those contaminated before the RMA took effect in 1991 and where no responsible party is present) is under public discussion.

Regional Government

The regional councils are responsible for regulating environmental issues of regional concern, such as stormwater runoff, surface water, groundwater, and air quality. They also have input on environmental site cleanups if regional issues are involved, or if they have been notified by the local authorities.[6] In the past, regional councils have also owned and operated transit systems, parks, refuse disposal sites, and sewerage and water systems. Some of these assets have been sold to local authority trading enterprises, leaving regional councils responsible mostly for regulation rather than direct management. The Auckland Regional Council is the entity for the Auckland area, which has seven local authorities. Of the local authorities, Auckland City is by far the largest in population and commercial activity.

Regulation of landfills is a relatively recent phenomenon in New Zealand. Most landfills were not properly contained (by U.S. standards) with barriers or liners and covered against erosion until 1989.[7] Regional governments also own and operate landfills, and regulate the upgrading of other landfills, including those held by local governments. Further, according to New Zealand law, contamination follows the material rather than the site. Therefore, burying materials at a landfill is no guarantee of reduced liability for the polluter. The only exception is if the landfill operator also provides an indemnification. Only one facility in North Island, however, is believed to offer this option, at substantial cost. The Auckland Regional Council keeps a map of known landfills and dump (tip) sites within its jurisdiction.[8]

The main way that regional agencies participate in the development of contaminated land is by issuing environmental discharge consents[9] through Section 15 of the RMA, which requires the regional authority to consider the environmental impacts of development if there are any potential off-site effects on storm- or groundwater contamination. If the regional authority finds that a discharge consent is needed, the developer or site owner must follow regional procedures. The regional council may also find that a discharge permit is not currently needed. The council considers background levels in determining whether or not a discharge consent is needed and how clean the site must be after remediation. The matter may be reconsidered in the future (that is, reopened) if standards or remediation technology changes. In early 1997, the Auckland Regional Council had about 15 discharge permits for contaminated sites pending or recently completed.[10]

Local Government

Local authorities are either city councils (in urban areas) or district councils (in rural areas). They often consult regional councils as a matter of course. Local authorities are responsible for maintaining property records, general planning and review of sites, determining whether a project complies with the appropriate environmental statutes, and regulating underground storage tanks (although some larger petroleum firms go through the regional council). As specified in the RMA, the Land Information Memorandum contains all pertinent data about a site, including any environmental factors and issues. Local authorities are responsible for the public health and for supplying a developer with all available information about known site problems, but they are not responsible for guaranteeing that sites are clean. Many local authorities own a large number of properties. Because it is liable for the accuracy of public records about potential property contamination, the Auckland City Council is developing a register of sites based on past land use. It reportedly contains about 4,000 sites, most of which contained industrial and commercial uses in the past.

Contaminated sites face these problems during planning review. The presence of environmental contamination on site requiring remediation is often determined to be a controlled situation subject to the city council's approval, similar to a variance or nonconforming land use in the United States. If the contamination has the potential for an off-site release that would affect water quality, then the regional council also must issue a resource consent under Section 15 of the RMA.

Sites are reviewed on an ad hoc basis, usually requiring the services of one or more private environmental consultants. No specific standard of cleanliness exists for most uses, and a developer or environmental engineering company may use any standards of cleanliness (usually from the Netherlands or the United States). The local authority may issue a certificate of compliance, similar to an NFA letter in the United States. Because of the complexity of the issues, limited staff resources, and relatively small amount of development, many local authorities lack the in-house expertise to evaluate a site's cleanliness and usually hire environmental consultants, who review each other's work. Often, these additional costs of project review are passed along to the developer. This peer review approach is similar to the one evolving in New South Wales, Australia, where the state's general approach is to set protocols for site investigation but not standards for final cleanup.

Partly because of the lack of specific standards for cleanliness, the approach taken for remediation of most Auckland sites has been to "dig and dump," comparable to "haul and bury" used in many parts of the United States.[11] Burial costs at landfills may be low, and many are run by local authorities, potentially putting them into a conflict of interest (one reason for creation of local authority trading enterprises). Excavation of hot spots, on-site treatment, and encapsulation are known but have been used in only a few cases.

Three Case Studies of Brownfield Development in Auckland

The following three case studies of contaminated land in Auckland involve a bulk retail center on the site of a former paint factory, a mid-rise residential project on a site used to store gasified coal, and a residential project on the site of a former tram and bus service garage. All three case studies describe the sites' background, development plan, history, and remediation process, and consider the importance of the contamination in light of the

FIGURE 15.1

LOCATION OF BROWNFIELD PROJECTS IN AUCKLAND

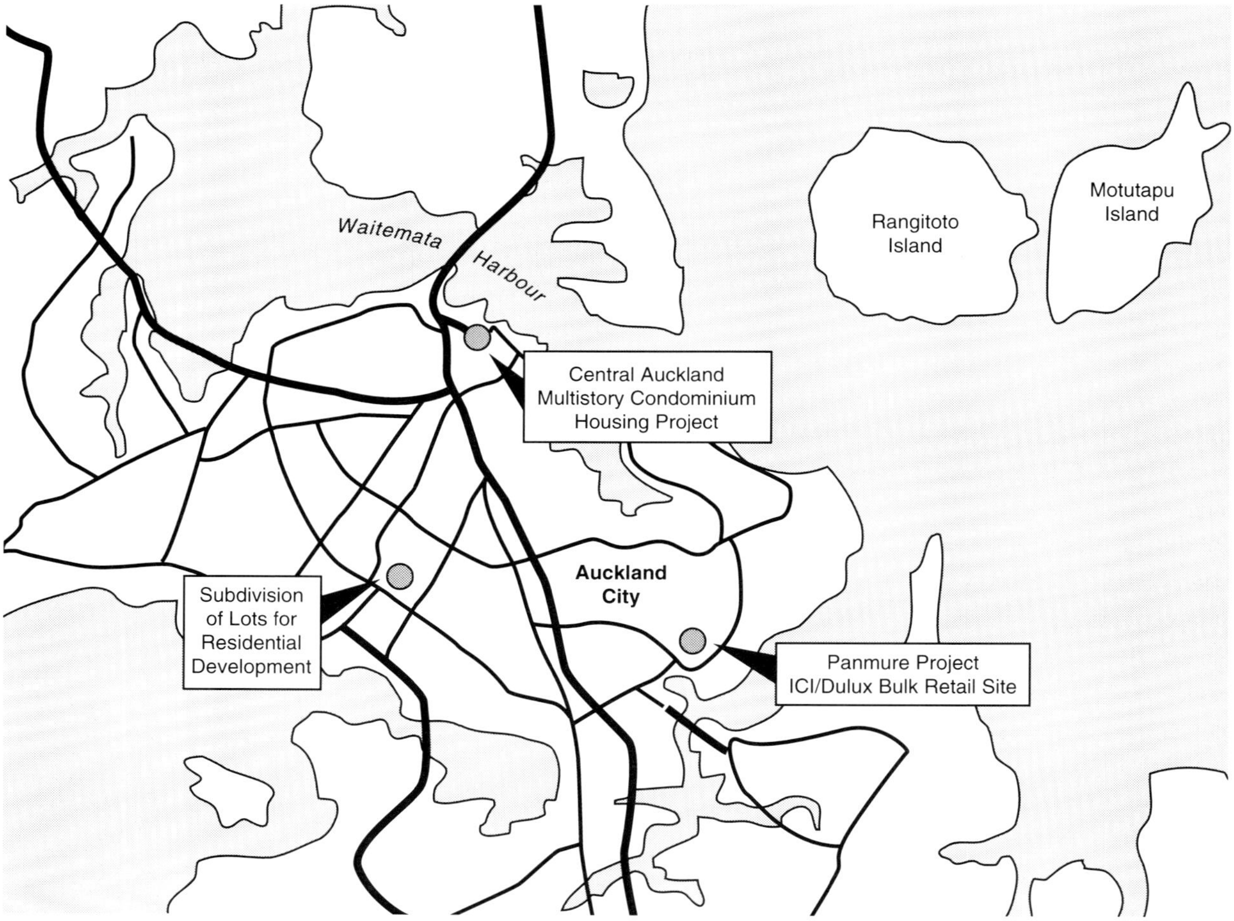

projects' end uses. Figure 15.1 shows an overview of Auckland and the general site locations.

ICI/Dulux Bulk Retail Site

Background. This site of a former paint manufacturer in Panmure, a suburb of Auckland at the foot of Mt. Wellington (one of the volcanic cones), has been remediated and sold to a developer for a power (bulk retail) center. It has received planning and remediation consents and is in the preleasing phase before development. ICI/Dulux, the former owner, remediated the site.

Development Plan. This 13-acre (5.4-ha) site is in an excellent suburban location on a major arterial road carrying 41,000 vehicles per day. The site has about 425 feet (130 m) of frontage on the main road and extensive access via road to the rear; it is on a gentle slope down toward the main road. The site has been rezoned for commercial retail use and may contain up to 226,000 square feet (21,000 m^2) of retail space when fully built out, a relatively dense retail FAR of 0.39. The slope of the site has been incorporated into the site plan to accommodate parking under the building. The intense use of the site is made more efficient by the local planning practice that takes into consideration the peaks and troughs of parking demand.

The project's tenant mix is designed to complement rather than compete with a nearby convenience retail district on the main road. Preleasing and land sales are going well, and according to the leasing company's representative, 40 to 50 percent of the space had firm commitments for lease or sale as of early 1997, including two pads for fast-food restaurants and several for big-box retailers near the back of the site. Land for the restaurant pads cost from \$18.60 to \$24.00 per square foot (NZ\$350 to NZ\$450/m^2), that for the big-box stores from \$10.60 to \$13.25 per square foot (NZ\$200 to NZ\$250/m^2). Leased space commanded market rents of \$7.45 to \$10.60 per square foot (NZ\$140 to NZ\$200/m^2) per year, double net.

The ICI/Dulux site in Panmure, a suburb of Auckland, from the main road. Mt. Wellington is in the background.

An overview of the ICI/Dulux site as seen from Mt. Wellington. The remediation of the site has been so thorough that all stigma of contamination has been removed, reflected in the project's acceptance at market values equivalent to projects on uncontaminated property.

History of the Site. The site's soil is typical for central Auckland, with volcanic topsoil over a layer of volcanic basalt and scoria on top of sedimentary rock. The volcanic material is fractured and porous. The site's previous tenant was the Dulux paint manufacturing complex, with more than ten separate buildings, which had operated there since 1956. Some of the past activity included putting unwanted materials that had undergone partial treatment into soak holes in the porous volcanic rock. Dulux's former owner, ICI Paints New Zealand, Ltd., remediated the site. ICI is a major international chemical company and has other plants in Australia and several other countries. ICI determined that paint operations on the site would cease in 1990, and the plant was leased for surface storage for several years.

According to ICI's corporate property manager in Sydney, Australia, ICI had three objectives in remediating the site: to eliminate future liability, to maximize sale prices, and to be environmentally responsible. Stringent laws governing landfills meant that maximizing on-site remediation would best accomplish these objectives. The property was remediated and granted all planning consents, including rezoning, during 1994 to 1996. All remediation was privately funded.

Once remediation was complete, the property was marketed through sealed bids in September 1996, with bids ranging from \$2.9 million to \$4.3 million (NZ\$5 million to NZ\$7.5 million). The successful bidder was The Hartford Group, a New Zealand developer, which is currently handling leases with tenants. Terms included cash to the seller at a sale price of \$4.3 million (NZ\$7.5 million), or \$7.30 per square foot (NZ\$138/m^2), with 10 percent down. ICI decided to remediate the site to a standard of "cleaner than clean"; that is, it would scientifically document that any remaining contamination on site is less than one might find at a comparable "clean" site without documentation. In doing so, ICI hoped to eliminate any stigma on prices after remediation.

Remediation. The manufacture of paints and related products left a residual contamination of hydrocarbons, including tetraphenylhydrazine, volatile organic compounds, and solvents, on site. Some hot spots contained heavy metals, including lead. The site of an underground storage tank also contained some concrete that had been dumped from other locations on the site. The buildings were removed at no cost to the owners by a salvage subcontractor. Woodward-Clyde, the project consultant, established the remediation plan and guided the segregation of the small amount of contaminated building concrete. Its recommendations for treatment were consistent with the seller's desire for total cleanup. Woodward-Clyde gathered soil and water samples from over 100 locations on site, finding concentrations of hydrocarbons in two main areas. Investigations revealed about 7,700 tons (7,000 metric tons) of soil contaminated with hydrocarbons and roughly 11,000 tons (10,000 metric tons) of soil contaminated with heavy metals.

For the hydrocarbons, Woodward-Clyde implemented an on-site treatment program that included soil aeration and forced air stripping. These techniques allowed the volatile hydrocarbon materials in the soil to be consumed by natural bacterial action through the inducement of

FIGURE 15.2

SITE OF THE ICI/DULUX PROJECT

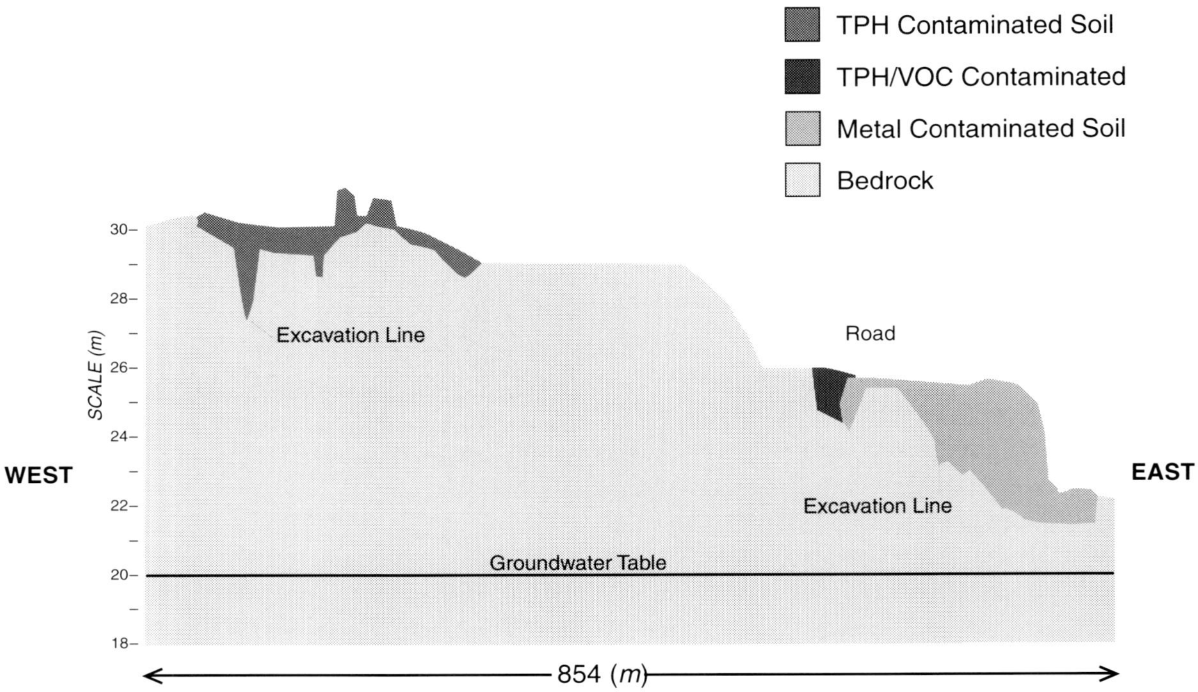

oxygen. The process took about six months, which went somewhat faster because of Auckland's temperate weather. As a result, levels of BTEX hydrocarbons were well below the stringent Dutch environmental standards Woodward-Clyde used. All soils were kept on site, saving the costs of transportation and burial. Final tests showed hydrocarbon levels so low that vehicles entering the site after a heavy rain could "contaminate" it by tracking in grease from the nearby road.

For the hot spots with heavy metals, Woodward-Clyde used different strategies for treatment, including separating metal-laden soils into "coarse" and "fine." The coarse soil was washed, purified, and validated (by testing samples) to contain certain amounts of inert metals. It was then used as clean fill on and off site. Fine soils were sterilized, bound on site, and taken to a landfill if necessary.

The Auckland Regional Council approved the developer's remediation plan in mid-1995. The developer received a final discharge consent from the regional council, and planning and resource consents from the Auckland City Council, in late 1996. The total cost of remediation was $1.7 million (NZ$3 million), or $3.00 per square foot (NZ$55.00/m^2). Of this amount, $400,000 (NZ$700,000) went for environmental consulting, testing, and laboratory fees, with the remaining $1.3 million (NZ$2.3 million) for actual remediation. The on-site remediation saved at least 50 percent of the cost of dig and dump and, because of New Zealand's regulations concerning liability and landfills, appears to have lower long-term liability for the seller. Figure 15.2 shows a map of the site and prior activity there.

Summary. As of early 1997, no financing had been extended for the site, but market acceptance has been very good, as evidenced by the number of bidders for the site and by the brisk leasing and land sales. Prices appear to be unaffected by the site's former contamination. Costs of remediation and environmental consulting represent 40 percent of overall gross land sales to the developer and will likely reflect 10 to 15 percent of the total value of the center at completion.

Multistory Condominium Housing in Central Auckland

Background. This well-located multistory residential project was built partly on top of and adjacent to a coal gasification storage site (a gasometer). The site has received its planning and remediation consents and was under construction as of early 1997. It obtained construction financing from a bank and has been well received in the marketplace. Part of the site was sold for commercial use.

Development Plan. The site is located on a small city block on the periphery of central Auckland, about 0.6 mile (1 km) from downtown. The overall site contains nearly 2.5 acres (1 ha), although the portion underlying the residential part of the project is just over 0.6 acre (0.25 ha). The four-story building contains about 40 units of upper-end for-sale residences. Residential owners receive freehold strata title (comparable to condominiums in the United States).

The one-, two-, and three-bedroom units range from 850 to 1,450 square feet (80 to 135 m^2), including balcony space. All units (except the three-bedroom units) have one bathroom and one parking space per bedroom. As of early 1997, more than 30 of the units were under contract, with typical prices of $154,300 (NZ$270,000) for one-bedroom units and $206,000 (NZ$360,000) for two-bedroom units. Marketing has proceeded well despite the clearly visible gasometer footprint directly adjacent to the project. Figure 15.3 shows the gasometer footprint superimposed on the building footprint.

History of the Site. The Auckland Gas Company (the original owner) used the site to store coal gas piped in from a coal gasification plant nearby. (Coal gas was commonly used in New Zealand for heating and fuel.) The 2.5-acre (1-ha) site (referred to as the larger site) also contained a sewer reserve, a garage and workshop, and an adjacent store. In 1993, a local developer bought 90 percent of the block, with gasometers still in place, for $1.9 million (NZ$3.3 million). The developer obtained planning and resource consents from the Auckland Regional Council and the Auckland City Council for the larger site, decontaminated most of it (at a cost of approximately $230,000 [NZ$400,000]), and subdivided the property into the land now underlying the residential structure (the residential site) and another parcel of about 1.6 acres (0.65 ha) (the commercial site). In 1996, the commercial site, with the concrete gasometer footprint still visible, was sold to an offshore developer for $2 million (NZ$3.5 million). The sales contract also included limited indemnification for the offshore developer, under which the seller could be held liable for a modest portion of the sale price. This sale left the local developer with a land cost of only $114,300 (NZ$200,000), after remediation, as its stake in the residential site, a savings of about 90 percent compared with residential land in the area. The commercial site may be developed as a retail or commercial property. The offshore developer

This well-located residential apartment building with 40 units was built on the site of former coal gas storage tanks. The base of one of the tanks can be seen in the foreground.

FIGURE 15.3

RELATIONSHIP OF GASOMETER FACILITY AND APARTMENT BUILDING

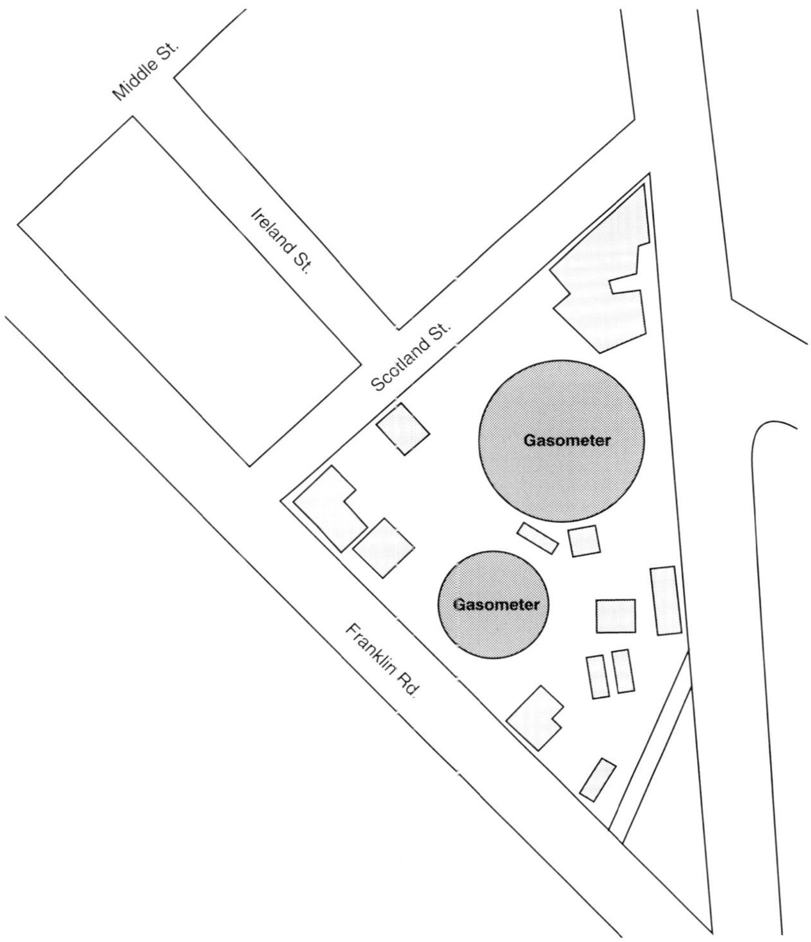

has since added two other smaller adjacent parcels to the commercial project and is marketing it for resale.

Remediation. The large steel tank cylinders of the two gasometers rose and fell within a concrete pit sealed with water, depending on the volume of gas inside. Over the decades of operation, a toxic sludge coagulated in the base of the gasometer pits. The site contained high levels of coal tar, volatile organic compounds, and lead. During 1994 and 1995, the site was remediated. Water and sludge were removed from the gasometer tank pits, the pits were filled with a gravel layer and then a clay barrier, and one tank (so far) has been backfilled with clean fill. Hot spots on other parts of the site were removed and buried in a landfill. A vapor barrier was put under the slab and around the footprint of the residential structure, below its basement parking deck. The developer obtained planning and resource consents in late 1995. Evidence of past remediation is recorded by reference to the resource consent on the property's title, one line of which refers to a section of the RMA. A more detailed search of this memorandum provides a description of a vapor barrier required under buildings and other nonenvironmental conditions (vehicular access, for example). Total cost of remediation was an estimated $286,000 (NZ$500,000), or $3.20 per square foot (NZ$60.00/m^2), or approximately 6 percent of current land value. The cost includes importing sand to backfill the first gasometer pit; the second could use excavated material from the additional parcels acquired. Environmental consulting fees, including several test pits and soil borings, were substantial. Apportioning the cost of decontamination to the condominium project's site area shows less than 1 percent of the total gross sales value at buildout, or less than 4 percent if the total cost (about $8 million [NZ$14 million]) is absorbed by the overall sales value of the residential project at full buildout.

Summary. Both developers obtained construction financing for the properties from major regional banks. The loan-to-value ratio for one of the loans was reportedly at the low end of the normal range of 0.5 to 0.6. Local lenders appear willing to finance the projects once they have obtained consents and after they have been remediated. Sales of the units have been brisk and market acceptance, evidenced by presales at the rate of about three units per month or more, good. No residual stigma is evident, and some purchasers of the units may be unaware of the site's history.

Housing in Suburban Auckland

Background. This residential subdivision is located along a major arterial road in a well-established, centrally located suburb of Auckland. A developer purchased the undeveloped parcel and buildings for $2 million (NZ$3.5 million). Formerly a tram and bus servicing facility, the property was mildly contaminated and the contamination removed along with the remaining structures. The project has received its planning and environmental approvals; it has been subdivided, and houses are under construction.

Development Plan. This 6.5-acre (2.7-ha) property has been approved for 21 lots for single-family detached houses, plus five larger parcels for future development as semiattached housing units. The smaller lots are about 4,300 square feet (400 m^2) each and sell for $125,700 (NZ$220,000), or $29.00 per square foot (NZ$550/m^2). Eight lots had been sold as of early 1997. Building covenants require that the houses built on the lots cost at least as much as the land, making the minimum completed value $251,400 (NZ$440,000). Several houses are under construction, none with basements, as is customary in New Zealand. Figure 15.4 shows a site plan for the project.

History of the Site. The site was formerly owned by the Auckland Regional Council and the operators of a tram and then bus garage, depot, and servicing facility. The buildings had bays with service pits the mechanics used to get under the trams and buses to work on them. Some fill had also been brought in to support the tram tracks. Like in much of Auckland, soils are volcanic. Solvents from the bus maintenance operation had been poured out at the site's borders. The regional council sold the site, in its unremediated condition and with some existing structures, to a developer for $2 million (NZ$3.5 million) in late 1995. The developer began to seek building demolition and subdivision consents, and then discovered the site was contaminated, which delayed the project by about a year. Local planning consents and regional approvals were obtained in late 1996.

Remediation. The tram and bus servicing facility left residual amounts of solvents, triphenylhydrazine, and volatile organic compounds on site. The developer conducted a dig-and-dump procedure on the hot spots with residual hydrocarbons. In addition, the volcanic soil on site indicated high levels of zinc, cadmium, and nickel, but further investigation revealed that levels were no higher than background soil. When levels of contaminants in the soil were deemed to be below the levels when health becomes a concern, the site was covered with 20 inches (0.5 m) of clean fill. The city council consented to and monitored cleanup, which took about a year. The developer's cleanup certificate does not require a notation on the titles of the lots about past contamination. The overall cost was about $57,000 (NZ$100,000) for consultants, plus $229,000 (NZ$400,000) for the dig and dump, new soil, and other remediation. The additional environmental cleanup expense (not counting delay) works out to approximately $0.95 per square foot (NZ$18.00/m^2).

Summary. The market appears to have accepted these lots, and sales have been brisk: about four per month in the first two months of sales. At completion, the project's total improved sales value is expected to be well over $9 million (NZ$16 million). Remediation costs represent approximately 5 to 7 percent of the overall value of gross land sales and approximately 3 percent of the value of gross building and land (combined) sales at buildout.

Lessons Learned

The Role of the Local Government in Regulating Brownfields. Development of contaminated land in New Zealand is an evolving issue. The environmental debate in New Zealand generally parallels that in eastern Australian states, such as New South Wales. Compared with the United States, New Zealand has delegated much power over environmental issues and permitting to local authorities. The potential for innovation is high, but as of now, local councils often find themselves without the expertise to evaluate complex environmental problems, and they rely heavily on private environmental consultants. Although local councils may receive assistance from the regional authority (which plays the role of oversight typical in most U.S. states with a VCP), site review is often ad hoc and coordination between local and regional authorities somewhat vague. Given the close relationship with Australian states just across the Tasman Sea, New Zealand may soon move to formalize an audit or peer review of environmental consultants. Although this additional oversight may be expensive for local councils or developers, it should provide satisfactory outcomes, subject to governmental certification of private consultants.

Because local authorities in New Zealand are compelled to keep a reasonable level of available data about contamination (and other property matters) on public land use records, many are developing property registers. In the long run, such registers could reduce the chance for inadvertent development of contaminated land.

On the other hand, New Zealand's approach (as of early 1997) involved possible local government conflicts of interest in several areas. For example, local government bodies wishing to dispose of real estate assets may

FIGURE 15.4

SITE PLAN FOR THE RESIDENTIAL SUBDIVISION

not have adequate information about the condition of prior contamination on site. Some local councils are still managing landfills where waste is taken while granting planning consents. Pressures to minimize costs may conflict with the public interest in some cases

Innovations by the Private Sector. Development of contaminated properties has attracted at least two developers to the Auckland market. Another market niche is being developed by environmentally conscious for-profit firms like ICI/Dulux Paints. As manufacturing operations are consolidated and sites become surplus, ICI finds itself with several sites having similar problems of contamination. The firm has developed the expertise to clean sites for the least cost by remediating over two-thirds of contaminated soil on site, saving dumping charges, and reducing long-term liability (and it could transport soil-washing equipment from place to place to save money and amortize its investment). In terms of marketing, ICI

This residential subdivision is located along a major arterial road in a well-established central Auckland suburb. After remediation, 20 inches (0.5 m) of clean fill was used to cover the soil and the low level of contamination that remained. None of the houses have basements, as is customary in New Zealand.

maintains that the stigma of remediation has negligible or no effect on prices, because ICI-remediated properties are "cleaner than clean" and have the scientific documentation to prove it. ICI also saved money on remediation and demolition, because demolition contractors removed structures at no cost to the company as a result of the market for recycled materials.

Because the developers picked areas with high potential property values, property values exceeded costs of remediation, and no state subsidies were required (or available, for that matter). Views of water or other green amenities like parks are compatible with value premiums. For nonresidential uses, good to excellent traffic access is a must. In general, property values in New Zealand are substantially higher than in depressed U.S. urban areas, which makes brownfield development more feasible without government subsidies. Moreover, getting the environmental and rezoning consents for higher density can increase returns to the developer.

Lenders readily grant brownfield loans, and some lenders in New Zealand and Sydney (many banks are in both markets) provide mortgages on remediated properties. They do not appear to be overly concerned about the stigma of formerly contaminated sites or standards of cleanliness that a typical brownfield lender or developer in the United States would consider insufficient. Although this attitude may be partly explained by the lack of litigation as a matter of common practice in New Zealand, it is remarkable because New Zealand has no liability exemptions for lenders, and lenders may be fully liable for cleanup expenses if they foreclose on a property in case of default. Lenders' risk managers generally seem to trust the ability of local authorities and appraisers to sort out environmental and valuation issues. Generally, banks in New Zealand view the environmental issue as just another business risk, typically based on a screening questionnaire that addresses environmental issues. Although none of the three lenders interviewed for this book would finance remediation of a site, they would consider a construction loan, generally at about 50 to 60 percent of a site's value (without explicitly accounting for remediation). One lender did indicate a much lower loan-to-value ratio, reflecting concern about the business risk of dealing with formerly contaminated property. One bank made a construction loan on property where the prior developer/owner provided partial indemnification.

The prevalence of long-term land leases can potentially play a role in financing the development of contaminated property. In some cases, liability for future cleanup may rest with a leasehold owner who has deep pockets rather than an operator or lessee, which could make lenders less reluctant to finance development.

Notes

1. Statistics New Zealand, *Population Trends in the City of Auckland*, 1996.

2. Cathy Dyer, manager, Contaminated Sites Section, New South Wales Environmental Protection Authority, Sydney, Australia, personal interview, February 1997.

3. New Zealand Ministry for the Environment, "Discussion Document on Contaminated Land Management," November 1995.

4. Eddie Grogan, Auckland Regional Council, personal interview, January 1997.

5. Kevin Wood, Worleys Environmental Consultants, Auckland, personal interview, January 1997.

6. Grogan, personal interview.

7. Wood, personal interview.

8. Grogan, personal interview.

9. A "consent" in New Zealand is similar to an approval or variance in the United States.

10. Ramon Scoble, Auckland Regional Council, personal interview, January 1997.

11. Wood, personal interview; and Mohammed Hassan, Woodward-Clyde Environmental Consultants, Auckland, personal interview, January 1997.

16 Brownfield Development in Manchester, U.K.

The United Kingdom has a long history of reusing land, dating back even before the industrial revolution of the 18th century. The need to reuse land is a factor of a limited supply of developable land in a highly populated island of about 60 million people. Moreover, development, since 1947, has been regulated by strict town planning controls. In many cases, town councils do not permit development of rural (greenfield) property on the periphery, which tends to promote brownfield development by supporting land prices within developed urban areas. And most urban residents of the U.K. are accustomed to higher density and smaller units than their counterparts in the United States. These factors have led to a substantial amount of development of previously contaminated urban land in the U.K.

The U.K. is part of the European Union, which is evolving into an entity roughly equivalent to the federal level in the United States,[1] although many people, especially in the U.K., oppose full federalization. The U.K. Department of Environment is responsible for environmental policy and funding guidelines in the country, subject in some instances to decisions taken by the European Union. These policies are then administered by the Environment Agency (a central, or national, government body) and by local authorities, including borough, county, and metropolitan councils. These local authorities are responsible for overseeing planning, providing planning consents, and addressing environmental issues. They consider environmental issues part of the overall development review process, consulting with their environmental health officer and the Environment Agency. Proposals for remediation may have to be approved by both bodies; such approval and any future monitoring are conditions of granting a planning consent. No regional or state levels of government are active in brownfield development in the U.K., although development agencies funded by the central government play an active role in urban regeneration.

Some industrial processes, which today are considered harmful to the environment, may not have been perceived that way at one time, and their waste emissions to land, air, and water may have been regarded just as the necessary byproducts of industrial progress. Similarly, the disposal of industrial wastes on manufacturing sites, perhaps even their use to prepare land to enlarge a factory or provide parking spaces, was regarded as normal practice, without any consideration given to the possibility that such acts could be polluting the land. Such actions were considered the prerogative of the landowner and usually considered of little concern to anyone else. Accidental spills and illegal dumping of wastes, known in the U.K. as "fly-tipping," have also contributed to the problem of contaminated land.

With an industrial history extending back over more than 200 years, it is impossible to estimate the number of contaminated sites in the U.K. and the total land area affected. Estimates of disused or underused industrial land vary from 50,000 to 100,000 sites, on a land area of 250,000 to 500,000 acres (100,000 to 200,000 ha). Not all of this land is contaminated, and estimates of the contaminated area range from 20 to 50 percent of the total land area affected by industrial dereliction.[2] In addition, certain sites that are still in full use as manufacturing plants, chemical storage depots, and waste treatment facilities, among other uses, may also contain contamination. Even then, not all the contaminated land is so seriously polluted as to require remedial action, and, under the U.K. government's risk-based approach to contaminated land, only a very small percentage of derelict or industrially damaged land is considered to need urgent treatment.

The Environmental Protection Act 1990 dealt with a wide range of environmental issues, but the section of greatest concern with regard to land currently or previously used for industrial purposes was Section 143. Section 143 proposed to establish registers of land used for "potentially contaminative purposes." The registers would not contain details of actual contamination, and all properties used for the specified purposes would be registered, whether actually contaminated or not. Even if it could be proved that no contamination was present on the site, properties could not be removed from the registers, because they were intended to be records of historical fact regarding land use. The registers also were not intended to differentiate the severity of possible contaminants or to identify potential receptors or targets at risk.

Following an extended consultation period and, at times, a very public debate, the government abandoned the proposal for registers in 1993, and the legislation was subsequently repealed in 1995. A debate continues on the usefulness and efficacy of brownfield registers, however.[3]

The Regulatory Environment in the U.K.

Environmental controls for waste disposal and the burning of rubbish in the U.K. date back to the 13th century, but the origin of modern environmental law is regarded as the Public Health Act 1848 and numerous subsequent laws enacted by Parliament, including the Public Health Act 1961, the Public Health (Recurring Nuisances) Act 1969, and the Control of Pollution Act 1974 in modern times.[4] Nevertheless, despite this long history of legislative controls—or perhaps even because of it—land has become contaminated by industrial activities. And although the first legislation specifically described as "environmental protection" was not enacted until 1990, Parliament has long been aware of the need to protect public health and the environment.

Since 1989, the government and the real estate industry have engaged in a debate about tackling the problem of contaminated land. In many respects, the problems and their solutions in the U.K. are similar to experiences in the United States, but there are some notable exceptions—perhaps the most important of which is a growing acceptance that contamination does not have to be removed in its entirety to facilitate development. Even for the most sensitive of all uses, private housing with individual gardens where young children might play, it has been accepted that some residual contamination may be left in the land. The U.K.'s official approach to contaminated land is that it should be remediated to the level of cleanliness necessary to make it suitable for its actual or proposed use, and no further (consistent with the notion of risk-based corrective action in the United States).

The general rule is that if the site is suitable for its existing, or proposed, use without treatment and there is no likelihood of harm to the wider environment, then cleanup is not required. This pragmatic approach, shortly to become effective through national legislation, requires there to be an unbroken link from contaminative source (say a manufacturing activity or a toxic substance) through a pathway (land, air, or water) to a receptor (or target) for a site to be classed as "contaminated." If the link is broken (say through an impermeable site cover) or one of the three elements, source, pathway, or receptor, is

FIGURE 16.1

DEFINITION OF SIGNIFICANT HARM IN THE U.K.

Type of Receptor	Description of Harm
Human beings	Death, serious injury, cancer or other disease, genetic mutation, birth defects, or the impairment of reproductive functions. Disease is to be taken to mean an unhealthy condition of the body or some part thereof.
Any living organism or ecological system within any habitat notified under section 28, declared under section 35, or designated under section 36 of the Wildlife and Countryside Act 1981, any European site within the meaning of regulation 10 of the Conservation (Natural Habitats, etc.) Regulation 1994, or any habitat or site afforded policy protection under paragraph 13 of Planning Policy Guidance Note 9 on nature conservation or Planning Guidance (Wales): Planning Policy (that is, Conservation, potential Special Protection Areas, and listed Ramsar sites).	Harm that results in an irreversible or other substantial adverse change in the functioning of the habitat or site. (In determining what constitutes a substantial adverse change, the local authority should have regard to the advice of English Nature, Scottish Natural Heritage, or the Countryside Council for Wales, as the case may be, and the requirements of the Conservation (Natural Habitats, etc.) Regulations 1994.)
Property in the form of livestock, of other owned animals, of wild animals that are the subject of shooting or fishing rights, or of crops.	Death, disease, or other physical damage such that there is a substantial loss in their value. For this purpose, a substantial loss should be regarded as occurring when a substantial proportion of the animals or crops are no longer fit for the purpose for which they were intended. In many cases, a loss of 10 percent of the value can be regarded as a benchmark for what constitutes a substantial loss.
Property in the form of buildings, where the "building" has the meaning given in section 336(1) of the Town and Country Planning Act 1990; that is, "building means any structure or erection, and any part of a building . . . but does not include plant or machinery comprised in a building."	Structural failure or substantial damage. For this purpose, substantial damage should be regarded as occurring when any part of the building ceases to be capable of being used for the purpose for which it is or was intended.

Source: "Consultation on Draft Statutory Guidance on Contaminated Land," Dept. of Environment, London, 1996.

missing (say because a site is disused and the contaminants are of a nonmigratory nature), then the land will not be legally classed as contaminated. This situation applies even if some alternative, more sensitive use of the site is regarded as highly toxic.

Perhaps one area where the U.K. has a smaller problem than the United States is leaking underground storage tanks. Petrol (gas) has always been a highly taxed commodity in the U.K., and its sale has been strictly controlled, with regular checks by weights and measures inspectors. Thus, any leaks are likely to be noticed quite early. LUSTs represent a substantial financial penalty to the operator of the filling station, as taxes would still have to be paid for product lost into the ground. Nevertheless, leaking aboveground tanks are still a major source of pollution, and transport operations can potentially contaminate through inadequate enclosure of aboveground road fuel (diesel) tanks and inadequate refueling practices.

No official definition of "brownfield" exists in the U.K., but an attempt was made to define such sites in 1994 as:

> . . . any areas of land [that] have previously been the subject of manmade or nonagricultural use of any type. This would include industrial uses such as chemical works, heavy engineering, shipbuilding, and textile processing, together with unfit housing clearance sites and docklands, both inland and coastal, as well as mineral extraction and those used for landfill purposes.[5]

In the U.K., whether or not such land is also "contaminated land" depends on the propensity of any materials in the soil or groundwater to cause "significant harm."

The word "brownfield," as used in the United Kingdom, is probably more closely associated with the Department of Environment's definition of "derelict land"— "land so damaged by industrial or other development that it is incapable of beneficial use without treatment."[6] Treatment of derelict land may include, for example, removal of underground obstructions such as old foundations and redundant services or consolidation of fill material, rather than any acts of decontamination.

Cleanup Standards

At the same time it announced abandonment of the registers, the government commissioned a comprehensive review of policy addressing contaminated land. This review, the details of which are contained in two documents by the U.K. Department of Environment and the Welsh Office, concluded that land affected by contamination should be remediated on the basis of "suitability for use." In other words, the less sensitive a proposed use, the lower the requirement to remove or treat contamination.

"Suitability for use" was embodied in legislation in the Environment Act 1995, which introduced a new part IIA to the Environment Act 1990. The new legislation defines "contaminated land" as:

> . . . any land [that] appears to the local authority in whose area it is situated to be in such a condition, by reason of substances in, on, or under the land, that
> (a) significant harm is being caused or there is a significant possibility of such harm being caused; or
> (b) pollution of controlled waters is being, or is likely to be, caused . . . .

The 1995 act defines "harm" as "harm to the health of living organisms or other interference with the ecological systems of which they form part." For humans, it is intended to include harm to property. The word "significant" is not defined in the act, and its use "in the main definition of contaminated land narrows its scope considerably."[7] A definition of "significant" has not yet been finalized, but the consultation draft of the statutory guidance to local authorities, which will determine how the legislation is implemented, contains the following definition of "significant harm":

> Only harm [that] is both to receptors of the type listed in [Figure 16.1], and within the description of harm specified for that type of receptor in that [figure], should be regarded as significant.

The draft statutory guidance also sets out the conditions that need to be satisfied so a local authority can determine that "a significant possibility of significant harm" exists within a time frame decided by the local authority. The consultation process has now been completed, and it is expected that the legislation will become effective soon.

These general principles are converted to specific guidelines for contamination that have been set by the Interdepartmental Committee on the Redevelopment of Contaminated Land (ICRCL), a government organization with representatives from different departments. ICRCL has established "trigger" and "threshold" levels for a number of contaminants according to uses of a site, such as open space, residences, and industry. It is considered reasonable to accept the presence of such substances if they are isolated by concrete bases, roadways, sidewalks, vehicle parking areas, or landscaping. These guidelines are continually being revised.

The Cleanup Process and Closure Documents

Developers of a typical brownfield project seek to obtain approval of the remediation plan from the local authority and, depending upon the nature of contamination, the Environment Agency. The developer's private environmental consultant typically prepares the remediation plan. Neither the Environment Agency nor the local council issues formal closure documents that are even roughly equivalent to an NFA letter or CNTS in the United States. Because final permission rests with the local council's health officer and planning consent is subject to consultation with the Environment Agency, however, approval is implicit.

Exemption from Liability for New Owners and Lenders

The central government has not passed any laws dealing specifically with an exemption from liability for new owners who successfully remediate property or for financial institutions who provide mortgage financing. In some cases, lenders have been forced into bankruptcy as a result of being forced to clean up contaminated property.

Like most of Europe, the U.K. has adopted the policy of "the polluter pays," but, given the country's long industrial history and the many changes of ownership that may have taken place during that history, it is not always feasible to track down the polluter. Nor is it always desirable, if that polluter can be found, to hold it accountable for actions that may have occurred decades earlier.

If, for example, the actions that contaminated the land 20 or more years earlier were accepted then as normal procedures in that particular industry, there may be no real benefit to be gained by bankrupting the polluter or causing it serious financial damage, with possible losses in employment. It is better to ensure that working practices are changed, with the objective of avoiding future contamination, and to use some public money to clean up the historic problem, often as part of a wider program of urban renewal—thus calling for a good working relationship between the public and private sectors. Current U.K. legislation includes provisions for hardship in considering the apportionment of responsibilities for cleanup. Equally important, the same legislation provides assurance that banks and other financial institutions are not unfairly penalized.

Financial Inducements

The U.K. has a coordinated funding support mechanism for assisting the development of contaminated property. The not-for-profit entity responsible for allocating these funds is English Partnerships, a quasi-autonomous nongovernmental organization (QUANGO) that is empowered to operate throughout England. The amount of grant aid allocated for most projects normally should not exceed the Department of Environment's guideline of one part public money to four parts private money.

The City Grant program (which has been discontinued but has been superseded by other central government initiatives) provided support to private sector capital projects that benefited run-down inner-city areas, similar to the Urban Development Action Grant program in the United States, which was also discontinued. The City Grant program was implemented in 57 English cities for projects exceeding $830,000 (£500,000),[8] which were required to generate tangible benefits such as jobs or private housing, with the secondary objective being environmental conservation.

Brownfield Development in Manchester

The Manchester conurbation is in the northwest region of England. Manchester was the home of the industrial revolution, and the wealth of the city and its neighbors rested on a diversity of industrial activities, including cotton import and processing, textiles and garment manufacturing, iron and steel production, heavy engineering, vehicle manufacture, and food processing.

In common with other manufacturing areas in the U.K., Manchester suffered severely from deindustrialization in the 1980s, resulting in widespread unemployment, depopulation of the inner-city areas, closure of many industrial manufacturing plants, and the creation of large areas of dereliction.

Some of the closed plants were major employers that occupied extensive areas of land, but, in common with other older industrial areas, many of the businesses were very small, employed only a few people, and occupied very small lots. Multiple ownership in inner-city industrial areas has presented major problems in treating contaminated soil; for example, the cleanup and development of a four-acre (1.6-ha) site in the Ancoats area of Manchester, only half a mile (0.8 km) from the city center, involved the purchase of as many as 19 small parcels of land, used for almost as many different purposes, to create a viable project.[9]

Despite economically depressed conditions, similar to the problems experienced in the United States's Rustbelt, over a dozen brownfield projects have been successfully developed in central Manchester, including two major industrial/office complexes, ten new housing projects with over 2,000 units, and several retail/mixed-use projects in and around the downtown. In addition, a number of buildings have been converted.

To provide an overview of how brownfield development has been tackled in the U.K., this chapter considers three very different case studies. The first is a major industrial area, including a former steelworks, in the metropolitan borough of Trafford, to the southwest of Manchester's city center (see Figure 16.2), which has been reclaimed for industrial use. The second is a small site, a former engineering works in east Manchester, reclaimed with low-cost housing for sale. The third site, also small, is a former tram and bus depot in the city of Salford, to the northwest of Manchester's city center. It has been developed for rental housing.

Trafford Park: Development for Industrial Use

Trafford Park was the world's first formally planned industrial estate (subdivision), and, for many years, it was the largest (at approximately 2,600 acres [1,052 ha]) industrial estate in Europe. The estate was developed after the opening of the Manchester Ship Canal in 1894, which, for the first time, brought ocean-going ships right to the heart of Manchester. Most of the land was under two ownerships, Trafford Park Estate Company and Manchester Ship Canal Company, which ensured that the area was laid out with the infrastructure required for major industrial development. As a result, by the end of World War II, Trafford Park contained one of the greatest concentrations of manufacturing industry in the world, providing jobs for around 75,000 people.

The era of prosperity was not to last, and by the 1970s, the canal and port facilities were no longer attractive to commercial shipping traffic. The area became increasingly run down and lost investment to areas with better road connections. By 1985, employment in Trafford Park had fallen to 24,500, and the area was caught in a spiral of disinvestment, extensive vacant areas, and underused land.

The Evolution and Role of TPDC. In an attempt to halt the decline, the U.K. government established the Trafford Park Development Corporation (TPDC) in February 1987, whose objective was to secure the regeneration of the Trafford Park Urban Development Area. TPDC is a QUANGO whose members are appointed by the central government.

FIGURE 16.2

TRAFFORD PARK SITE PLAN

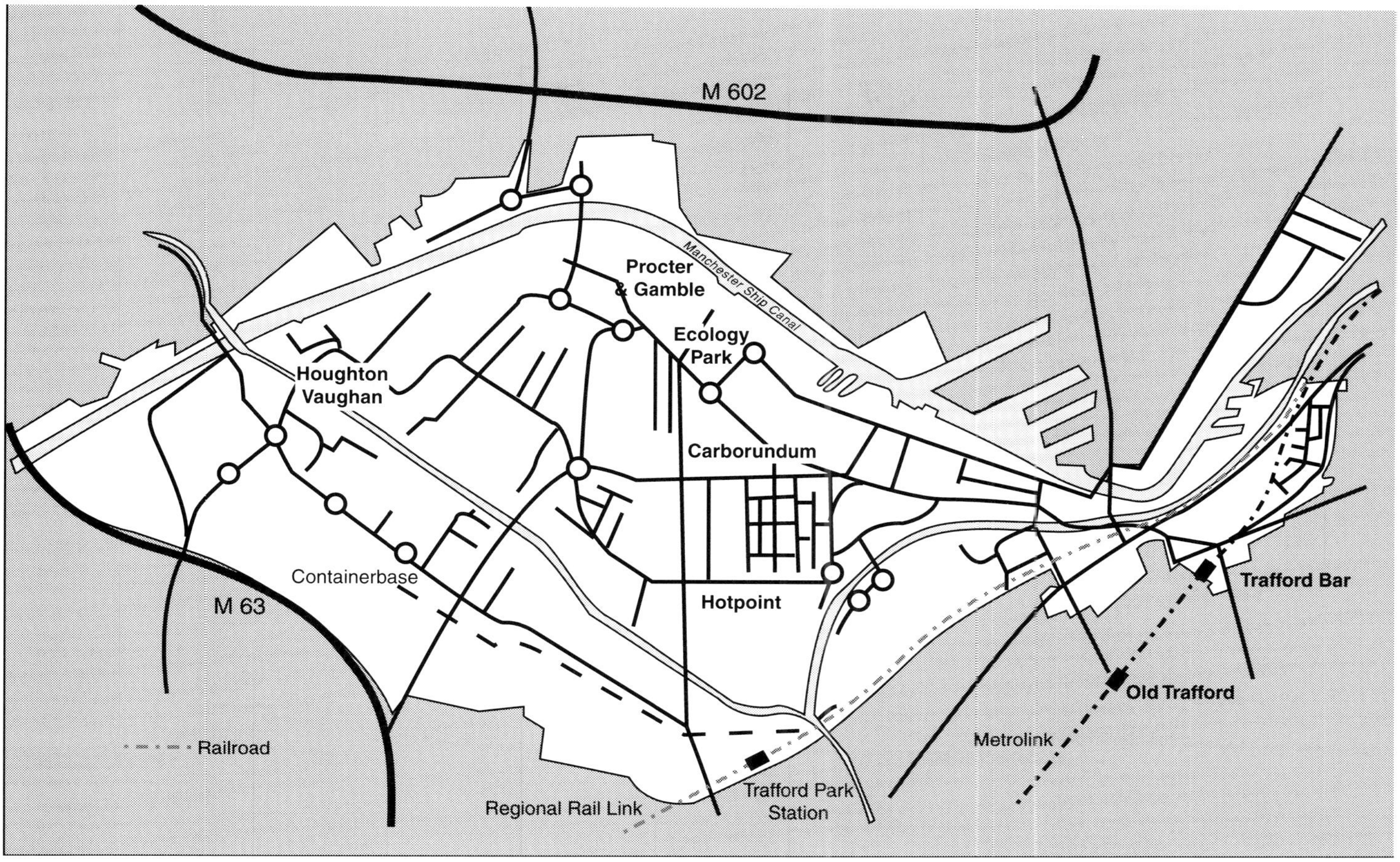

QUANGOs have been used as instruments of the government in the U.K. as a means of directing central government funds to specific local issues for a variety of purposes, from health care to urban renewal. For development corporations, some of the powers and duties of elected local authorities (for example, those with regard to town planning and economic development) are placed in the hands of nonelected board members. These board members work only part time, in some cases less than one day a week, and include local business leaders and professionals such as architects. Elected representatives, councillors, from the local authority may also be appointed, but they would almost certainly be a voting minority. The board of a QUANGO is responsible to the sponsoring government department, the Department of Environment for development corporations, and a chief executive and staff drawn from both the public and private sectors are responsible for day-to-day management. The spatial extent of urban development areas is predefined, and the corporations can operate only within those identified boundaries.

TPDC's output has been impressive. According to its 1995 annual report, TPDC has reclaimed 350 acres (142 ha) of land since 1987. Over the same time, over 16,000 jobs (gross) have been created, and $1.5 billion (£915 million) in private sector investment has been attracted to the industrial park. TPDC has attracted over 700 new companies and provided 19 miles (30 km) of new roads within the park.[10] These impressive achievements have been well leveraged: TPDC's public investment was $328 million (£197 million), or about 18 percent of the overall investment figure.

Northbank Steelworks Site. Included within Trafford Park Development Corporation's urban development area was the former Northbank Steelworks, Irlam. Although within the area of the Trafford-based development corporation, the steelworks was in fact situated in the city of Salford, on the opposite side of the Manchester Ship

FIGURE 16.3

NORTHBANK INDUSTRIAL PARK SITE PLAN

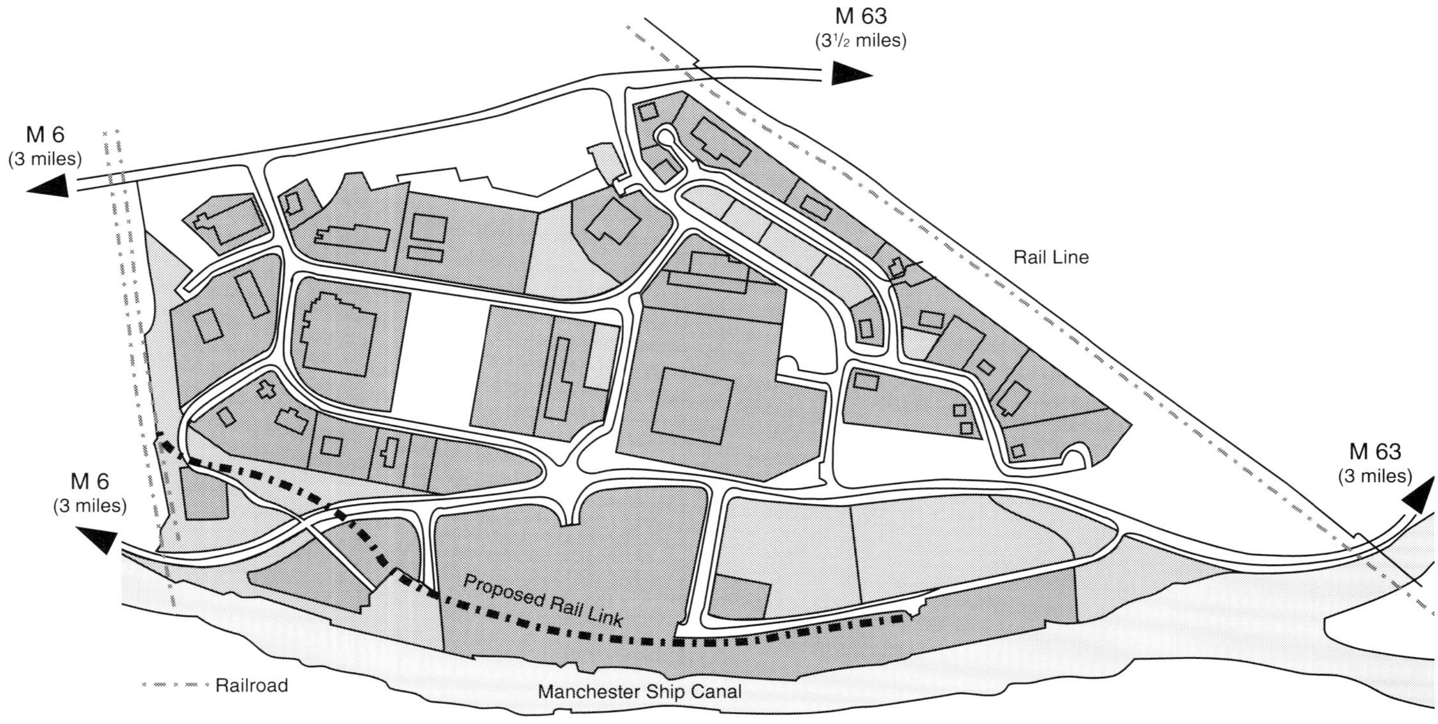

Canal to Trafford. Thus, the QUANGO's control extended across city boundaries.

The site of the former steelworks totaled approximately 250 acres (101 ha), and the works themselves had been demolished to ground level between 1972 and 1978—long before TPDC came on the scene. As a consequence of the demolition work, the site was left with approximately 20 inches (0.5 m) of demolition rubble over the original site surface. While it gave the appearance of a level site, it was incapable of supporting development. Moreover, no attempt had been made to remove underground foundations and redundant services.

The task of acquiring, reclaiming, and developing this derelict site fell to TPDC. Acquiring the land from 11 former owners and occupants cost $0.45 per square foot (£3 million, or £12,000 per acre). After TPDC obtained title, it undertook the following actions:

- Site investigations, including bore holes and trial pits, to ascertain the geotechnical nature of the ground and to chart the buried obstructions, as well as to sample and analyze possible contaminants;
- Consulting with engineers and specialists to determine the results of investigative reports and appropriate remedial action;
- Civil engineering work to begin remediation, on a speculative basis, as well as to provide new above- and belowground infrastructure.

The objective of the investigative work and the subsequent site remediation was to reduce the economic legacy of the steelworks and to provide a relatively level site, ready for industrial development. Light foundations and other buried obstructions were removed to a predetermined depth, together with any other unsuitable material below that depth. The entire operation was controlled by appropriately qualified engineers and chemists, with the location and depth of all material left in the ground carefully recorded. Any material considered unsuitable for reuse on the site, for geotechnical or contamination reasons, was removed to a licensed landfill. Environmental consulting costs for the 250-acre (101-ha) site were only $38,000 (£23,000).

Some materials containing elevated levels of contaminants (those over ICRCL's guidelines) were left on site.

Construction operations at the site had to be carried out under controlled conditions to protect the workers, but the safety procedures were no more onerous than those applied to the construction industry in general. So far as those areas intended for soft landscaping were concerned, a break layer of coarse material was incorporated into the covering layer to prevent the upward migration of contaminants through capillary action. As with site clearance, a detailed record was maintained of all remediation work. The overall cost to remediate the site was approximately $16.7 million (£10 million), or about $1.50 (£1.00) per square foot of land. Future site development costs are to be borne by developers of those sites.

The search for an occupant for part of the Northbank site began before remediation was complete. In 1990, the commercial director of TPDC visited Omega Engineering of Stamford, Connecticut, which was looking for a 15- to 20-acre (6- to 8-ha) site on which to base its European operations. The company was prepared to consider locating on the site of a former steelworks, possibly because its headquarters in Connecticut was also built on the site of a former steelworks that it had reclaimed.

The issue of indemnification was raised during the course of negotiations, when Omega asked for a warranty from TPDC against any future problems encountered, over and above the remediation specification. As QUANGOs have only short lives, the development corporation was unable to provide warranties, but it did obtain collateral warranties from the consultants and contractors who undertook the work (although these warranties may be of limited value).

The deal with Omega was signed in October 1993, but, during the course of site remediation, additional problems were discovered that caused a delay in commencement of the construction project. They included a culvert, whose presence was previously unknown, that had to be grouted and a further area of contamination beneath the culvert. TPDC paid the additional costs of dealing with these problems. In June 1995, more than five years after the first contact between TPDC and Omega Engineering, work began on the construction of a 350,000-square-foot (32,500-m^2) industrial plant on a 21-acre (8.5-ha) site that will employ 500 people.

Public Investment. Overall, TPDC and other public agencies incurred costs of just over $49.5 million (£29.7 million) on the Northbank site, mostly for site acquisition, remediation, and site preparation. The project, which is only partially built out, has created a total of 872 jobs (including the 500 at the Omega plant) since 1987, and over 550,000 square feet (51,000 m^2) of building space has been erected. In addition, TPDC was able to recoup $7.2 million (£4.3 million) in land sales; the estimated future rental income stream is up to $3.8 million (£2.3 million).

Lessons Learned. One lesson from this case is to think *big*. TPDC has undertaken development of an enormous scale, building on an industrial area that has some potential but also had been in severe decline for several decades. TPDC worked on fundamentals, creating the infrastructure, and road, rail, water, and highway transportation links to make the area competitive. TPDC also developed expertise in managing site remediation. Further, once established, it prepared some of the sites for development on a speculative basis (in the sense that land was remediated before users were identified). TPDC aggressively marketed the site overseas, bringing Omega and other users into the park. It leveraged public money with private investment, roughly four parts private money to one part public. Finally, a QUANGO, unlike not-for-profit entities in the United States, has a finite lifespan (ten years). While this factor does have some disadvantages (for example, TPDC could not provide indemnification), these entities must work hard to sustain themselves or go out of business.

The Carriages at Openshaw: Redevelopment Of a Factory Site for Residential Use

This former factory site is located in an area that, until 1980, was totally dominated by heavy industry, especially engineering for building machinery. Today, virtually all of the industrial businesses have closed, either going out of business and reducing the number of plants needed

The Carriages at Openshaw comprises terraced and semidetached townhouses (two- and four-unit structures) similar in size to existing dwellings in the neighborhood. Four models are offered, ranging from about 600 to 750 square feet (55 to 70 m^2) of floor area.

or relocating to greenfield sites, but a factory building is still located adjacent to the site. This economic decline has left behind a legacy of redundant buildings, mostly vandalized, or cleared but contaminated sites. Parts of the area have been developed for housing, including the subject property. Most existing houses in the locality are two-story terraced buildings built in the latter part of the last century. In good condition, these houses sell for around $42,000 to $50,000 (£25,000 to £30,000), about the same as the construction cost for similarly sized new houses. The sale price for mildly contaminated land suitable and zoned for attached and semiattached residential use, depending on condition and availability, is $8.00 to $15.00 (£5.00 to £9.00) per square foot.

History of the Site. The 7.2-acre (2.9-ha) site was the location of a long-running industrial dispute in the early 1980s, when management locked out the workforce. After many months of bitterness, the matter was brought to an end, the factory demolished, and the demolition material used to level the site. This procedure eventually gave the appearance of a green and level site.

In 1989, the site was subsequently sold for residential development. The price paid by the original developer, which did not directly consider the knowledge of contamination but did reflect the industrial character of the locality, was substantially below residential development land values in other parts of the city. In reality, up to 10 feet (3 m) of fill material covered more than one-third of the site area. Following the sale, investigation revealed extensive contamination caused by the previous industrial use. Parts of the site had been used to dispose of waste materials from the former metal finishing operations, while other areas were filled with demolition rubble, some of which contained contaminants from the same source.

There was no recourse. The purchaser had neglected to investigate the site before entering into the contract. In time, the original developer fell into financial difficulties, and the bank stepped in as mortgagee in possession.

After more than two years and many abortive negotiations, the bank agreed in 1993 to sell the site to the current developer, Maunders Urban Renewal Ltd., for about $620,000 (£370,000), or $2.00 (£1.20) per square foot, which was significantly below the price paid by the original developer. Maunders is one of the country's most successful homebuilders and has been in the business for over 80 years. The developer for this project is a division within the company that specializes in all as-

FIGURE 16.4

THE CARRIAGES AT OPENSHAW SITE PLAN

FIGURE 16.5

PROJECT DATA—THE CARRIAGES AT OPENSHAW

Land Use Information
Site Area: 7.2 acres (313,600 square feet)
Floor/Area Ratio: 0.30
Building Area: 91,125 square feet (135 units @ 675 square feet per unit)

Development Cost Information		
Land Acquisition Cost	$617,000	($1.97 per square foot)
Site Preparation Costs		
Demolition	0	
Remediation	$888,000	($2.83 per square foot)
Construction Costs		
Building hard costs	$5,667,000	($62.20 per building square foot)
Soft Costs		
Architect, legal, planning	$533,000	
Environmental consultants	65,000	
Other costs (agents, financing)	833,000	
Total Development Cost	**$8,603,000**	($63,700 per unit)
Minus Public Subsidy	–1,275,000	City grant/English Partnerships
Net Cost to Developer	**$7,330,000**	($54,300 per unit)
Cash Flow at Completion		
Number of Sales	135	
Average Sale Price	$61,700	
Total Proceeds from Sales	$8,333,000	Net after market
Gross Profit	**$1,005,000**	
Financing and Investment		
Value of Sales	$8,333,000	
Gross Profit from Sales	$1,005,000	
Equity Requirement	$7,328,000	Net cost
Return on equity	13.5%	

pects of urban renewal projects. The firm is vertically integrated and handles many development-related functions in house.

To make the project financially feasible, the Department of Environment offered a city grant of $1.3 million (£765,000) to ensure the site's development. The amount of the grant exceeded the cost of site remediation and included an element of commercial subsidy, supporting the provision of new housing in a depressed part of the city. The development unit is the company's urban renewal subsidiary. The required private sector financing was provided from the construction group's internal resources. The developer's in-house team undertook all the design work other than site remediation.

Development Plan. The development plan for the housing project calls for 135 new for-sale units. The new development includes terraced and semidetached townhouses (two- and four-unit structures) similar in size to the existing dwellings in the neighborhood. Four models are offered, ranging in size from about 600 to 750 square feet (55 to 70 m^2) in floor area. The overall density is 19 units per acre, with an approximate floor/area ratio of 0.30. These two- and three-bedroom starter houses sell for $58,300 to $70,000 (£35,000 to £42,000), excluding central heating and a garage, which add $1,700 to $5,000 (£1,000 to £3,000) to the sale price. All houses have off-street parking and access to small, semi-private gardens. As is fairly common in the U.K., the units are leasehold, with a nominal ground rent of about $165 (£100) paid annually. Ground leases on new developments are usually for a period of 125 years, without rental reviews, and are used to enable the developer to retain a degree of management control over the completed development. Over two-thirds of the units have been sold and occupied.

Remediation. The entire site was covered with demolition rubble and industrial waste, up to ten feet (3 m) thick, over a layer of ash material on top of the natural clay. The site had been leveled following completion of the demolition work and banked along the roadside to prevent fly-tipping and use of the site by itinerants, then left to vegetate naturally. An unused canal forming the western boundary of the site had been filled with a variety of material of unknown origin and then landscaped.

A site investigation commissioned by the bank and developer over the period from 1990 to 1993 found the fill material to be contaminated with a wide range of heavy metals and mineral oils. Most of the contaminants were at levels below the "trigger concentrations" for domestic gardens, as set out in ICRCL guideline 59/83,[11] but elevated levels of lead, arsenic, copper, zinc, nickel, and boron were found. The highest concentrations of all these contaminants were found in two discrete areas of the site. The developer subsequently retained the consulting engineer responsible for carrying out investigation of the site for the bank to supervise remediation. The Manchester City Council Environmental Health Department periodically inspected the site during remediation, at the consulting engineer's request.

Site remediation in this case study was based on the safe containment of a residue of contaminated material (at concentrations considered safe) under the development itself. Contaminated hot spots were removed to a landfill, and the remaining contaminated fill material was regraded to fill the voids left by removal of the hot spots. Doing so had the effect of lowering the ground level throughout the site and reducing the remaining contaminants to concentrations below ICRCL's trigger levels. The site was then covered (capped) with three feet (1 m) of clean clay and topsoil. Remediation was completed in May 1994, and the site was deemed suitable for residential development by the consultant. The Manchester City Council Environmental Health Department subsequently approved the remediation.

The alternative of removing all the contaminated material to a landfill and backfilling the site with clean material would have cost over $2 million (£1.2 million). In contrast, the total cost of remediation for the project, including environmental consulting fees, was an estimated $953,000 or $3.00 per land square foot (£572,000 or £1.80/sf). The level of aid required for total removal of the contaminated soil would have substantially exceeded the Department of Environment's guideline of one part public money to four parts private money. The site therefore would not have received a grant.

Construction Costs. The developer is expected to incur substantial expenses in addition to site acquisition, remediation, and environmental consulting fees. Direct construction costs for the units and other site work are an estimated $5.7 million (£3.4 million). Professional fees, including costs allocated to in-house services and outside sources, are expected to be $530,000 (£320,000). Legal, marketing, and financing expenses are expected to total $830,000 (£500,000) by the end of the project. Total project costs, before subsidy, are $8.7 million (£5.2 million).

Deal Structure and Financing the Project. As indicated earlier, the developer financed the project out of internal cash flow; no development loans were required. Virtually all aspects of project development and marketing, except for site remediation, were handled in house. The advantages of direct coordination were reflected in better communication and a shorter development time period, resulting in lower cost. Overall, remediation of the site (including consulting fees) represented 11 percent of the value of the project at completion. After deducting the city grant of $1.3 million (£765,000), the developer's net costs are expected to be just under $7.3 million (£4.4 million). Expected sales revenues of $8.3 million (£5 million) for the units yields a gross profit of $1 million (£600,000), or 14 percent. Figure 16.3 summarizes the financial information for this case.

Market Acceptance. As indicated earlier, the houses have sold briskly, and buyers have accepted the product. As of year-end 1996, 95 houses had been sold and occupied. Moreover, users can readily obtain mortgage loans, something that would be difficult for first-time homebuyers in the United States because of the ground leases, which are generally unacceptable to secondary mortgage markets in the United States.

According to the developer's market research, virtually identical houses in other parts of the Manchester conurbation unaffected by industrial dereliction and older, terraced houses were selling for prices up to 10 percent higher. The generally lower selling prices in east Manchester may not be entirely the result of possible blight from contamination but to some extent reflect the depressed economy in that part of the city.

Lessons Learned. The developer has found a niche in developing urban sites. The firm's vertical integration enables more control over the project, retains funds in house, and may shorten the development period.

Developing brownfields into moderate-density housing can be feasible because of relatively high land values. In general, land values in urban areas in the U.K. are higher than in the United States, partly because strong local planning authorities can discourage development of greenfield sites. Moreover, urban residents in the U.K. appear comfortable with higher-density development and smaller units than their counterparts in the United States. Having lived in an industrial society for many generations, they may also be less sensitive about living next to factories or other land uses that would be buffered more in the United States.

Coordinated financing is another important component of this case. English Partnerships is a major player and can subsidize projects effectively with a predetermined maximum amount of leverage. It is easier for the developer than in the United States, where funds may need to come from several sources.

The city grant enabled the developer to take control of the property at a price that represented a discount of at least 70 percent against the value of an uncontaminated site. Much of the reduction in the price paid was attributable to the expectation of lower selling prices, but at least part of the discount is attributable to the developer's perception of increased risk. The developer also considered that an increased marketing budget was required to overcome the possible stigma attached to the previous use.

Townhouses for Rent in Salford

This low-income rental project is located in one of the highest crime areas in greater Manchester and the scene of much urban deprivation. It was therefore deemed to have considerable import in terms of urban renewal. When the site became available, its complexity required two developers and almost a decade to bring the project to fruition. It is currently partly occupied and is actively being developed.

History of the Site. The site, originally used as a tram depot, is located along a major street. About 70 percent of the site was covered by buildings, which had been used primarily as maintenance workshops. The buildings contained maintenance pits, extending over almost half the total floor area, above which trams were driven on rails supported by cast-iron columns. The pits were an average of five feet (1.5 m) deep.

When trams ceased to operate in the streets of Manchester and Salford, the depot was converted for use by motor buses. The conversion involved filling the pits and constructing at least four groups of "finger pits." The origin of the fill material is unknown but is assumed to have contained industrial wastes, mainly ash or slag from nearby metal treatment and finishing works. Following closure of the bus depot, all buildings on the site were demolished down to the floor slabs, and some of the demolition material appears to have been used to fill the finger pits.

The site was subsequently sold to a developer for the construction of a housing project containing 119 units. A site investigation was commissioned, and, based on the information then available, the Department of Environment awarded a city grant. The development was not started, and the developer eventually went into receivership. Four years later, a second developer agreed to purchase the site, provided that grant aid was still available, and to carry out the original scheme. That developer paid about $505,000, or $2.75 per land square foot (£303,000) for the site. This price represented a discount of about 20 percent against the price paid by the original developer.

Development Plan. The 4.2-acre (1.7-ha) site has been approved, and construction of 119 rental units has begun. The density is 28 units per acre (11.5/ha). The one- to three-story townhouses have two to four bedrooms, with one bath or 1½ bathrooms. They range from 500 to 800 square feet (50 to 75 m^2). The development backs up on a river. Established residential areas are adjacent to the project on two sides. Most of the existing housing in the neighborhood is public housing owned by the city council or social housing owned by not-for-profit housing associations. A large community park is located nearby.

Remediation. The original site investigation had not tested the fill material for chemicals, and a second investigation was commissioned to identify the nature and extent of any contamination. This investigation revealed that the fill material in the maintenance pits was

As the city council guarantees the rents of people on social security, the waiting list for these units includes 500 families The developer intends to acquire more land in the area to expand the project. This acceptance by renters is remarkable, because the project is actively being remediated while units are being leased.

FIGURE 16.6

Project Data—Salford Residential Rental Project

Land Use Information		
Site Area: 4.2 acres (183,000 square feet)		
Floor/Area Ratio: 0.40		
Building Area: 71,400 square feet (119 units @ 600 square feet per unit)		
Development Cost Information		
Land Acquisition Cost	$505,000	($2.76 per square foot)
Site Preparation Costs		
Demolition	0	
Remediation	$908,300	($4.96 per square foot)
Construction Costs		
Building hard costs	$6,250,000	($87.54 per building square foot)
Soft Costs		
Architect, legal, planning	$397,000	
Environmental consultants	53,000	
Other costs (agents, financing)	863,300	
Total Development Cost	**$8,977,000**	($75,400 per unit)
Minus Public Subsidy	–2,000,000	City grant/English Partnerships
Net Cost to Developer	**$6,977,000**	($58,630 per unit)
Cash Flow (stable year)		
Number of Tenants	119	
Average Monthly Rental	$600	Per unit, future year
Total Annual Revenues	$860,000	

heavily contaminated with heavy metals, including arsenic, boron, chromium, mercury, nickel, lead, selenium, and zinc, and with polyaromatic hydrocarbons. A formal, quantified risk assessment by a consultant subsequently classified the site as "high risk."

The site is adjacent to a river and was at risk from flooding from a 100-year flood. The National Rivers Authority, now part of the Environment Agency, had therefore recommended that the finished floor level of the ground floors of the dwellings be raised by at least 40 inches (1 m) above the existing levels. Remediation required the removal of contaminated hot spots and the sealing of residual contamination within the original maintenance pits, with the entire site then covered with at least 40 inches (1 m) of clean material. Upon completion of the work, the risk assessment will be reduced to "low risk." Remediation and construction are occurring simultaneously on different parts of the site. Remediation is expected to cost $908,300 (£545,000), and environmental consulting fees are $37,000 (£22,000), plus $17,000 (£10,000) for site investigation. Additional environmental issues will add 11 percent to total project costs (see Figure 16.4).

Construction Costs. In addition to site acquisition, remediation, and environmental consulting fees, the developer is expected to incur substantial other expenses. Direct construction costs for the units and other site work are an estimated $6.25 million (£3.75 million). Professional fees are expected to be $397,000 (£238,000). Legal, marketing, and financing expenses are expected to total $863,300 (£518,000) by the time the project is completed. Total project costs, before subsidy, are $9 million (£5.4 million).

Public Subsidy. The entire cost of site remediation, abnormal foundations work, and selected other expenses was covered by an offer of investment funding from English Partnerships for a maximum of $2 million (£1.2 million). This public funding was approximately $833,000 (£500,000) more than the estimated cost of dealing with contamination-related issues, and represents a substantial commercial subsidy for the project because it is in a targeted area and serves a low-income group. The total grant amount reflects 20 percent of the completed project's value.

Deal Structure and Financing of the Project. After deducting this subsidy, the developer's net costs are expected to be just under $7 million (£4.2 million), or $58,600 (£35,200) per unit. When the time came to obtain a mortgage loan, the development finance lender was hesitant because of concerns about the site's cleanliness. The lender was more comfortable when the man who coordinated remediation and the city grant told them that a 50-pound child would have to eat several pounds of soil each day to be at risk from the contamination left on site. The lender then provided the requisite short-term financing.

The housing development is closely managed by an on-site team, which will continue after construction is completed. Long-term investment funding is being provided by six or seven building societies and banks, which have offered more than enough funding to complete the development. The developer has decided to rent the units and to retain them in his own investment portfolio.

Market Acceptance. As of early 1997, about 50 of the 119 houses were occupied, many of them by people on social security whose rents are guaranteed by the city council. The waiting list contains more than 500 families for the remaining units. The developer intends to acquire more land in the area to extend the project. This acceptance by renters is even more remarkable, because the project is actively being remediated while units are being leased.

Lessons Learned. Very few of these developed sites have presented problems for subsequent owners or occupants of buildings constructed on them. In many instances, it has not been considered necessary to remove all contaminants from the site, even for residential use. Experience has shown that the occupants of residential properties, and their funding institutions, are often more prepared to accept some residual contamination than their counterparts dealing with commercial investments.

Public funding is the key to this project. It received a subsidy of 20 percent of the project's value from English Partnerships, enabling investors to obtain an adequate rate of return.

Translating scientific details to an understandable level (how many pounds of soil a 50-pound child would have to eat in one year) is a necessary step in making lenders and other reluctant, cautious players agree to participate in development of contaminated land.

Notes

1. Peter Meyer, Richard Williams, and Kristen Yount *Contaminated Land: Reclamation, Redevelopment, and Reuse in the United States and European Union* (Brookfield, Vt.: Edward Elgar Publishing Co., 1996).

2. See Paul Syms, *Contaminated Land: Its Assessment and Treatment. A Guide for Valuers, Surveyors, and Developers* (Oxford, U.K.: Blackwell Science Ltd., 1997).

3. Robert A. Simons and Paul M. Syms, "Contaminated Land: Do Property Registers Do More Harm Than Good? An Analysis of the U.K. and U.S.A. Approaches to Public Management of Brownfield Sites," paper presented at a conference of the Pacific Rim Real Estate Society, January 1997, Palmerston North, New Zealand.

4. D. Hughes, *Environmental Law*, 2d ed. (London Butterworths, 1992).

5. Paul M. Syms, "The Funding of Developments on Derelict and Contaminated Sites," in *Industrial Property: Policy and Economic Development*, edited by R. Ball and A.C. Pratt (London: Routledge, 1994).

6. Univ. of Liverpool, Environmental Advisory Unit *Transforming Our Waste Land: The Way Forward* (London: Dept. of Environment, 1986).

7. J. Denner and M.F. Lowe, "U.K. Contaminated Land Policy Developments," in *Contaminated Soil '95*, edited by W.J. van den Brink, R. Bosman, and F. Arendt. Proceedings of the Fifth International FZK/TNO Conference on Contaminated Soil, Oct. 30–Nov. 3, 1995, Maastricht, The Netherlands.

8. As of early 1998, $1.00 equaled £0.6.

9. Paul M. Syms, "Piccadilly Village, Manchester: A Case Study in Waterside Urban Renewal," in *Urban Regeneration: Property Investment and Development*, edited by J. Berry, S. McGreal, and B Deddis (London: E & F N Spon, 1993).

10. Trafford Park Development Corp., "Annual Report," 1995, p. 9.

11. Interdepartmental Committee on the Redevelopment of Contaminated Land, *Guidance on the Assessment and Redevelopment of Contaminated Land*, London, 1987.

Appendices

APPENDIX A
Methodology for the Economic Base Analysis

City-County Data Book, published by the U.S. Bureau of the Census, is a good resource to analyze decreases in firms, employment, and housing in major cities. Another Census Bureau publication, *County Business Patterns,* is an adequate backup source for selected items. The analysis for this study was conducted on the 76 largest cities in the United States, those with a population in 1992 of over 200,000 and a combined population of over 47 million, plus a few smaller cities in New England. Over half these cities had substantial increases in land area and population through annexation or absorption of adjacent communities. Because the methodology for cities with substantial increases in land area would underestimate the number of brownfields (they would be masked by growth), most of these cities were dropped from the analysis. For the 31 cities studied, changes in industrial, commercial, and residential activity between 1963 and 1987 were noted, with net contraction (negative numbers) interpreted as potential brownfields.

The net decrease in the number of transportation, manufacturing, and wholesale trade firms and employment was used to estimate the number of industrial brownfield sites, and the net decrease in the number of retail firms and employees to estimate commercial brownfield sites. Standard industry estimates of square footage per employee and floor/area ratios were used to "back into" estimates of acreage. These factors were adjusted to "fit" the cities where good data are available, such as Cleveland. The assumptions used were 600 square feet per employee for industrial sites, 1,000 square feet for wholesale trade, 450 square feet for transportation employment, and 400 square feet for retail trade. Floor/area ratios ranged from 0.30 for wholesale trade to 0.45 for manufacturing and retailing. Average lots for closed wholesale trade, industrial, and transportation firms were assumed to be one to one-and-a-half acres. For commercial uses, the assumption was 0.25 acre per site. Finally, changes in employment and firms for each category were averaged to determine the total average of nonresidential brownfields.

To determine residential brownfields for cities with less than 25 percent of their housing stock in single-family detached units in 1987, the average was determined of the net reduction in the number of single-family houses and of the net change in occupied housing units. For cities with higher-density housing, only net change in occupied units was used. Each residential single-family lot lost was assumed to be 4,000 square feet.

Because this analysis does not include all U.S. cities, the methodology has some shortcomings. For most—but not all—cities, it will lead to an underestimation of the total number and acres of brownfields. Moreover, changing municipal boundaries are likely to mask (underestimate) the presence of brownfield sites in areas of growth. The study also ignores land that was vacant before 1963 or was developed after 1987. In addition, the average figures for nonresidential acreage do not account for large sites, and, although many observers consider landfills brownfields, they are not considered here.

Some assumptions could overestimate brownfields. Some unlisted sites in this group are also probably on some federal or state lists. Moreover, this economic base analysis uses no direct evidence of contamination for these sites, but given building materials and processes used during the time used in the analysis, many of the sites would be suspect and, at a minimum, would be *perceived* to be contaminated. It must be acknowledged that not all the properties estimated using this approach are necessarily financially abandoned, derelict sites.

This methodology assumes that space-per-employee ratios have not substantially changed over the study's time frame. Further, it does not explicitly consider changes in land use on brownfields or their development. For example, if residential growth were high (as was the case in New York City), then it could consume some of the excess industrial land or it could just go to a higher-density residential use. Nor are changes in public infrastructure or other public space, such as buffer zones around airports, considered. While figures for individual cities may vary substantially from the current reality, the big picture and the cities' ordinal rankings are consistent with expectations. Despite these caveats, these estimates of brownfields are consistently applied across the communities, and they form a valuable starting point for discussing the magnitude of the problem.

APPENDIX B
Market Demand for Brownfields

Forecasts of demand for several types of land use, including industrial, office, and residential development, were prepared. The primary focus was on industrial demand because of the role of old-line manufacturing firms in creating brownfields and because of the major economic significance of manufacturing firms and employment to Great Lakes urban economies. For each city real estate market, the best available, locally generated real estate data were collected and historical trends for 1990 to 1995 obtained. Generally, this information included existing inventory by type at year's end and vacant space by type. In most markets, data permitted a breakdown of geographic area as well as product type. Some real estate firms also made available information on new construction, lease rates, and leasing activity.

Industrial Building Space. To standardize the analysis for all markets, estimates of past absorption were based on the net change in standing inventory (existing buildings in place, net of change in vacancy) over the period from 1990 to 1995. This figure can be interpreted as the net demand for new space, which assumes the existing inventory does not decrease. This method may somewhat understate future demand, because it assumes no new brownfields will be created.

Past trends in absorption, by industry type (manufacturing, warehouse/distribution, office/showroom, and high-tech space) were prepared for major geographic submarkets in each metropolitan area, using two approaches to forecasting. First, an average annual absorption rate for each type of product and each submarket over the five-year period was prepared. Second, an alternative approach was used that extended the trend over the period 1991 to 1994 to reflect the more aggressive growth coming out of the 1992 recession. Overall metropolitan market absorption was held constant for both forecasting techniques. The two approaches were then averaged and used for the "continuation of past trends" scenario of demand for industrial land.

The continuation of past trends scenario may plausibly be considered a "worst case" for several reasons. First, the major contraction in center-city manufacturing jobs from 1960 to 1990 (which caused much of the abandonment of industrial land in the first place) appears to have stabilized. Second, because the national recession in 1992 was part of the study period, the past five years should generally reflect future economic trends. Moreover, the North American Free Trade Agreement, an external factor affecting the departure of some manufacturing jobs from the country, was implemented during the time span under consideration. Finally, no comprehensive state legislation was enacted to encourage the development of brownfields, except perhaps in the last six months of the analysis period.

Industrial Land. Demand for industrial space by geographic subarea was converted to demand for industrial land by assuming a floor/area ratio of 0.4:1.0, suitable for high-density industrial development in a land-constrained market. In other words, for each 10,000 square feet of industrial demand, 25,000 square feet, or about 0.6 acre, of land would be required. These figures were carried forward to the supply/demand analysis for brownfields.

Best-Case Scenario. The best-case scenario assumes that newly implemented state voluntary cleanup programs and improved local marketing of brownfields can substantially increase the share of metropolitan industrial demand that can be captured by the center city. For each industrial market, the center city's share in the best-case scenario was determined by looking at the best-performing suburban submarket in each metropolitan area and assigning its share to the center city. Doing so implies that newly enacted state voluntary cleanup programs can level the playing field for brownfield sites. It was accomplished by redistributing the remaining shares among the other markets, thereby holding constant overall metropolitan demand. Typically, this method served to approximately double the center city's share.

Office Space. For office space, the methodology was the same as for industrial space, except that the floor/area ratio for space in the CBD was assumed to be 5.0:1. The FAR for suburban office space was assumed to be 0.4:1. Because of the stringent requirements for location of most office development projects, no best-case scenario was developed, so the results are the same as the past-trends scenario. The demand for office space is small compared with industrial demand.

Housing. Demand for housing is important because the housing sector is very large and, with generally low density, consumes large quantities of land. Residential land is also very flexible compared with industrial land or office space. It requires smaller parcels, and, while complete land assembly is desirable, it is not a necessary condition for successful housing development. On the other hand, the costs of environmental remediation for housing are likely to be higher than for industrial uses.

The analysis of demand for housing was much less elaborate. For each metropolitan area, the total number of building permits issued between 1988 and 1995 was collected and an annual average determined. Data were collected for the center city and the primary metropolitan statistical area, and the center city's share determined. These shares were generally very low, ranging from 0.25 percent for Detroit to 5.8 percent for Chicago. One- to four-family dwelling units were assumed to be developed at a density of 3.5 units per acre to generate the demand for residential land in each center city. Demand ranged from 46 acres in Detroit to 1,420 acres in Chicago over five years.

The more aggressive approach to demand for residential land assumes that the center city could triple its share of housing starts in the metropolitan area through aggressive marketing, the encouragement of land assembly, financial incentives, better amenities, and more straightforward and workable legislation. Cleveland has managed to attain this increased output through aggressive financial inducements such as tax abatement, low-interest loans, donation of building lots, and investment in infrastructure.

APPENDIX C
Supply of Brownfields

Cleveland's Supply of Brownfields. The city of Cleveland has not generated a list of brownfields, although the Cuyahoga County Planning Commission is currently attempting to develop a computer mapping database of available property, including brownfields.[1] An estimate of the location and type of brownfields was developed for Cleveland and surrounding Cuyahoga County (1990 population about 1.7 million).

Listed sites in the county include 172 NFRAP and 50 CERCLIS sites. They averaged eight acres, based on a sample of 78 out of 222 sites with usable addresses where records were available. Of these sites, 134 known CERCLIS- and NFRAP-listed sites were in the city. The county contained 1,800 LUST sites (average size of 0.1 acre), 363 of which were in the city, excluding the one-third that were assumed not to be covered in the computerized analysis of unlisted sites.[2] These listed brownfield sites in the city of Cleveland are estimated to cover 1,108 acres.

In Cleveland and Cuyahoga County, local property tax assessment records from the Cuyahoga County auditor's office were used to identify potential unlisted brownfield properties. These records were expected to reflect properties likely to be contaminated based on prior use, showing evidence of financial distress. Unlisted brownfields could include vacant industrial land (no virgin land) in the city, vacant commercial land (again no virgin land) in the city, vacant industrial land in the suburbs that is more than two years delinquent in property taxes, all municipally owned land-banked lots (formerly residential) that have been foreclosed because of delinquent property taxes, standing industrial buildings of very poor quality at best, commercial buildings in very poor condition used as automotive repair shops or dry cleaners, and any of these types of buildings in fair or poor condition where the ratio of land to building value is less than one that are also two years or more behind in property taxes.

This approach resembles Milwaukee's in many ways. It excludes vacant, privately owned residential land, landfills, municipally owned property larger than 0.15 acre, state-owned land (some of the Superfund sites are in the category), all standing commercial buildings not associated with automotive repair or dry cleaning, and standing industrial buildings of fair quality or better where the owners are paying property taxes. While municipal authorities know generally about these sites (which are often more than 30 acres), no formal list is believed to be available. Thus, the overall number of brownfields and the acreage are likely to be higher than shown here. A cross-check of the CERCLIS and NFRAP lists with the unlisted sites shows that only about 5 percent of these listed sites (six out of 115 where data on parcels could be attached) would have met the economic conditions of a brownfield.

For unlisted sites, the city of Cleveland is estimated to contain more than 3,100 vacant parcels of industrial and commercial land on 1,400 acres, approximately 2,800 properties with standing, substantially underused industrial and commercial buildings on 260 acres, and more than 7,200 formerly residential lots on 800 acres that have been foreclosed because of delinquent property taxes and are publicly owned. Of the 14,100 unlisted brownfield sites on 2,730 acres in the county, 93 percent of the sites, with 91 percent of the acreage, are in the central city.

According to the definition used here, the city of Cleveland contained 3,565 acres of brownfields in 1996. Cleveland's total was 77 percent of the total brownfield acreage in Cuyahoga County and 88 percent of total brownfield sites in the county. Sites over one acre, prime for industrial development, represent about 40 percent of all brownfield acreage in the county and 60 percent in the city.

Detroit's Supply of Brownfields. Detroit has not prepared overall estimates of brownfields, so we assumed the 28 CERCLIS sites and 55 NFRAP sites in the city were the size of EPA-listed sites in Cleveland. Total acreage was estimated to be 664 acres. The city also has 1,765 LUST sites, which we assumed indicated 177 acres. Thus, the total amount of listed brownfield sites in Detroit was estimated to be 841 acres. Data on unlisted sites were more difficult to estimate. Local planners are developing a system that may be capable of generating estimates of brownfields within a year, but no total figures are presently available. Therefore, the figure shown on Table 1 of the U.S. Conference of Mayors study (which cited 2,500 industrial brownfields in the city of Detroit) was used.[3] Detroit planners indicated that an industrial parcel in the city is typically two to three acres.[4] Using an average size of 2.5 acres and subtracting the 83 EPA-listed sites and one-third of the LUST sites to avoid double counting (588 sites) leaves an estimated 1,829 industrial sites on 4,573 acres not counted elsewhere. Thus, a conservative estimate of industrial brownfields (excluding formerly residential property) in Detroit is 5,414 acres, say 5,400 acres.

Milwaukee's Supply of Brownfields. Milwaukee has developed and is maintaining an ongoing list of brownfields, but it is very narrowly defined (excluding properties whose property taxes are current) and excludes EPA-listed sites. We looked at the 14 CERCLIS sites and 30 NFRAP sites in the city of Milwaukee and, assuming eight acres per site, estimated their total size to be 352 acres. The city contains 870 LUST sites. Again, we assumed each site was 0.1 acre, making 87 acres of LUST sites. Thus, the total amount of listed brownfield sites in Milwaukee is an estimated 439 acres. Milwaukee's tax assessor has developed a database for brownfields based on property tax records that features a do-not-acquire list, which combines delinquent properties with those believed to be environmentally contaminated. As of mid-1996, this list (which is frequently updated) contained 489 properties whose average size was 0.48 acre. This list is believed to be free of CERCLIS and NFRAP sites.[5] One-third, however, are believed to have USTs on site. Subtracting this number leaves 325 do-not-acquire sites not counted elsewhere, for a total of 156 acres on the do-not-acquire list. Therefore, total known brownfield sites in Milwaukee was 595 acres, excluding residential properties.

Chicago's Supply of Brownfields. Chicago has not developed a database of brownfields, and our estimates were drawn from known EPA-listed sites. The city contained 56 CERCLIS sites and 158 NFRAP sites, yielding a total size of 1,712 acres. It also contains 1,310 LUST sites, which were assumed to cover 131 acres. Thus, the total amount of listed brownfield sites in Chicago was estimated to be 1,843 acres. Data on unlisted sites were more difficult to estimate. No estimates of total brownfield sites or acreage were available, but Table 1 of the U.S. Conference of Mayors study notes 2,000 industrial brownfield sites in the city.[6] Assuming an average size of 2.5 acres per site (comparable with the figure for Detroit and the average of 2.6 acres per site in the U.S. Conference of Mayors report) and subtracting the 214

EPA-listed sites and one-third of the LUST sites to avoid double counting (437 sites) leaves an estimated 1,349 industrial sites on 3,373 acres not counted elsewhere. Thus, a conservative estimate of industrial brownfields (excluding formerly residential property) in Chicago would be 5,216 acres, say 5,200 acres.

Notes

1. Virginia Aveni, Cuyahoga County Planning Commission, personal interview, April 1996.

2. Arthur Sementelli and Robert A. Simons, "Regulation of Leaking Underground Storage Tanks: Unintended Side Effects," *Economic Development Quarterly*, August 1997, pp. 236–48.

3. U.S. Conference of Mayors, "Impact of Brownfields on U.S. Cities: A 39-City Survey" (Washington, D.C.: Author, 1996).

4. Debbie Fisher, Detroit Planning and Development Dept., telephone interview, November 1996.

5. M. Morgan, commissioner, and R. Salcedo, City of Milwaukee, personal communication, July 1996.

6. U.S. Conference of Mayors, "Impact of Brownfields on U.S. Cities."

APPENDIX D
References

Adair et al. v. *Chevron et al.*, Case no. B-152440, filed in 60th Judicial Circuit, Jefferson County, Texas, 1995, pp. 32–33.

AIG Environmental. *1997–1998 Product Directory. Innovative Environmental and Casualty Coverages*. New York: Author, 1997.

Apogee Research, Inc. *Achieving Environmental Justice: Examining the Potential Role for the Empowerment Zone/Enterprise Community Program*. Bethesda, Md.: Author, May 1995.

Archer, Dennis W., et al. *Jump-starting the Motor City: With New Ideas, New Relationships, and New Technologies for the Detroit Empowerment Zone*. Vol. 1 and 2. City of Detroit, June 1994.

Arulanantham, R., D.W. Charlton, and S.I. Morse. *Using Net Benefit Analysis to Manage Risk and Value of Groundwater Resources*. White paper. San Francisco: San Francisco Bay Regional Water Quality Control Board, 1995.

"Area Stands to Benefit from Brownfield Tax Relief." Cleveland *Plain Dealer*. March 12, 1996.

Auckland City Council, Strategic Development Group. *Economic Trends*. Auckland: Author, 1996.

Bartsch, Charles. "Financing Brownfields Cleanup and Redevelopment." *Northeast Midwest Economic Review* 8(5), June 1995: 4–9.

Bartsch, Charles, and Elizabeth Collaton. *Coming Clean for Economic Development: A Resource Book on Environmental Cleanup and Economic Development*. Washington, D.C.: Northeast Midwest Institute, 1995).

—. "Industrial Site Reuse and Urban Development: An Overview." *Cityscape* 2(3), September 1996: 17–61.

Benjamin, John, ed. *Megatrends in Retail Property*. Boston: Kluwer, 1996.

Bier, Tom. "Survey of Cleveland Home Sellers." Cleveland: Cleveland State Univ., Housing Policy Research Program, 1991.

Black, Thomas J. "Brownfields Cleanup." *Urban Land,* June 1995: 47–51.

California EPA, Dept. of Toxic Substances Control. "Environmental Renewal and Economic Revitalization Successes." March 1996.

—. "Fact Sheet: Brownfields Initiatives." February 1997.

—. "Fact Sheet: Prospective Purchaser Policy." October 1996.

—. "Fact Sheet: Senate Bill 923." January 1997.

—. "Update: Redevelopment and Revitalization of Brownfields." *DTSC Initiatives.* August 1996.

Church, Thomas, and Robert Nakamura. *Cleaning Up the Mess: Implementation Strategies in Superfund.* Washington, D.C.: Brookings Institution, 1993.

City of Chicago. *Brownfields Forum: Recycling Land for Chicago's Future.* Final report and action plan. 1995.

Commerce and Industry Insurance Company. *1996 Commerce and Industry Insurance Producer's Guide.* Washington, D.C.: Author, 1996.

Cuyahoga County Planning Commission. "The Brownfields Report." January 1995.

—, Brownfields Group. "Cuyahoga County Brownfields Reuse Strategies." July 1993.

Davis, Todd, and Kevin Margolis, eds. *Brownfields: A Comprehensive Guide to Redeveloping Contaminated Property.* Cleveland: Hemisphere Corp., 1997.

Denner, J., and M.F. Lowe. "U.K. Contaminated Land Policy Developments," in *Contaminated Soil '95,* edited by W.J. van den Brink, R. Bosman, and F. Arendt. Proceedings of the 5th International FZK/TNO Conference on Contaminated Soil, October 30–November 3, 1995, Maastricht, The Netherlands.

Dinsmore, Clement. "State Initiatives on Brownfields." *Urban Land,* June 1996: 37–42.

Dept. of Environment and Welsh Office. *Framework for Contaminated Land: Outcome of the Government's Policy Review and Conclusions from the Consultation Paper* Paying for Our Past. London: Author, 1994.

—. *Paying for Our Past: The Arrangements for Controlling Contaminated Land and Meeting the Costs of Remedying the Damage to the Environment.* London: Author, 1994.

Emeryville, California. Pilot Grant Application to U.S. EPA, 1996.

Environmental Financial Advisory Board. "Financing Brownfields Redevelopment: Linkages to the Empowerment Zone/Enterprise Community Program." Draft Report. Washington, D.C.: Author, June 1995.

—. *Financing Brownfields Redevelopment: Linkages to the Empowerment Zone/Enterprise Community Program.* Brownfields Report No. 1. Washington, D.C.: Author, September 1995.

—. *Financing Strategies for Brownfields Redevelopment.* Report No. 4. Washington, D.C.: Author, August 1995.

—. "Information Needs of Capital Providers in Brownfields Redevelopment." Draft Report. Washington, D.C.: Author, July 1995.

Green-Leigh, Nancey, Robert D. Swartz, and Peter B. Meyer, eds. "Focus: Environmental Constraints to Brownfields Redevelopment." *Economic Development Quarterly: The Journal of American Economic Revitalization* 8(4), November 1994. Special Issue.

Holden, Tim, et al. *How to Select Hazardous Waste Treatment Technologies for Soils and Sludges: Alternative, Innovative, and Emerging Technologies.* Park Ridge, N.J.: Noyes Data Corp., 1989.

Hughes, D. *Environmental Law.* 2d ed. London: Butterworths, 1992.

Kinnard, William, and Elaine Worzala. "Attitudes and Policies of Institutional Investors and Lenders toward On-site and Nearby Transactions." Paper presented at an annual meeting of the American Real Estate Society, April 1996, Lake Tahoe, California.

Interdepartmental Committee on the Redevelopment of Contaminated Land. *Guidance on the Assessment and Redevelopment of Contaminated Land.* London: Author, 1987.

LaGrega, Michael D., Phillip L. Buckingham, Jeffrey C. Evans, et al. *Hazardous Waste Management*. New York: McGraw-Hill, 1994.

Lederman, Peter, and William Librizzi. "Brownfields Remediation: Available Technologies." *Journal of Urban Technology* 2(2), Spring 1996: 21–30.

Lee, Philip W. "Environmental Site Assessments: The Impact of the ASTM Site Assessment Standards on Environmental Risk Management." Paper presented at the Seventh Annual Conference and Business Meeting of The Building Environment Council of Ohio, April 28 and 29, 1994, Cleveland, Ohio.

McGrath, Daniel T. "An Investigation into the Impact of Hazardous Waste Contamination Liability on Urban Industrial Land Redevelopment in the City of Chicago." Working Paper. Chicago: Great Cities Institute, 1995.

Meyer, Peter, Richard Williams, and Kristen Yount. *Contaminated Land: Reclamation, Redevelopment, and Reuse in the United States and European Union*. Brookfield Vt.: Edward Elgar Publishing Co., 1995.

Miller, William G. *Managing Environmental Mandates for Multifamily Housing: 1997. A Compendium of Federal Laws and Regulations*. Washington, D.C.: ULI–the Urban Land Institute, 1996.

Mukatis, W. Alfred, and James Nielsen. "Real Estate Lending Activities of Commercial Banks under Superfund." *Real Estate Law Journal*, Spring 1996: 358–67.

Mundy, Bill. "Intermediaries Influence Buyer Behavior: The Role of Banks and Environmental Firms." *Brownfield News* 1(1), 1997: 29–30.

Nestor, Anthony S., and Scott J. Adamowski. "Financing Remediation by Delisting and Selling Clean Portions of Affected Property." *Remediation,* Summer 1995: 33–44 (New York: John Wiley & Sons, 1995).

New Jersey Dept. of Environmental Protection. "Performance Partnerships in Environmental Management." 1995 Annual Report.

—. "Revitalizing New Jersey's Brownfields: Industrial/Commercial Contaminated Site Reuse." Trenton: Site Remediation Program, July 1996.

New Zealand Ministry for the Environment. "Discussion Document on Contaminated Land Management." Wellington: Author, November 1995.

New Zealand Resource Management Act 1991.

Nunno, Thomas, Jennifer Hyman, Peter Spawn, John Healy, Clay Spears, and Margaret Brown. "International Technologies for Hazardous Waste Site Cleanup." Park Ridge, N.J.: Noyes Data Corp., 1990.

O'Brien, James. "Brownfields Redevelopment: Successful Voluntary Cleanups." *Environmental Insights* Chicago: Chapman & Cutler, 1994.

Patchin, Peter. "Contaminated Properties and the Sales Comparison Approach." *Appraisal Journal,* July 1994: 402–9.

Pepper, Edith. *Brownfield Case Studies: Lessons from the Field*. Washington, D.C.: Northeast Midwest Institute, 1997.

Poindexter, Georgette. "Addressing Morality in Urban Brownfield Redevelopment: Using Stakeholder Theory to Craft Legal Process." *Virginia Environmental Law Journal* 15: 37–76.

Porter, Michael. "The Competitive Advantage of the Inner City." *Harvard Business Review,* May/June 1995: 55–72.

Sementelli, Arthur, and Robert A. Simons. "Regulation of Leaking Underground Storage Tanks: Unintended Side Effects." *Economic Development Quarterly,* August 1997: 236–48.

Simons, Robert A. "BUSTR Orphan Tank Analysis in Cuyahoga County." Cleveland: Cleveland State College of Urban Affairs, The Urban Center, 1995.

—. *Financing Contaminated Land in the Great Lakes Empowerment Zones*. Cleveland: Cleveland State Univ., Great Lakes Environmental Finance Center, 1996.

—. "Supply and Demand for Brownfields in Great Lakes Cities: Implications for Community Involvement." Paper presented at the Brownfields '96 Conference, September 1996, Pittsburgh, Pennsylvania.

Simons, Robert A., W. Bowen, and A. Sementelli. "The Effect of Leaking Underground Storage Tanks on Residential Sales Price." *Journal of Real Estate Research,* forthcoming.

Simons, Robert A., and John Brennan. "Development and Issues of Inner-City Retail Niche Markets," in *Megatrends in Retail Property,* edited by John Benjamin. Boston: Kluwer, 1996.

Simons, Robert A., and D. Iannone. "Brownfields: Supply and Demand." *Urban Land,* June 1997: 36–38+.

Simons, Robert A., and David Sharkey. "Jump-Starting New Housing Markets: Do Public Housing Subsidies Justify the Cost?" *Housing Policy Debate,* Spring 1997: 143–71.

Simons, Robert A., and P.M. Syms. "Contaminated Land: Do Property Registers Do More Harm Than Good? An Analysis of the U.K. and U.S.A. Approaches to Public Management of Brownfield Sites." Paper presented at a conference of the Pacific Rim Real Estate Society, January 1997, Palmerston North, New Zealand.

Statistics New Zealand. *Population Trends in the City of Auckland.* 1996.

Syms, Paul. *Contaminated Land: Its Assessment and Treatment. A Guide for Valuers, Surveyors, and Developers.* Oxford, Eng.: Blackwell Science, 1997.

—. "Effects of Industrial Contamination on Residential Land Values in the United Kingdom." *Land Contamination and Reclamation* 4(1), 1996: 49–56.

—. "The Funding of Developments on Derelict and Contaminated Sites," in *Industrial Property: Policy and Economic Development,* edited by R. Ball and A.C. Pratt. London: Routledge, 1994.

—. "Piccadilly Village, Manchester: A Case Study in Waterside Urban Renewal," in *Urban Regeneration: Property Investment and Development,* edited by J. Berry, S. McGreal, and B. Deddis. London: E & F N Spon, 1993.

Trafford Park Development Corporation. "Annual Report." Manchester: Author, 1995.

ULI–the Urban Land Institute. "Collinwood Neighborhood, Cleveland, Ohio: Retooling an Older Industrial Community." Case Study. Washington, D.C.: Author, 1996.

U.S. v. *Fleet Factors Corp.,* 901 F.2d 1550, 1557 (11th Cir. 1990), *cert. denied,* 498 U.S. 1046 (1991).

U.S. General Accounting Office. "Community Development: Reuse of Urban Industrial Sites." GAO\RCED 95-172. Washington, D.C.: Author, June 1995.

U.S. Conference of Mayors. "Impact of Brownfields on U.S. Cites: A 39-City Survey." Washington, D.C.: Author, 1996.

U.S. Bureau of the Census. *Census of Population and Housing.* Washington, D.C.: U.S. Dept. of Commerce, 1990.

—. *Census of Retail Trade.* Washington, D.C.: U.S. Dept. of Commerce, 1992.

—. *City-County Data Book 1963.* Washington, D.C.: U.S. Dept. of Commerce, 1963.

—. *City-County Data Book 1994.* Washington, D.C.: U.S. Dept. of Commerce, 1994.

—. *Social and Economic Characteristics of the United States.* CP-2-1. Washington, D.C.: U.S. Dept. of Commerce, 1990.

U.S. Environmental Protection Agency. "EPA Announces a Total of 29 Brownfields Redevelopment Projects." EPA Press Advisory. November 1995.

Univ. of Liverpool, Environmental Advisory Unit. *Transforming Our Waste Land: The Way Forward.* London: Dept. of Environment, 1986.

Voinovich, George V., and Nancy P. Hollister. "Jobs Bill III: Proposed Legislation, Interagency Initiative." State of Ohio, June 1995.

Wagner, Wendy. "Overview of Federal and State Law Governing Brownfield Cleanups," in *Brownfields: A Comprehensive Guide to Redeveloping Contaminated Property,* edited by Todd Davis and Kevin Margolis. Cleveland: Hemisphere Corp., 1997.

White, Michael R., et al. "Cleveland Empowerment Zone Application: A Comprehensive Strategy for Economic Development in a Context of Community Building." Cleveland: Dept. of Community Development, January 1994.

Yin, Robert. *Case Study Research: Design and Methods.* Thousand Oaks, Calif.: Sage, 1994.